TUDORS

G. J. Meyer is a former Woodrow Wilson and Harvard University Fellow with an M.A. in English literature. His other books include *The Tudors: The Complete Story of England's Most Notorious Dynasty, Henry VII to Henry VIII* and *A World Undone: The Story of the Great War* ('Magnificent... researched to the last possible dot' *The Washington Times*, 'Masterful... has an instructive value than can scarcely be measured' *Los Angeles Times*, 'A worthy counterpoint to Hew Strachan's magisterial three-volume scholarly project' *Publishers Weekly*). He lives in Goring-on-Thames.

The TUDORS

Lady Jane Grey to Elizabeth I

G. J. MEYER

AMBERLEY

For Rosie

This edition published by arrangement with Delacorte Press, an imprint of the Ramdon House Publishing Group, a division of Random House, Inc.

Amberley Publishing Plc
Cirencester Road, Chalford,
Stroud, Gloucestershire, GL6 8PE

www.amberleybooks.com

British Library Cataloguing in Publication Data.
A catalogue record for this book is available from the British Library.

ISBN 978 1 4456 0144 1

Typesetting and Origination by Amberley Publishing.
Printed in Great Britain.

Contents

THE WORLD OF THE TUDORS

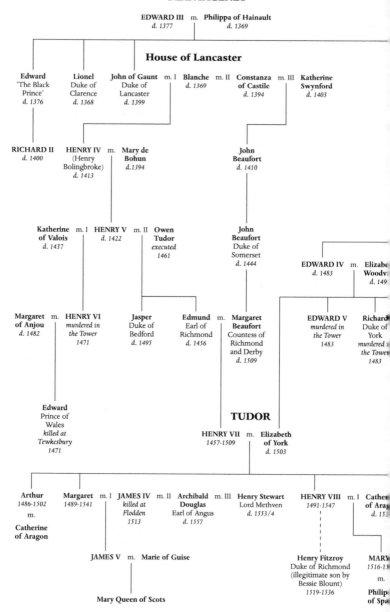

PLANTAGENET

EDWARD III m. **Philippa of Hainault**
d. 1377   *d. 1369*

House of Lancaster

Edward   **Lionel**   **John of Gaunt** m. I **Blanche** m. II **Constanza** m. III **Katherine**
'The Black   Duke of   Duke of   *d. 1369*   of Castile   Swynford
Prince'   Clarence   Lancaster   *d. 1394*   *d. 1403*
d. 1376   *d. 1368*   *d. 1399*

RICHARD II   **HENRY IV** m. **Mary de**   **John**
d. 1400   (Henry   **Bohun**   **Beaufort**
         Bolingbroke)   *d.1394*   *d. 1410*
         d. 1413

Katherine m. I **HENRY V** m. II **Owen**   **John**
of Valois   *d. 1422*   **Tudor**   **Beaufort**
d. 1437   *executed*   Duke of
                  1461   Somerset
                              d. 1444

                                       EDWARD IV m. **Elizabe**
                                          d. 1483   **Woodv**
                                                  d. 149

Margaret m. **HENRY VI**   **Jasper**   **Edmund** m. **Margaret**   **EDWARD V**   **Richard**
of Anjou   *murdered in*   Duke of   Earl of   **Beaufort**   *murdered in*   Duke of
d. 1482   *the Tower*   Bedford   Richmond   Countess of   *the Tower*   York
             1471   *d. 1495*   *d. 1456*   Richmond   *1483*   *murdered*
                                     and Derby   *the Tower*
                                     d. 1509   *1483*

         Edward
         Prince of
         Wales
         killed at
         Tewkesbury   **TUDOR**
         1471
                       HENRY VII m. **Elizabeth**
                       1457-1509   **of York**
                                  d. 1503

Arthur   **Margaret** m. I **JAMES IV** m. II **Archibald** m. III **Henry Stewart**   **HENRY VIII** m. I **Cathe**
1486-1502   *1489-1541*   *killed at*   **Douglas**   Lord Methven   *1491-1547*   **of Ara**
      m.   *Flodden*   Earl of Angus   *d. 1553/4*   *d. 153*
                   1513   *d. 1557*
Catherine
of Aragon

            JAMES V m. **Marie of Guise**   **Henry Fitzroy**   **MAR**
                                         Duke of Richmond   *1516-1*
                                         (illegitimate son by   m.
                                         Bessie Blount)
               Mary Queen of Scots   *1519-1536*   **Philip**
                                                               of Spa

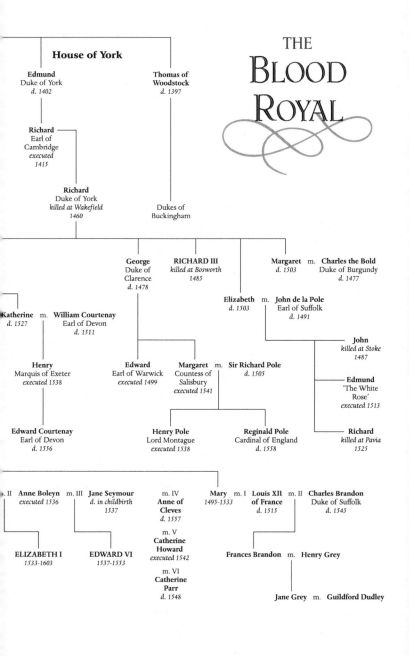

THE BLOOD ROYAL

House of York

Edmund
Duke of York
d. 1402

Thomas of Woodstock
d. 1397

Richard
Earl of Cambridge
executed 1415

Richard
Duke of York
killed at Wakefield 1460

Dukes of Buckingham

George
Duke of Clarence
d. 1478

RICHARD III
killed at Bosworth 1485

Margaret m. **Charles the Bold**
d. 1503   Duke of Burgundy
              d. 1477

Elizabeth m. **John de la Pole**
d. 1503   Earl of Suffolk
              d. 1491

Katherine m. **William Courtenay**
d. 1527   Earl of Devon
              d. 1511

John
killed at Stoke 1487

Henry
Marquis of Exeter
executed 1538

Edward
Earl of Warwick
executed 1499

Margaret m. **Sir Richard Pole**
Countess of   *d. 1505*
Salisbury
executed 1541

Edmund
'The White Rose'
executed 1513

Edward Courtenay
Earl of Devon
d. 1556

Henry Pole
Lord Montague
executed 1538

Reginald Pole
Cardinal of England
d. 1558

Richard
killed at Pavia 1525

m. II **Anne Boleyn**   m. III **Jane Seymour**
executed 1536   *d. in childbirth 1537*

m. IV **Anne of Cleves**
d. 1557

Mary m. I **Louis XII** m. II **Charles Brandon**
1495-1533   of France   Duke of Suffolk
              d. 1515   *d. 1545*

m. V **Catherine Howard**
executed 1542

ELIZABETH I   **EDWARD VI**
1533-1603   *1537-1553*

m. VI **Catherine Parr**
d. 1548

Frances Brandon m. **Henry Grey**

Jane Grey m. **Guildford Dudley**

A Tudor Timeline

1547	*February 20*	Coronation of Edward VI
	March 31	Death of Francis I of France
	September 10	At the Battle of Pinkie English forces commanded by Edward Seymour, new lord protector and Duke of Somerset, defeat the Scots
1549	*July 8*	Start of Kett's Rebellion in Norfolk
	September 5	Execution of Thomas Seymour
1551	*October 11*	Arrest of Edward Seymour, Duke of Somerset; John Dudley, new lord president of Edward VI's council, is elevated to Duke of Northumberland
1552	*January 22*	Execution of Somerset
1553	*May 21*	Marriage of Lady Jane Grey to Guildford Dudley
	July 6	Death of Edward VI
	July 10	Jane Grey is proclaimed queen
	August 3	Mary I enters London in triumph two weeks after being proclaimed queen
	August 21	Execution of John Dudley, Duke of Northumberland
	October 30	Coronation of Mary I
1554	*February 12*	Execution of Jane Grey and Guildford Dudley
	April 11	Execution of Sir Thomas Wyatt
	May 19	Release of Elizabeth after two months of confinement in the Tower
	July 25	Marriage of Mary I to Philip II of Spain
1555	*October 16*	Execution of Nicholas Ridley and Hugh Latimer
	November 12	Death of Stephen Gardiner, chancellor

1556	*March 21*	Execution of Thomas Cranmer; Reginald Pole becomes archbishop of Canterbury
1558	*January 5*	Fall of Calais to France
	April 24	Marriage of Mary Queen of Scots to future Francis II of France
	November 17	Deaths of Mary I and Reginald Pole; appointment of William Cecil as Queen Elizabeth's secretary of state
1559	*January 15*	Coronation of Elizabeth I
	May 8	Elizabeth signs Act of Uniformity
	September 18	Mary Queen of Scots becomes Queen of France with accession of Francis II
1560	*December 5*	Death of Francis II
1561	*August 19*	Arrival of Mary Queen of Scots in Scotland
1564	*September 29*	Robert Dudley is created Earl of Leicester
1565	*July 29*	Mary Queen of Scots weds Henry Stuart, Lord Darnley
1566	*June 19*	Birth of future James VI of Scotland and James I of England
1567	*February 10*	Murder of Darnley
	May 15	Mary Queen of Scots is married to James Hepburn, Earl of Bothwell
	July 24	With Mary a prisoner, her son is proclaimed King James VI
1571	*February 25*	William Cecil is raised to nobility as Baron Burghley
1572	*June 2*	Execution of Thomas Howard, fourth Duke of Norfolk
	August 24	Start of St. Bartholomew's Massacre in Paris
1584	*June 9*	Death of Francis, Duke of Alençon
	July 10	Assassination of William of Orange
1585	*August 20*	With Treaty of Nonsuch, England commits to sending troops to the Netherlands
1586	*January 15*	Earl of Leicester takes the oath as governor-general of the Netherlands
1587	*February 8*	Execution of Mary, Queen of Scots
1588	*July 27*	Spanish Armada arrives off Calais
	September 4	Death of Robert Dudley, Earl of Leicester

1593	*February 25*	Robert Devereux, Earl of Essex, becomes a member of the Privy Council
1596	*July 5*	Robert Cecil is appointed secretary of state
1598	*August 4*	Death of William Cecil, Lord Burghley
	September 13	Death of Philip II
1599	*April 14*	Earl of Essex arrives in Ireland as lord lieutenant
1600	*June 5*	Arrest of Essex
1601	*February 25*	Execution of Essex
1603	*March 24*	Death of Elizabeth I

Introduction

The Tudors ruled England for only three generations, an almost pathetically brief span of time in comparison with other dynasties before and since. During the 118 years of Tudor rule, England was a less weighty factor in European politics than it had been earlier, and nothing like the world power it would later become. Of the five Tudors who occupied the throne—three kings, followed by the first two women ever to be queens of England by right of inheritance rather than marriage—one was an epically tragic figure in the fullest Aristotelian sense, two reigned only briefly and came to miserable ends, and the last and longest-lived devoted her life and her reign and the resources of her kingdom to no loftier objective than her own survival. Theirs was, by most measures, a melancholy story. It is impossible not to suspect that even the founder of the dynasty, the only Tudor whose reign was both long and mostly peaceful and did not divide the people of England against themselves (all of which helps to explain why he is forgotten today), would have been appalled to see where his descendants took his kingdom and how their story ended.

And yet, more than four centuries after the Tudors became extinct, one of them is the most famous king and another the most famous queen in the history not only of England but of Europe and probably the world. They have become not merely famous but posthumous stars in the twenty-first-century firmament of celebrity: on the big and little screens and in popular fiction their names have become synonymous with greatness, with *glory*. This is not the fate one might have expected for a pair whose characters were dominated by cold and ruthless egotism, whose careers were studded with acts of atrocious cruelty and false dealing, and who were never more than stonily indifferent to the well-being of the people they ruled. It takes some explaining.

At least as remarkable as the endlessly growing celebrity of the Tudors is the extent to which, after so many centuries, they remain controversial among scholars. Here, too, the reasons are many and complex. They begin with the fact that the dynasty's pivotal figure, Henry VIII, really did change history to an extent rivaled by few other monarchs, and that appraisals of his reign were long entangled in questions of religious belief. It matters also that both Henry and his daughter Elizabeth were not just rulers but consummate *performers,* masters of political propaganda and political theater. They created, and spent their lives hiding inside, fictional versions of themselves that never bore more than a severely limited relation to reality but were nevertheless successfully imprinted on the collective imagination of their own time. These invented personas have endured into the modern world not only because of their inherent appeal—it is hard to resist the image of bluff King Hal, of Gloriana the Virgin Queen—but even more because of their political usefulness across the generations.

Henry, in the process of forcing upon England a revolution-from-above that few of its people welcomed, created a new elite that his radical redistribution of the national wealth made so rich and powerful so quickly that within a few generations it would prove capable of overthrowing the Crown itself. No longer needing or willing to tolerate a monarchy as overbearing as the Tudors had been at their zenith, that new elite nevertheless continued to need the *idea* of the Tudors, of the wonders of the Tudor revolution, in order to justify its own privileged position. It needed to make the mass of English men and women see the Tudor century as the supreme forward leap in England's history, a sweeping away of the dark legacy of the Middle Ages. (This whole "Whig" view of history requires a smug certainty that the medieval world was a cesspit of superstition and repression.) It demanded agreement that the Tudors had put England on the high road to greatness, and that to say otherwise was to be not only extravagantly foolish or dishonest but actually unfit for participation in public life. Centuries of relentless indoctrination and denial ensued, with the result that England turned into a rather curious phenomenon: a great nation actively contemptuous of much of its own history. One still sees the evidence almost whenever British television attempts to deal with pre-Tudor and Tudor history.

It was not until the second half of the twentieth century, really, that historians of some eminence in England and the United States began, often slowly and grudgingly, to acknowledge that the established view of the Tudor era was essentially mythological and could never be reconciled with a dispassionate examination of the facts. Not until even more recently was the old propaganda pretty much abandoned as indefensible. Tudor history remains controversial because, quite extraordinarily for a subject now half a millennium old, its meaning is still being settled. The truth is still being cleared of centuries of systematic denial.

With the academy still bringing sixteenth-century England into focus, we should not be surprised that much of the reading public and virtually the entire entertainment industry remain in the thrall of Tudors who never existed. Whether this will ever change—whether the cartoon versions of Henry VIII and Elizabeth I that now shine in the celebrity heavens alongside James Dean and the Incredible Hulk will ever give way to something with a better connection to reality—is anybody's guess. Perhaps such a change is no longer possible. It is certainly not going to happen as a consequence of this book. I do entertain the more modest hope, however, that a single volume aimed at introducing the entire dynasty to a general readership might prove useful in two ways: by helping to show that the true story of the Tudors is much richer and more fascinating than the fantasy version, and by showing also that the whole story is vastly greater than the sum of its parts. That it contains depths and dimensions that cannot be brought to light by focusing exclusively on Henry VIII, Elizabeth I, or any other single member of the family. That if it is as deeply tragic as I believe it to be—as I hope I have shown it to be—the extent of the tragedy can become clear only when the five reigns are joined together in a narrative arc that begins with Henry VII building a great legacy out of almost nothing, moves on to his son's extravagant abuse of a magnificent inheritance, and follows the son's three children as, one after another and in their joltingly different ways, they attempt to cope with what their father had wrought. If a writer should have an excuse for adding to the endless stream of Tudor literature, I therefore offer these: that not enough has been done to deal with the Tudor dynasty as a continuum, a unity, and that popular perceptions of the family have fallen so far behind scholarly understanding that it is necessary to try, at least, to narrow the gap.

I disavow any claim to competing with, never mind replacing, the many splendid biographies of the Tudor monarchs and their spouses, agents, and victims that have appeared over the last half-century or so. To the contrary, I have drawn heavily on many such works in assembling the facts with which to weave my story, and I am not merely in their debt but could scarcely have even begun without them. And I am mindful that my approach carries a price: dealing with five reigns obviously makes it impossible to provide the depth of detail available in (to cite just one distinguished example) J. J. Scarisbrick's magisterial *Henry VIII*. But it seems fair to question whether so much detail is necessary or even desirable in a work aimed at a general readership, and in any case forgoing it brings a gain too. The story of the whole dynasty is not only bigger in obvious ways than any biography—encompassing more personalities, more drama, more astoundingly grand and ugly events—but also, if paradoxically, *deeper* in one not-insignificant sense. The story of any one Tudor becomes fully rounded only when set in the context of what had come before and what followed, with causes and effects sketched in.

Not being a work of scholarship in anything like a strict and academic sense—not the fruit of deep tunneling into original source materials—this book is not intended for professional Tudor scholars. I can only express my gratitude to the members of that community, most of whom will be familiar with my facts and my arguments and some of whom (any still attached to the old conception of the Tudors as "builders of England's glory," certainly) are likely to reject my conclusions. In any case those conclusions, based on years of reading and reflection, are my responsibility entirely and not to be blamed on anyone else.

I am indebted to my editor, John Flicker, whose suggestions unfailingly prove to be perceptive and helpful (even and perhaps especially the ones I don't welcome at first), to my agent, Judith Riven, for her unflagging support and encouragement, and above all to my partner, Sandra Rose, who cheerfully shared and endured the whole years-long, life-devouring process.

G. J. Meyer
Goring-on-Thames, England
June 2009

PART ONE

*A King Too Soon and
a Queen Too Late*

1547–1558

1

A New Beginning

With the death of Henry VIII, the supreme headship of the church in England, the authority to decide what every man and woman in the kingdom was required to believe about God and salvation and the nature of ultimate reality, passed to a nine-year-old child. Little Edward Tudor, upon becoming King Edward VI, was recognized by church and state alike as the one person empowered by God to resolve conflicts over doctrine and practice that divided the most powerful and learned of his subjects.

It would have been a challenging situation under the best of circumstances. England's experience of being ruled by boys had been mercifully limited but not very happy. Even in the days before the Crown was responsible not only for the government but for a fractured and fractious church, it had been an experience of struggles for power punctuated with betrayal, bloodshed, and disorder. In the late 1540s, under the circumstances that Henry had created with his jumble of innovations, rule by a child-king was a recipe for trouble, little better than an absurdity. With a restless population kept quiet only by the threat of armed force, and with court and church divided into factions that hated each other mortally, the chances that Edward's minority could be passed without serious difficulty must have seemed slim indeed.

The church of Henry's making was, at the time of his death, emphatically not Roman Catholic but just as emphatically not Lutheran (the

king having made it a capital crime to follow Luther in denying free will
or believing in justification by faith alone). The new theology contradicted itself so boldly on so many points as to border on incoherence: in
the King's Book of 1543, for example, Henry had forbidden the very use
of the word *purgatory,* but then in his will he made provision for thousands of masses to be said for the repose of his soul (which could only
have benefited if it were in something like purgatory). The result was
confusion, contention, and division on a scale without precedent.

The main points of dispute were familiar by now. They ranged from
free will to justification by faith, from whether the eucharistic bread and
wine were literally the body and blood of Jesus Christ (Henry and
Luther had both affirmed this, but increasingly influential Swiss theologians denied it and were winning over Englishmen as eminent as Archbishop Cranmer) to whether religious statues and pictures should be
destroyed as idolatrous and practices that had been at the center of English religious life for a millennium should be banned as superstitious.
Disagreement was almost boundless, debate smoldered just below the
surface of public life in spite of Henry's readiness to condemn anyone
who disputed his truth, and the dangers of the situation were compounded by the fact that so many people believed the questions at issue
to be matters of eternal life and death. People in every camp, if not always prepared to die in defense of their positions, were prepared to kill
to prevent others from luring the population into the fires of hell.

In the final weeks of Henry's life, as the various organs of his huge
body began to malfunction and he became incapable even of rising from
his bed, he had focused the last of his strength on arrangements for
holding the kingdom together until his son grew old enough to take
charge. Someone, or some group, was going to have to manage the
kingdom in Edward's name, probably for almost a decade. Finding such
a person would not be as simple as it had been in similar situations in the
past. The royal family was small: Henry had no brother or uncle entitled
by blood to rule on the boy-king's behalf, and his only adult child, Mary,
the former princess, remained illegitimate in consequence of the annul-
ment of her parents' marriage. Mary's legal status would have made her
an unsuitable candidate to serve as regent during her half-brother's minority even if Henry had trusted her on the supremacy, which he rightly
did not.

The central contest continued to be between the traditionalists, who wanted the religion of their ancestors regardless of whether they secretly accepted the leadership of the pope, and the evangelicals, a diverse party united by its contempt for the old church and a determination to restore what its adherents believed to have been the purity and simplicity of earliest Christianity. Henry, whether by craft or good luck, had since his break with Rome been able to maintain a balance between the two sides, dividing the highest offices of church and state between them while leavening his own conservative pronouncements on doctrine and dogma with enough reformist measures to keep both sides insecure. The traditionalists, the most prominent of whom were by the mid-1540s Thomas Howard, Duke of Norfolk, and Stephen Gardiner, bishop of Winchester, undoubtedly represented by a wide margin the greatest part of England's population. Though evangelicals hostile to the old ways had been prominent at court at least since the days of Anne Boleyn, King Henry's conservatism had always required them to tread carefully and appear more conservative than they actually were. This had become more true than ever after Thomas Cromwell began to fall out of favor; it was then that Henry lost his appetite for religious innovation and made it a crime punishable with death to reject Catholic orthodoxy in favor of the Lutheran beliefs he despised. By the early 1540s it must have seemed inevitable that, if Henry ever made provision for the governing of England after he was dead and before Edward attained his majority, he would reinforce the position of the traditionalists. Even if he made no such provision, conservative dominance after his death must have seemed practically certain. Most of England's clergy, most of the bishops included, belonged to the traditionalist camp. So did most of the population, the nobles, and the gentry. On their side they had the law of the land: the Six Articles, with which Parliament had upheld the real presence and clerical celibacy. On their side, too, they had the King's Book, which to the horror of the evangelicals had affirmed the traditional creed and all seven of the Catholic sacraments. As a final bulwark they had Henry's heresy laws, which made it a capital crime not to believe as the king believed.

Thus the evangelicals could preach as they believed only at the risk of their lives. Even if they had been left free to express themselves, they would have been a tiny and scorned minority almost everywhere except at the universities and in London and southeastern England, and even in those places they remained a minority, though not such a tiny one or nearly so scorned. Remarkably, however, from the start of Edward's reign they assumed a position of such complete dominance that with astonishing speed the official religion became more radically evangelical and reformist than Henry could ever have intended or imagined. And it was Henry, improbably enough, who had made this possible. How did it happen? The answer is almost certainly not to be found in anything like an end-of-life shift in the king's thinking in favor of justification by faith or any of the other foundation stones of evangelical thought. It lay, more likely, in the fact that in the last years of his life Henry was a solitary and profoundly lonely man.

Henry was alone as only a man can be who is feared by nearly everyone with whom he has contact, who believes that he alone has the truth on every subject of real importance so that there is no need to converse or listen but only to pronounce, and who has cast away or even destroyed one after another of the people to whom he had been closest earlier in his life when he was still capable of being close to anyone. At the end of his life he was no longer capable of any such thing. He exalted his little son as the jewel of England but rarely saw him. If he dined with his daughters, they sat not at the same table as their father but beneath him, and at a distance. He had threatened the life of his sixth and last wife, Catherine Parr, for her reformist religious views and summoned neither her nor any of his children to be with him for his last Christmas or the beginning of what would turn out to be his last year.

Still, the very fact that he had married Catherine despite being far along in his physical decline is suggestive of neediness, and the marriage was significant even if it produced no offspring and in all likelihood was never consummated. Catherine like Anne Boleyn before her was a fervent evangelical, and as the king's wife she was able to take a hand in the education of his children. Thus was the child Edward placed in the care of tutors who began the process by which he became an evangelical of an exceptionally militant bent. Thus, too, Queen Catherine's brother William Parr, an elegant gentleman of deficient judgment but like her a supporter of religious reform, was made Earl of Essex (the same title that Cromwell had been given not long before his death) and joined the increasingly influential evangelical faction on the Privy Council, the innermost circle of royal advisers.

The king's neediness helps to explain the survival, almost alone among the men who had been important in church or state when Henry was still married to Catherine of Aragon, of Thomas Cranmer. Cranmer's religious views had never meshed well with Henry's, really, and for years he had to conceal the fact of his marriage from a king who to the end of his life insisted on a celibate clergy. But Cranmer became and was able to remain archbishop of Canterbury because no matter what happened, no matter what the king demanded, he was always compliant. Though he had his own beliefs and his own agenda for reform, and though those beliefs became increasingly radical with the passage of the years and he became increasingly ambitious in pursuit of his agenda, the side of himself that he allowed the king to see was unfailingly submissive. He lived in a style reminiscent of Wolsey's, with four palaces and a small private army, but he was unfailingly careful never to do anything that might be construed as a challenge to royal authority. Thus Henry found it possible to trust Cranmer as he trusted no other man, perhaps even, in a way, to love him. And thus the senior bishopric of the English church remained in the hands of a confirmed enemy of the old religion, a man who in his innermost being utterly rejected many of the things that the conservatives, his royal master among them, believed most strongly. Cranmer was infinitely easier to work with, to manage, than the most prominent of the conservative bishops, Stephen Gardiner. Gardiner was *too* conservative, too proud, too firm in his beliefs ever to coexist comfortably with a ruler as self-willed as Henry even though the two of them were never far apart in doctrine. Gardiner came as close to displaying a mind of his own as it was possible for a bishop to do while retaining his position (and staying alive) in the England of the 1530s and 1540s. He never seemed as dependable as Cranmer made himself appear. And so it was almost inevitable, when Henry began to plan seriously for the succession, that Gardiner would be dismissed and Cranmer would prosper.

The same sort of dynamic worked to the advantage of other men whose religious opinions had little in common with Henry's. The excellent family connections that had brought Jane Seymour to Henry's court as a lady-in-waiting first to Catherine of Aragon and then to Anne Boleyn also created opportunities for her brothers Edward and Thomas. The elder of the pair, Edward, was about thirty-five years old when his sister became queen and had been in royal service almost from childhood. He had had some success, being knighted while with the English army in France in 1523 and later becoming master of horse to King Henry's illegitimate son the Duke of Richmond, but he was still a mere esquire of the body when his sister was chosen as the king's third bride. The marriage changed his life completely. In 1536, the year of the wedding, he was made a gentleman of the privy chamber—one of the privileged few with free access to the king's private apartments—and raised to the nobility as Viscount Beauchamp. The following year, the year of Prince Edward's birth and Jane's death, he was made Earl of Hertford and given a number of coveted offices including a seat on the Privy Council.

Little is known of whether Edward and Jane Seymour had a close relationship—before her death she showed herself to be attached to the old religion, while he was strongly inclined in the other direction—but in any case her death did nothing to interrupt his rise. He retained the confidence of the king, who, when he resumed his wars in 1544, appointed Seymour lord lieutenant in the north and gave him an army with which to invade Scotland. Seymour proved a capable commander, hesitantly at first but then energetically carrying out the king's instructions not only to capture Edinburgh but to lay waste to it and everything surrounding. Later that same year he was with Henry at the capture of Boulogne, which he was rumored to have made possible by bribing the commander of the French defenders. In 1545 he was in command at Boulogne, routing a superior French force that attempted to retake it. He then returned to Scotland, where he conducted a scorched-earth campaign even more devastating than the one of the previous year. In 1546, yet again in command at Boulogne, he negotiated a treaty under which England was to retain possession of that city until 1554 and then allow the French king to buy it. By this point it was clear that Henry had come to rely heavily on his brother-in-law in war and diplomacy, and that Seymour was not unworthy of the king's confidence.

Henry had another reason to put his trust in Seymour. Born a commoner though with a tincture of royal blood, Seymour could never possibly aspire to the throne. He owed his place in the world, his title and position and the wealth he was rapidly accumulating, entirely to the fact that he was uncle to the Prince of Wales, who of course had no uncles on the paternal side. Seymour had every reason to want Edward to live and prosper, and everything to lose if Edward were to die or somehow be removed from the throne. In searching for someone who seemed capable of managing the kingdom during his son's minority, of waging war if necessary and holding the government together, Henry had to look no further than to Seymour. Best of all, it was not necessary to fear that in a crisis Seymour would subordinate his nephew's interests to his own. Seymour could never become a Richard III. He could help himself, save himself from the enemies that his rapid rise and his unfriendliness to the conservatives had inevitably created, only by preserving the child. The interests of the two were inextricably intertwined.

It was much the same in the case of the leading lay conservative, the leader of one of the last of the grand old noble families that for centuries had possessed so much land and had at their command so many armed men as to make them an effective counterweight to royal power. Thomas Howard, Duke of Norfolk, was seventy-three in 1546, still tough and vigorous though nearly old enough to be the father of a king supposedly dying of old age, and he had spent his long life serving the Tudors at home and abroad, in peace and in war. Grandson of the Duke of Norfolk who had died fighting on the side of Richard III at Bosworth Field in 1485, son of the Howard who was restored to the Norfolk title after destroying a Scots army at Flodden in 1513, he himself had led his father's vanguard at Flodden and had gone on to serve as lord lieutenant in Ireland and commander of English armies in the north and in France. His shrewd if unscrupulous management of the Pilgrimage of Grace may very well have saved King Henry from ruin. Though the Howards like the Seymours (and, for that matter, like a number of noble and gentry families) had a touch of royal blood from generations back, and though Norfolk's first wife had, like Henry VIII's mother, been one of the numerous daughters of Edward IV (she died young, and none of their four children survived), the family had no plausible claim to the throne and no illusions on that score. Three times in the space of a decade, marriages had created the possibility that the Tudors and the Howards would be permanently linked by blood. Norfolk's daughter

Mary had been wed to Henry Fitzroy, the king's bastard, but that had come to nothing as a result of Fitzroy's early death. King Henry's disastrous marriages to two of Norfolk's nieces, Anne Boleyn and Catherine Howard, had served as persuasive reminders of the dangers of aspiring too high. As an ambitious but sensible dynast, Norfolk would have been content to remain first among the peers of the realm and a faithful servant first of Henry and then of his son.

That did not, however, turn out to be possible. To the Seymours and other "new men" around the king—men who had not inherited their high places, but had been elevated to them in consequence of winning Henry's favor—Norfolk was like Gardiner a rival, an obstacle, and a threat. Both had to be neutered, removed if possible, if the Seymour faction were to achieve and maintain control. From about 1544 events began to turn in the Seymours' favor. Norfolk found himself criticized by the king for not conducting his military operations more aggressively in France. (He replied, not unreasonably, that he had been given neither the men nor the munitions to accomplish what Henry demanded.) Edward Seymour, at almost the same time, was ravaging Scotland and delighting the king with his reports of devastation. Two years later, in the last year of Henry's life, Norfolk's son Henry, Earl of Surrey, was replaced by Seymour as commander of the garrison at Boulogne. Upon negotiating his settlement with the French, Seymour returned to court, where he found himself in higher favor than ever with the failing king and therefore easily able to win the friendship of the most well placed of the evangelicals. Among them were William Paget, the king's principal secretary; Queen Catherine and her brother Essex; second gentleman of the privy chamber Anthony Denny; and—most fatefully for the long term—a hitherto obscure soldier named John Dudley, recently elevated to the Privy Council and to the post of lord high admiral. Even conservatives as prominent as Thomas Wriothesley, the new lord chancellor, sought to establish good relations with Seymour as they saw which way the political winds were blowing, and with what force. Seymour's importance even before the death of the king is apparent in the fact that the Privy Council began holding its meetings at his home rather than at any of the royal palaces.

Norfolk and his son Surrey found themselves elbowed aside by the very men who wanted to persuade the king that the entire Howard clan was not to be trusted. The enmity between the two groups was bitter and had deep roots: as early as 1537, Surrey, then only about twenty, had been taken into custody for striking Edward Seymour, who that very year became King Henry's brother-in-law and a viscount with a place on the council. This happened at Hampton Court Palace, and the pre-scribed penalty for such an act of violence on royal premises was loss of the right hand. Surrey, whose hopes for a military career hung in the bal-ance, was saved by the intervention of Cromwell. As recently as 1546 an argument around the Privy Council's table had ended with Seymour striking Bishop Gardiner, who as a leading conservative was linked to the Howards, in the face. Two years before that, with the council in-creasingly under Seymour domination, the bishop's personal secretary and nephew, Germaine Gardiner, had been put to death after being charged with denying the royal supremacy. Much more than political advantage was at stake here, obviously. These were men who hated and feared each other intensely and had good reason to do so.

No one was more intense than Surrey, who shared his father's high pride in their family's ancient lineage (actually far more ancient and noble in the female than in the male line, the Howards themselves being rather recent upstarts who had married well) and his disdain for the new men by whom they saw themselves being supplanted. What he lacked, tragically, was the political savvy, the craftiness, that had made it possi-ble for his grandfather to erase the stigma of having fought on the wrong side at Bosworth Field and finally claw his way back to preemi-nence among the noble families of England. Surrey was brilliant—an ac-complished classicist, a poet of very nearly the highest order—but also arrogant and reckless almost to the point of madness. He had an obses-sive, anachronistically medieval conception of personal honor. His life-long pursuit of military glory had been punctuated with pridefully self-destructive acts; his striking of Edward Seymour, whom he was in-capable of accepting as an equal, much less as senior in rank, was merely a remarkably vivid example.

With the king visibly failing and increasingly susceptible to their sug-gestions, Seymour and his following saw an opportunity to finish off their rivals. They ensnared Gardiner in a clumsy but effective trap, telling the king that the bishop had refused a request that he exchange some properties belonging to his see of Winchester for lands belonging to the Crown. It is understandable if Gardiner had in fact been reluctant to agree to such a deal—trades advantageous to the Crown had become a subtle way of plundering the dioceses—but it is unlikely that he would have flatly refused. Gardiner himself protested that he had simply expressed a wish to discuss the matter with the king. In the end he had to submit an apology and surrender his seat on the council. If there had ever been any chance that he would figure in the king's plans for the management of the kingdom after Prince Edward succeeded, that chance was now lost. He did, however, survive. He remained not only free but bishop of Winchester.

The Howards were not so fortunate. On December 12 father and son were confined in the Tower amid rumors that they had been planning to seize control of the government in the event of the king's death, planning to abduct Prince Edward, and other, similar nonsense. When in January 1547 they were charged, however, it was for no such offense. Surrey was accused of committing high treason by using the heraldic emblems of Edward the Confessor, a Saxon monarch whose reign had preceded the Norman Conquest, and thereby staking a claim to the crown. Norfolk was charged with being aware of his son's treason and failing to report it. When put on trial, Surrey defended himself vigorously and at length, pointing out that his ancestors had displayed the same arms that were now alleged to be treasonous and had experienced no difficulty as a result of doing so. It was by no means clear that the jury was prepared to convict until Secretary Paget brought word that the king demanded a guilty verdict. Surrey was beheaded six days later. Thereafter Norfolk, in an effort to save himself, sent the king a letter of submission in which he pleaded guilty to "keeping secret the acts of my son, Henry earl of Surrey, in using the arms of St. Edward the Confessor, which pertain only to kings." It did no good. Norfolk was attainted by Parliament, so that he had no opportunity to answer the charges against him, all his possessions became the property of the Crown, and the king could order his execution whenever he wished. On January 26 Henry signed the necessary order, which was to be carried out the next day; but when the sun rose on January 27, Henry was dead and the council became afraid to proceed. The old duke, a pauper now, paced his cell waiting to learn his fate.

Henry's Third Succession Act had authorized him to appoint a Regency Council to govern if his son inherited while still a child. Many of the king's last hours of consciousness were spent in consultation first with his secretary Paget, then with Paget and Edward Seymour, and finally with a wider circle to decide who would be named executors of his will and the new king's regents. Gardiner and Norfolk were out, absolutely. So was anyone too closely associated with either of them—the bishop of the new see of Westminster, for example, because he had been "schooled" by Gardiner, whom Henry described as being of "so troublesome a nature" that if he were included no one would be able to control him. The Regency Council was by no means uniformly evangelical; Henry ensured a measure of balance by appointing such figures as Cuthbert Tunstal, the bishop of Durham who, a decade and a half before, had made himself a nuisance with his objections to the royal supremacy. But when all the names had been filled in, the list was dominated on the clerical side by Archbishop Cranmer and bishops affiliated with him, and on the lay side by Seymour and his cohorts. The evangelicals had won the last throw of the dice, the one that decided the long contest for control of policy that the whole final decade of Henry's reign had turned into.

Under the terms of Henry's will, the sixteen members of the Regency Council were to be equals and all decisions were to require approval of the group as a whole. If this is really what Henry intended, he was being exceedingly unrealistic: his arrangement left not only the council but the kingdom in desperate need of a chief executive. Edward Seymour recognized this need and put himself forward to fill the void, and his friends on the council were so quick to support him that the public learned of his appointment as lord protector of the realm and governor of the new king's person almost before they knew that the old king was dead. It is not certain that this was a usurpation; Charles V's ambassador reported seeing a letter bearing King Henry's signature that bestowed the duties of lord protector upon his brother-in-law.

Nor is there any way of knowing whether Seymour and his cohorts were, as they claimed, simply carrying out the king's wishes when they made it almost their first matter of business to heap rewards upon themselves. Henry's will instructed his executors to make good on any promises that he had made before his death, and when the Regency Council sought to find out what was intended by this, it could turn only to the three of its own members who had been most in the king's company during the last weeks of his life: Anthony Denny, William Paget, and Seymour himself. They reported that "the king, being on his death-bed put in mind of what he had promised, ordered it *to be put in his will* [emphasis added], that his executors should perform everything that should appear to have been promised by him." They then went on to provide details. What they disclosed was, if a true statement of Henry's intentions, an act of extraordinary generosity on the part of a king who knew all too well that he was leaving his son an empty treasury, heavy debts, and ruined credit. If it was not true, Seymour and the others were thieves on a breathtaking scale. Certainly it is reasonable to suspect that the whole thing had been fabricated for their benefit. The statement that Henry was on his deathbed when he added to his will instructions for the carrying out of his promises is not easily squared with the fact that the will itself was almost certainly completed and signed weeks before he died and well before he or anyone else had reason to think that death was imminent. But the entire record of the king's final weeks—of what he actually did and said, and when he did and said it—is an impossible tangle of contradictions and ambiguities.

What is certain is that, well before Henry's body was put to rest, the closest associates of his last days declared that among the "unfulfilled gifts" he would have bestowed if he had lived were new titles for them and their friends. Thus, supposedly in keeping with the king's wishes, Edward Seymour was elevated from Earl of Hertford to Duke of Somerset, William Parr from Earl of Essex to Marquess of Northampton, and Seymour's henchmen John Dudley and Chancellor Wriothesley to the earldoms of Warwick and Southampton respectively. Six knights, Thomas Seymour, Richard Rich, and Paget among them, were made barons, and to all these men and to others besides (Cranmer, for example, who as a clergyman could not receive a title, and Anthony Denny, who for some reason got no title) there were munificent disbursements of money and land. The new Duke of Somerset—we will use that name for Edward Seymour henceforth, to distinguish him from his brother Thomas Lord Seymour of Sudeley—did best of all. He was given four manors previously belonging to the Diocese of Lincoln, seven from the Diocese of Bath and Wells, and tracts of church land at Westminster on which he would soon begin building the magnificent Somerset House with stones hauled in from ruined monasteries. He was also granted the incomes of the treasurership of one cathedral, the deanship of another, and prebends (chapter memberships) at six others. Overall this splendid payday transferred lands generating income of £27,000 annually to private hands, nearly half in the form of gifts for which the recipients paid nothing. If these benefactions were in fact expressions of the late king's wishes and not merely an act of plunder by which Somerset enriched himself and rewarded his allies, they did in fact accomplish the second purpose as well as the first.

There was trouble all the same. Thomas Seymour was as ambitious as his elder brother, he would soon show himself to be every bit as ruthless, and now he was unable to see why he—no less an uncle of the king than Somerset—should not have a more important part in the new regime. Somerset, in addition to being lord protector and governor, had taken for himself the offices of high steward, great chamberlain, lord treasurer, and earl marshal. Thomas Seymour regarded it as an indignity that he was only a baron, and that his only office—aside from his seat on the council—was that of master of ordnance, a job he had been given more than two years earlier, when King Henry was still alive and active. He argued that the posts of protector and governor should not be held by one man, and that he, by virtue of his blood relationship with the king, should have one of them. Somerset refused but attempted to appease his brother by surrendering the office of great chamberlain (a lucrative one involving custodianship of royal lands) to John Dudley, the new Earl of Warwick, who in turn resigned the office of lord high admiral in favor of Thomas Seymour. But Seymour was not at all satisfied, turning his attention and energy not to his new naval responsibilities but to securing the kinds of honors to which he thought himself entitled. Later in the year, when Somerset and Dudley went north to resume the war on the Scots, Seymour remained behind in London to make mischief in his brother's absence and pay court to Dowager Queen Catherine, with whom he had had a budding romance years before until the king took an interest in the lady.

A more pressing problem emerged in the person of Thomas Wriothesley, lord chancellor and new Earl of Southampton. During the last half-decade of Henry's reign Wriothesley had been one of the chief instruments through whom the king discouraged religious innovation and tried to achieve a national uniformity based on the kind of conservatism set forth in the Six Articles. He himself was as conservative a major figure as was to be found on the Regency Council, and though he had offered no objections to Somerset's appointment as lord protector (his share in the "unfulfilled gifts" must have helped to make him cooperative), soon thereafter he began to make a nuisance of himself. He insisted that there should be no significant departures from the terms of the late king's will and that no religious reforms should be undertaken until the new king reached his maturity and could act in his own right. What gave particular offense was his insistence that Somerset must—as had been stipulated when he became lord protector—take no action without the approval of a majority of the council.

Somerset had no intention of accepting any of these strictures, but he quickly ran up against a complication. Wriothesley, as chancellor, had custody of the king's Great Seal, without which no order that Somerset might issue or have issued over the king's signature could be binding. And, being a strong-willed politician who knew how to use the powers of his office to good advantage, Wriothesley would allow no use of the seal in matters of which he did not approve. The solution proved to be relatively simple. Judges subservient to Somerset declared Wriothesley guilty of having abused his office. (The charge was transparently trumped up; Wriothesley was technically guilty, but only of the previously acceptable practice of delegating judicial responsibilities that his duties at court left him with no time to perform.) He was stripped of his office and placed under arrest. The newly ennobled Richard Lord Rich, ready as always to do whatever was required by whoever was in power, was dispatched to collect the seal. Somerset then used the seal to stamp and thereby make official a letter of patent, signed by his nephew the king, by which he was given the power to appoint and remove members of the Privy Council, into which the Regency Council was now absorbed. He also empowered himself to assemble the council (or just as important, decline to assemble it) "as he shall think meet . . . from time to time."

This was all Somerset needed to begin exercising the authority of a king. He secured Rich's appointment as chancellor, thinking that this would ensure his control of the Great Seal. He began to live in royal fashion, ordering that two gold maces be carried before him wherever he went. That his rule would be less savage than Henry's was signaled when Wriothesley was freed, excused from paying the heavy fine that had been levied against him, and allowed to keep most of the winnings of his long career at court. He was even allowed to return to the council where, while taking care not to go so far as to put himself at risk, he continued to resist the majority's efforts to shift the church in a markedly evangelical direction.

At the center of all this turmoil, sometimes seen but almost never heard, was the small figure of King Edward VI. He was a solitary figure: a boy who had never known a mother, had grown up worshipping a distant father who appeared to be the mightiest man in the world, and had spent most of his life in a household separate from those of his father and two half-sisters. Though Catherine Parr appears to have been an attentive and even affectionate stepmother, soon after Henry's death her attention was drawn in other directions. Edward was a lad of above-average intelligence (all the Tudors were that), if not necessarily the prodigious genius that some of his tutors and courtiers claimed. He was also an exceptionally conscientious child, so serious about the rigorous course of study to which he was subjected from the earliest possible age and his responsibilities as a great king's heir that in learning about his upbringing one begins to wish for more evidence of play, and playfulness. Probably it would have been better, if only for Edward himself, if he had been less obedient to the learned men who were always on hand to direct his development into a great, good, and wise ruler worthy of his father. If he had been given more time and space in which to be a child.

His coronation, the first of a king of England in nearly four decades, was an outsize event, grandiose but rather sadly overwhelming for a child to have to endure alone. It was preceded, three weeks after Henry's death and just days after his embalmed corpse had been lowered into a crypt beneath the floor of St. George's Chapel at Windsor Castle, by a four-hour parade during which the new king, dressed in cloth of silver and gold and mounted on a horse draped with satin and pearls, was put on display for the people of the metropolis. The next day, February 20, Edward entered Westminster Abbey at the center of a vast procession, a bishop flanking him on one side and an earl on the other, the long train of his crimson robe carried by John Dudley, William Parr, and his uncle Thomas Seymour. There he was anointed king. The ceremony was conducted according to a formula that had been used on every such occasion since 1375. Cranmer, however, in his capacity of master of ceremonies, had introduced changes underscoring the new powers that Henry VIII had gathered to the Crown and the fact that for the first time in history a new king was becoming not only head of state but also head of the church. A traditional promise to respect the laws and liberties of the English people was expunged from the coronation oath; henceforth the king would decide which laws and liberties to grant and which to deny. "Peace and concord" were promised to the church and the people but not, as in the past, to the clergy; now it was for the king to decide whether the clergy deserved peace. Somerset and Cranmer together placed three crowns in succession on Edward's head—one each for England, France, and Ireland, Henry VIII having been the first English king to fashion himself king of Ireland. Then all the bishops and nobles came forward in pairs to pay homage, lowering themselves to their knees and swearing in unison to be loyal. Finally Cranmer delivered a sermon that he addressed not to the whole assembly but to Edward alone. The boy was told that nothing he had just sworn should be interpreted as limiting the right that God had bestowed on him to rule in whatever way he thought best. There was a half-concealed message in this, and it was unmistakably evangelical: the king was not bound by law. Emphatically he was not bound by such laws as Henry VIII's Six Articles. To the extent that the king was bound by anything, Cranmer said, he was bound by a duty that was primarily religious, and religious in an evangelical way. It was, "as God's viceregent and Christ's vicar, to see that God be worshipped and idolatry be destroyed; that the tyranny of the bishop of Rome be banished and images be removed." Cranmer, who by this time had abandoned whatever belief he might once have had in transubstantiation, then went through the elaborate motions of the traditional solemn high mass.

He had placed a heavy burden on the shoulders of a boy of nine, one that many normal and healthy boys might have cheerfully ignored. But the melancholy fact is that Edward regarded such matters with a solemnity that would have seemed more fitting in a pious cleric deep into middle age. His early education, under the supervision first of his stepmother Catherine Parr and then, from age six, of Archbishop Cranmer, had provided intense exposure to evangelical doctrine along with inoculation against what he was taught to see as the monstrous absurdities of the old religion. Cranmer placed him in the hands of scholars as accomplished and committed as any that evangelical England had produced up to that time. Hugh Latimer, who in 1539 had lost his position as bishop of Worcester because his insistence on radical reform had put him too far out of step with Henry's orthodoxy, was brought to court soon after Edward became king. From a special pulpit installed for the purpose, he delivered hour-long sermons that Edward dutifully watched from one of the windows of his privy chamber, taking detailed notes. The boy embraced what he was taught, forming firm opinions on immensely complex subjects at a prodigiously early age. It is more pathetic than impressive to see him, at age ten, producing under the approving eyes of his tutors a lengthy treatise in which he considers the claims of the pope to headship over the church and concludes not only that these claims are invalid but that the bishop of Rome is "the true son of the devil, a bad man, an Antichrist and an abominable tyrant." By this time he was certain, as he would remain for the rest of his life, that the religion of his father with its seven sacraments and toleration of images and purgatory and free will was nearly as great an abomination as Roman Catholicism itself. If he rebelled, it was against the traditionalism of his dead father, not against his own mentors.

All of which was entirely acceptable to his uncle Somerset, most of whose supporters in the court and council were zealous reformers genuinely committed to the evangelical cause. The coronation of the new king had been a thrilling event for these people, promising an outlet for their contemptuous opinion of the old dogmas and an opportunity to cast off the dead weight of the past in favor of something cleaner, something capable of remaking the world. They wanted a religious revolution vastly more ambitious than anything Henry VIII had attempted, a replacement of idols and false sacraments and empty superstitious practices with the direct authority of Scripture. If they also had a hearty appetite for whatever riches it might still be possible to extract from the church, that did not mean they were necessarily less than sincere in their convictions.

They faced formidable obstacles—so much so that, in spite of controlling the person of the king and the principal levers of power in both

state and church, they continued to think of themselves as a beleaguered and even oppressed minority. Virtually all the laws and pronouncements of Henry VIII were against them: the Six Articles, the
King's Book, and the heresy statutes that put their lives at risk at least
theoretically every time they gave voice to what they believed. Most of
the people of England, even most of the clergy, had no liking for their
ideas. Throughout the first year of the new reign, therefore, they had to
proceed carefully. They began the process of imposing their theology
on the kingdom, but always with an eye to keeping their adversaries off
balance. When accused of preaching what was unlawful, they replied in-
genuously that they were merely saying what the late king had believed
at the time of his death but had not lived long enough to express in law.
To complaints that they were advocating change of a kind that should
not be attempted before Edward came of age, they responded in tones
of innocence that they were doing no such thing—that they accepted
the Six Articles as the law of the land and recognized that heresy remained a capital crime. Meanwhile they were actively carrying out their
revolution, but by such small steps that it was difficult for the traditionalists to know where to lay down a challenge. Even as they advanced
their agenda, the evangelicals continued to insist that they wanted nothing more than peace and continuity and the unity of the church.

That they actually wanted nothing of the kind first became plain in
August 1547, seven months after the old king's death, when Somerset
sent official "visitors" to every diocese. These representatives of the
Crown delivered to the bishops a set of sermons to be read in every
church every Sunday. This was provocative: the sermons were the work
of Cranmer, who by now had abandoned any pretense of believing
what he had professed during the reign of his master Henry, and their
content was in direct contradiction not only to Henry's Articles but to
what an overwhelming majority of the clergy and indeed the population still believed. Even more provocatively, the visitors had oral instructions that went far beyond their written commissions, and in pursuit of
those instructions they launched a campaign—shocking to most people
in every part of the country—of physical destruction. Magnificent
stained-glass windows, an irreplaceable part of England's medieval
legacy, were condemned as idolatrous and smashed to bits. The same
thing happened to statuary, to paintings, and to the ancient adornments

of church buildings everywhere. Whole libraries of Latin works, even the library of Oxford University, were put to the torch. Barbaric as such acts may seem today, to the radical evangelicals they were something to be celebrated, a necessary step in freeing England from a filthily papist past.

For Stephen Gardiner, the disgraced bishop of Winchester, all this was too much to be borne. Protesting that the Cranmer sermons contradicted the doctrines of the English church as established by Parliament under the late king, he accused the archbishop of contradicting what he himself had claimed to believe when Henry was alive. For this he was thrown into prison; clearly the evangelicals no longer saw any point in trying to seem conciliatory. Neither Somerset nor Cranmer could afford to have Gardiner at liberty to rally the forces of tradition when a new Parliament was called later in the year. The evangelicals had big plans for that Parliament—plans that Gardiner was likely to oppose to his last breath.

First, however, Somerset wanted to deal with Scotland, which had been almost an obsession for him since his two invasions in the closing years of Henry's reign. Scotland at this time was in a state approaching civil war, with an evangelical faction friendly to England fighting a Catholic, pro-French faction for control of Edinburgh and custody of Queen Mary, still a child of four. Somerset assembled an army of twenty thousand men, many of them mercenaries recruited at great cost from distant parts of Europe, and started north with John Dudley as his second in command. They crossed the River Tweed early in September, and on the tenth day of that month they met and destroyed the Scottish defenders at the Battle of Pinkie, a rout that ended in the slaughter of nearly ten thousand Scots. Edinburgh remained in the hands of England's enemies, however, and Somerset surprised those enemies and his own followers by declining to exploit the tremendous advantage his victory had given him. Instead he allowed his troops four days of pillaging and then hurried back to London.

He was now England's greatest living military hero in addition to having control of the Crown, Parliament, and the church. England was his to do with as he chose. It was also his to lose. Everything now depended upon his ability to manage what fate and his own boldness had put into his hands.

INSTRUMENTS OF POWER

THE REGENCY COUNCIL THAT HENRY VIII HAD CREATED TO manage England until the boy Edward grew up was a new variation—the latest of many variations—on an old, old theme. The rulers of England had always had councils, weak kings no less than strong ones all the way back to Saxon times, but the makeup and importance of those councils had varied drastically from one reign to the next. The idea of the royal council was a kind of blank slate on which each generation was free to write as it chose according to its own circumstances.

Why councils at all? Because history offers no examples of leaders of nations, even tyrannical leaders of nations, who were able to survive without finding competent advisers and listening to them, sharing some portion of their power with *somebody* and accepting the fact that, no matter how much they may have wanted to do everything themselves, that was simply impossible. For many hundreds of years, until the evolution of more modern instruments of government, royal councils were the best mechanisms available for dealing with that reality.

Even that flinty old killer William the Conqueror, after he crossed over from Normandy in 1066 and by brute force turned the whole of England into his personal property, immediately put a council in place. The most important men in the kingdom sat on it—the bishops, the half-civilized warlords who were William's tenants-in-chief—but everyone understood that it was the *king's* creature and existed to do his bidding. That would remain the rule for more than half a millennium, and England would depart from it only when something was deeply, seriously wrong. When the king was insane, for example, or otherwise unable to maintain control. Or when he was, like Edward VI, simply too young to take command.

The earliest Norman councils did everything: executed the king's orders, heard and passed judgment on complaints and appeals, settled disputes, and offered as much advice as the king was willing to take. But as the population grew and the economy developed and society grew more complicated, such a workload became unmanageable. Various functions were spun off one by one—an exchequer to manage the Crown's money, courts for the handling of different kinds of cases—and turned into governmental departments. One function, however, was never spun off: that of advising the king, of having a voice when policy was being decided. That was what made a seat on the council a prize. Always in principle and almost always in fact, being a councilor meant having access to the king, being able to speak directly with the king, having a chance to influence the king and win his favor.

The value of this access fluctuated, increasing at times to the point where councils became more powerful than the monarchs they formally served. This happened late in the fourteenth century, after Richard II came to the throne as a half-grown boy, and again in the fifteenth during the reign of Henry VI, the half-brother of Edmund and Jasper Tudor, who became king as an infant and even when grown was too weak a character to take back control of the council from magnates who were using it to bend the government and the judicial system to their own advantage.

Under the Tudors, the flexibility of government by council was put to new tests and not found wanting. In the course of his twenty-four-year reign the wily Henry VII appointed upward of 150 men to his council, but his doing so was an exercise in public relations intended to win the support of different interest groups—merchants, lawyers, soldiers—by allowing them to think that they were represented at the highest level. Real power was limited to an inner circle of perhaps a dozen men, many of them officers of the royal household and therefore the king's dependents, and council meetings were typically attended by only between six and ten members. Henry VII used the council's adaptability to devise a quick and simple solution to one of the most serious problems inherited from the Yorkists: England's sclerotic, cumbersome, and too-often-corrupt courts of law. He resurrected the council's aboriginal judicial function, encouraging subjects to bring their suits to it with the promise of receiving an impartial hearing at tolerable cost. Thus the councilors' traditional meeting place, the room at Westminster called the Star Chamber because of the decorations on its ceiling, became a famous and, for a long time, a respected source of royal justice. The lord chancellor, as the Court of the Star Chamber's presiding officer, would gradually be so burdened with its caseload that he was unable to function as the king's chief minister as in the past and became what he is today: Britain's senior law officer.

We saw earlier how young Henry VIII, when he first became king, had no interest in the routines of administration and so left the business of governing in the hands of his father's councilors, and how this ended when Thomas Wolsey became chancellor and drew the reins of power into his own hands. Throughout the decade and a half of Wolsey's ascendancy the council sank into unimportance, a development much resented by those nobles and others who felt excluded from decision-making. The workaholic Wolsey performed the considerable feat, never to be repeated by his successors, of simultaneously overseeing both the entire government *and* the courts, continuing to preside at sessions of the Star Chamber and giving high priority to improving the delivery of justice to ordinary subjects. On the negative side, he displayed an occasional tendency to use the Court of the Star Chamber as an instrument of discipline, a political weapon with which to punish people perceived as enemies. A century on, under the next dynasty, this tendency would become so pronounced that hatred for the court finally caused it to be destroyed.

Another action of Wolsey's that merits attention in this connection is his unprecedented capture of all the royal seals, the coinlike bas-relief carved figures that, when pressed into a blob of hot wax, certified the authenticity of documents such as grants, writs, warrants, subpoenas, and correspondence. In becoming chancellor, the cardinal had automatically taken custody of the king's Great Seal, which since its origins in pre-Conquest times had become so essential to the operations of government that its removal from the chancery at Westminster was forbidden. This had led to the creation of what was called the Privy Seal; it was smaller, simpler (it showed the king's arms rather than his picture), lawfully transportable, and so useful to the peripatetic monarchs of the Middle Ages that by the early fourteenth century its official keeper was one of the court's most important members. As administrative machinery was erected even around the Privy Seal, again the need arose for something simpler. Hence the signet, at first a "secret" seal, which was kept by the king's secretary and by the advent of the Tudors was even more important than the older, grander seals in the origination and authentication of important documents. It is a measure of Wolsey's unprecedented power that he became the first minister ever to achieve control of all three seals and thus of every item of official business.

It was however Thomas Cromwell, not Wolsey, who broke the patterns of the past and found genuinely new uses for old institutions including the council. He was content to allow Thomas More and then his own protégé Thomas Audley to occupy the office of lord chancellor and disappear into its judicial responsibilities. Instead he transformed the unencumbered position of king's principal secretary into a power base from which he made himself chief executive and, on the king's behalf, managed everything from the treasury to the church, from diplomacy to military affairs. Though Cromwell was far too canny to ignore the seals—as secretary he had possession of the signet, and in 1536 he took over the office of Lord Privy Seal from the ruined Thomas Boleyn—he demanded obedience on the basis of his own signature and by doing so allowed the use of seals to become an almost empty formality.

It was however in his use of the Royal Council that Cromwell displayed the full reach of his political genius. Wolsey had treated the council much as he treated Parliament: as a nuisance to be ignored when possible, bullied when necessary. Cromwell, by contrast, saw that the council, like Parliament, could be shaped into a tool of enormous value. In the mid-1530s he carved out of Henry VIII's excessively large and essentially useless council what would become one of the principal institutions of government: a *Privy Council* of purposely limited size (only nineteen members in the beginning and thereafter never many more than that). This new council was no longer too big to function but did have enough size to carry an important load of work. And it was, most importantly, a *working* council: each of its members brought either influence or special expertise to the table, and various members were put in charge of various activities—always, of course, under Cromwell's careful supervision—almost like a modern cabinet. In selecting the membership Cromwell strove for, and to a considerable extent achieved, a balance of power among the leading factions. Cranmer sat as representative of the religious reformers, Gardiner and Tunstal for the conservatives. There were members of the ancient nobility—the Duke of Norfolk, the Earl of Sussex—and of families recently raised to the peerage. Among the commoners were representatives of the old landowning gentry and men (solicitor-general Sir Richard Rich being once again among the favored) who had risen from obscure origins to positions of prominence in the royal service. Together they formed an instrument beautifully engineered to perform exactly as Cromwell, and the king, desired.

When Cromwell fell and no one emerged to take his place, the Privy Council simultaneously grew in importance and became the cockpit within which the factions suddenly found themselves free to fight for dominance. And fight they did, with the results we saw in the last chapter: by the start of Edward's reign, chiefly as a result of King Henry's choices, the evangelicals had overcome long odds and routed the conservatives. Norfolk was in prison, Gardiner was in prison, and Tunstal and his kind had been utterly marginalized. The kingdom and the future were in the hands of the new and evangelically inclined nobility of whom Edward Seymour had made himself chief. The power of that new nobility, in turn, was rooted in the council.

2

England's Second Reformation

Despite the Duke of Somerset's great victory at Pinkie—it might be just as fair to say *because of* that victory, or because of Somerset's failure to follow up on his success—Scotland remained as big a headache as it had ever been. The death of Henry VIII had been followed, just weeks later, by that of his old friend and rival and enemy Francis I. In his final days, enfeebled by syphilis and wandering miserably from palace to palace in search of a peace that he seemed unable to find, the king of France had displayed not only a willingness to come to terms with the English but a kind of paternal solicitude for the child who now wore England's crown. At the end he seemed accepting even of the Treaty of Greenwich, by means of which Henry had provided for the marriage of Edward VI to Mary, Queen of Scots, and the eventual union of England and Scotland.

Francis's son, Henry II, was far less amenable. He saw what his father would have had no difficulty seeing when he was younger and more vital: that a Scotland unfriendly to England was a precious asset, a back door through which to threaten the English whenever they came out of their front door to threaten France. Henry disavowed the Greenwich agreement, and when the Scots asked for his help after Pinkie he sent shiploads of fighting men. His troops were soon making life a misery for the forces that Somerset had positioned in Scottish lowland garrisons, and his fleet took the five-year-old Scottish queen to France, where she was soon betrothed to the heir to the throne and Henry could proudly declare that "France and Scotland are now one." Fighting continued in the border country between England and Scotland, but the whole situation had been turned into a humiliation for England and especially for Somerset, whose judgment was inevitably brought into question.

But Somerset clung stubbornly to his idea of controlling Scotland by maintaining a string of fortresses there, and in doing so he destroyed any possibility of coming to grips with the financial and economic problems inherited from Henry VIII. The magnitude of his blunder is evident in a few numbers. In the six years following Henry VIII's death, a total of £335,000 was raised through parliamentary taxation, but during just the first three of those years Somerset's government spent £580,000 on its campaign to subdue Scotland—£350,000 on manpower alone. Somerset found it necessary to import mercenaries—nearly 7,500 of them, by common reckoning—from Ireland, Spain, Germany, and Italy, even from Hungary and Albania. The treasury being empty and the Crown deep in debt when Somerset became protector, financing his wars (not only in Scotland but also in France, where the virtually useless city of Boulogne could be defended only at great expense) was totally beyond the Crown's capacity. Thus the duke found himself unable to reverse Henry's debasement of the coinage and in fact was driven to worsen the problem, skimming £537,000 from the mint in four years. The hundreds of thousands of additional pounds needed to meet the government's obligations were secured through the plundering of pockets of church wealth that had remained untouched until now (more about that shortly), extensive sales of Crown lands, and further borrowing at the high rates of interest that lenders demanded because of the sorry state of the treasury and the shriveling value of English coins.

Another problem that the lord protector encountered, one far less avoidable than the conflicts with Scotland and France but at least as dangerous, was the kingdom's ever-more-serious division along religious lines. Statistical precision is impossible, but at midcentury perhaps 20 percent of the population of London was in some meaningful sense evangelical, while the new religion had scarcely penetrated many other parts of the kingdom. Though radical reformers from Cranmer down had the approval of the Somerset faction and were therefore increasingly influential in the setting of Crown policy, and though the dispersion of the monastic lands was creating a new landowning gentry class that would have felt threatened by any move in the direction of Rome, the Pilgrimage of Grace had demonstrated the dangers of imprudently aggressive reform. The fall of Norfolk and Gardiner—both remained in prison—had sealed the ascendancy of the evangelicals, who responded to their victory not with satisfaction but with redoubled determination to rid the kingdom of papistry. Having supported Edward Seymour when he set out to make himself protector, governor, and duke, they now demanded to be repaid. And what they wanted was the dismantling of all the legal defenses that King Henry had erected around traditional doctrine. One of Somerset's greatest challenges was to maintain the support of his radical allies without sparking a reaction akin to the Pilgrimage of Grace.

He proved unequal to the task. What he lacked above all was firmness—the ability to face his problems cleanly and decisively, lay down clear policies, and thereby secure the acquiescence if not the active support of people who might themselves have preferred a different course. He appears to have believed that it was possible to be all things to all people. As a result, he left uncertainty in his wake and allowed difficulties that might have been dispatched quickly to linger and grow worse.

His brother Thomas was quick to exploit his weakness. In the first weeks of the protectorate, smarting from Somerset's failure to bestow upon him offices and honors commensurate with what he saw as his deserts, the fortunate but sullenly ungrateful Baron Seymour of Sudeley set out to advance himself through matrimony. According to various reports he set his sights on Princess Mary (now a mature woman and unlikely to have any interest in an upstart evangelical), on Princess Elizabeth (barely more than a child, quite young enough to be impressed), and even on poor Anne of Cleves, now living quietly on her estates and enjoying her status as a peripheral member of the royal family. He found, however, that his best prospects lay with the Dowager Queen Catherine Parr, whom he probably would have married years earlier if the king had not swept her up first. Catherine for her part was eager enough: childless after three marriages (all of them to men much older than herself), yoked most recently to a fat, sick, and prematurely aged king whose every word and act was overhung with menace, she must have seen in the virile, wolflike Seymour a last chance for something like a normal life. Soon he was paying secret visits to her residence, arriving late at night and slipping away quietly before sunrise.

When Somerset learned of his brother's activities, he reacted angrily, declaring that neither of them was a suitable mate for the daughters or widows of kings. The council, too, found the proposed marriage to be unthinkable. But Seymour had been currying favor with his nephew the king, supplying him with money—as much as £40 at a time—with which he could confer gifts on the preachers, musicians, and other retainers to whom he wished to show favor. At Seymour's direction, Edward wrote a letter worded, cleverly, to suggest that he was *asking* Catherine to take his uncle as her husband—not only expressing his approval but allowing the queen to believe that if she agreed she would be doing her sovereign a favor.

Under this canopy of royal protection the wedding was allowed to take place, but it solved little. Soon the Seymours' wives—one a duchess and wife of the lord protector, the other a former queen but now the spouse of a mere baron—were squabbling over which should have precedence at court. Seymour, insatiable, took control of his bride's considerable wealth and tried to resist when she was ordered to return the jewels that Henry had given her during their marriage. He also began scheming to take from his brother the title of governor of the king's body, and again he was able to make the king his accomplice. This led to his being called before the council and accused of plotting to overthrow the government. He refused to recognize the council's authority until threatened with arrest, at which point his nerve failed him and he acknowledged that he had in fact done wrong.

His brother the duke, who might have spared both of them much future grief by seeing to it that Seymour was thoroughly chastised, instead not only forgave him but arranged for his income to be increased by £800. It is understandable if the younger brother came away from the episode believing that, almost whatever he did, the consequences would turn out to be greatly to his advantage. He was soon back at his old tricks, looking for ways to make himself more important and his brother less. When he and Catherine, who was now pregnant, took Princess Elizabeth into their household, Seymour was soon raising eyebrows by entering the girl's bedchamber when she was still in her nightclothes and engaging in intimacies that went at least as far as playful slaps on her backside. The onetime queen, told of these high jinks, made light of them, but a storm erupted when she found the pair embracing. The rumor mill said that Seymour regretted marrying the king's widow when he might have had a bride of royal blood. It said, too, that Elizabeth was not averse to her host's advances.

When Parliament convened late in 1547, Somerset and the council presented it with a legislative agenda that was largely religious in content and aimed primarily at dismantling Henry VIII's church. The Act of Six Articles, which the late king had labored to make a definitive statement of his theology, was repealed outright, as was the Act for Advancement of True Religion, which had offended the evangelicals by curtailing freedom to read the Bible. Also expunged were every one of the many felonies created during Henry's reign, every one of his heresy laws, every treason law passed in the two centuries since the reign of Edward III, and the act that had given royal proclamations the force and legitimacy of parliamentary statutes. It was a thorough housecleaning, but it is not plausibly interpreted as a birth of religious liberty. Its effect was to free Cranmer and his fellow evangelicals not merely to preach and worship as they wished but to suppress all beliefs and practices of which they disapproved. One crucial piece of Henrician orthodoxy remained intact: it was still a capital crime to deny that the king was supreme head of the church.

But with the evangelicals now dominant, the young king supportive of everything they were doing, and England becoming a haven for continental reformers who would have risked their lives by entering the kingdom during the previous reign, supremacy now meant much more than separation from Rome. Now it was a tool to be used in the destruction of almost everything that remained of the old religion. Cranmer, confident of the backing of the lord protector and the king, forbade ceremonies that had been part of community life in England for so long that to most people they seemed eternal: the carrying and blessing of candles on Candlemas Day, for example, and of ashes on Ash Wednesday and palms on Palm Sunday. King Henry himself had inveighed against religious images—statues, pictures, whatever—where these were deemed to have become objects of worship, but few such images had been destroyed. Cranmer now ordered their wholesale removal. It was one of the earliest outbreaks of Puritanism in England, though the word *Puritan* had not yet been coined.

The most notorious act of the Parliament of 1547, one that Henry probably would have admired, transferred to the Crown two of the few repositories of church wealth not already expropriated: the endowments of chantries (small chapels that over the centuries had been established in almost incalculable numbers for the purpose of offering prayers for the dead) and the assets of guilds, fraternal associations of individuals and families designed to provide benefits such as burial insurance and funding for schools and charitable activities. By any reasonable reckoning the property of the chantries—much of it income-generating land—was private. If prayers for the dead made no sense to people with no belief in purgatory, the Crown's claim on the money that generations of donors had provided for the saying of such prayers (as Henry VIII himself had done, on a characteristically lavish scale, in anticipation of his own demise) made even less. To argue that the property of the guilds did not belong to their members, or that the existence of the guilds was not of significant benefit both to their members and to the community, was equally implausible. The confiscation bill, when presented to Parliament, was defended as a way of making funds available for education, the relief of the poor, and the support of vicars and preachers. What had already happened to the wealth of the monasteries made such arguments so utterly incredible that even Cranmer objected at first, but when he saw which way the political winds were blowing he swiftly fell silent. The government was desperate for cash as usual, everyone from the lord protector down to the lowliest member of Parliament was eager for a share in fresh spoils, and cities that objected vigorously were bought off with promises of special exemption.

And so the bill passed. Commissioners rushed out to gather the gold and silver plate belonging to the chantries and deliver it to the mint to be melted down, blended with base metals, and thus converted into still more of the debased currency with which the government was—just barely—fending off bankruptcy. Much chantry and guild land went the way monastic land had gone earlier: into the possession of the Crown, then out again either to buyers or to those influential enough to claim such munificent gifts. All this was accomplished by the same Parliament that, as noted earlier, enacted a statute providing for the branding and enslavement of anyone found guilty of vagrancy. The English Reformation was hardening into the shape that would one day cause G. K. Chesterton, in his *Short History of England,* to call it "the revolt of the rich." The target of this revolt was not established authority but the common people, the poorest definitely included.

Once Parliament had finished its business, the authorities deemed it safe to release Stephen Gardiner from prison. But the bishop refused to behave himself; the abrupt swerve toward evangelicalism that began with the new reign had exhausted his considerable reserves of malleability. After his release he remained such an outspokenly disgruntled critic of this latest religious settlement that he was called before the council, of which he had long been a leading member. There he was ordered to appear outside St. Paul's Cathedral on an appointed day and, in the presence of King Edward, deliver a sermon expressing his acceptance of the latest official orthodoxy. He was given a script and invited to use it instead of drafting his own, but he refused. Invited to show his text to the council before delivering it, he again refused, promising however that he would deal with the subjects that the council had prescribed. He was admonished to say nothing that could be considered controversial, but his sermon when he delivered it proved to be exactly what the council least wanted: an explanation of the traditional understanding of the mass and the Eucharist—possibly the first time in his life that Edward had been exposed to such ideas. The young king must have been horrified by such compelling evidence that the Antichrist had not yet been expelled from England.

Gardiner, accused of disobeying his instructions, replied that what he had said could not possibly be considered controversial because it expressed the beliefs of their late, great king and in fact was exactly what Cranmer himself had often preached during Henry's life. Cranmer, outwitted, was no more amused than the king. Gardiner was sent back to prison, this time to stay. The number of bishops who followed his lead was surprisingly large in light of how he had been treated and how few had followed John Fisher less than two decades before; the innovations introduced under Somerset's protectorate proved to be too radical even for many who had accepted the separation from Rome. Edmund Bonner was stripped of the see of London and joined Gardiner in prison. The bishops of Chichester, Durham, Exeter, and Worcester also were removed. Their dioceses, before successors were appointed, were stripped of much of their income.

But blood was no longer flowing. The English reign of terror was, at least for the time being, at an end. This has to be attributed to Somerset, who with all his faults (which were numerous and serious enough) was utterly lacking in the bloodthirstiness of the late king. He was scarcely less proud or greedy than Henry, and he became increasingly autocratic as problems pressed in on him, but he was never viciously and rarely unnecessarily cruel. This is perhaps the most attractive feature of his complex, almost inscrutable personality. It may also—one hesitates to say such a thing, because it can seem to excuse the enormities of Henry VIII's reign—have been the most serious of his weaknesses. He lacked the toughness that his situation required.

He may also have lacked the needed intelligence. This would explain the tenacity with which he persisted in his bellicose approach to Scotland, where there was nothing to be gained after the removal of the child Mary Stuart to France, and his determination not to allow the French to have Boulogne in spite of the ruinous cost of defending it. It would also explain his fumbling and ill-conceived efforts to deal with England's economic problems, notably the growing discontent over high inflation and declining wages. Somerset took a simplistic view of the economy, believing that the worst of its ills were rooted in the practice of enclosures, which had first become a cause of unrest long before he was born. Wolsey and Cromwell among others had attempted to stop them, but the profits of the wool and cloth trade made conversion difficult to resist and political power lay in the hands of those who owned the land.

Somerset decided to give it another try. He sent out commissioners to enforce the laws against enclosure and to look for evidence of corruption in their enforcement. Some of these commissioners were evangelists of a crusading bent, men committed not just to law enforcement but to creating a new and ideal England in which the pursuit of money would be replaced by brotherly love. Though they accomplished little or nothing in practical terms, the speeches in which they condemned the greed of the rich excited hopes and inflamed resentments among the common folk. This had different effects at different levels of society.

Among the working poor, whose livelihoods were being jeopardized by changes in rural life of which the enclosures were just one aspect, Somerset came to be known as "the good duke," the champion of the oppressed. There were scattered riots and attacks on property by mobs who thought their actions would be approved by the lord protector. The nobility and gentlemen farmers, the greatest of whom owned tens of thousands of sheep, naturally took a drastically different view. They were alarmed by the disturbances and angered by the protector's role in fomenting them. They were angered, too, by a new tax on sheep and wool—a government attempt to encourage a return to the growing of crops. If the duke's motives were noble, if he was really motivated by a desire to relieve the suffering of the rural poor, his actions were ineffectual. If on the other hand his intention was to make himself widely popular, he was successful in the most immediate sense but ultimately deeply foolish. The same gestures with which he was winning the affection of the impotent were costing him the trust of the classes with real power, the ones he needed in order to survive. Those classes would not have been impressed by expressions of sympathy for the peasantry under any circumstances, but when such expressions came from an upstart duke who was using his position to make himself the greatest private landowner in England, they could only snort in derision. Somerset was certainly vulnerable on that score. Ownership of a "manor"—the term refers to an estate of indeterminate size, originally large enough for the support of a feudal lord and his retinue—was generally sufficient to put a family well up among the gentry. Somerset, in just a few years as protector, helped himself to more than two hundred manors.

A kingdom broken into religious factions was now in danger of class warfare as well—or so it seemed, at least, to many of those with most to lose—and Somerset responded as indecisive men in positions of authority often will: by trying to please everyone. Arriving at some new kind of unity continued to appear as necessary as it had under Henry VIII, though that goal would remain unachievable as long as the government tried to enforce beliefs that most of the population found incomprehensible if not repugnant. Cranmer was instructed to bridge the gap between the conservatives and the radicals by doing something that no one could possibly have done in mid-sixteenth-century England— produce "one convenient and meet order, rite and fashion of Common

Prayer" that everyone in the kingdom could accept. It was probably inevitable that the result—the first version of the Book of Common Prayer, a volume of prayers and church services so ambiguous in its treatment of controversial questions that no one was satisfied but not even the conservatives could find reason to reject it outright—led to rancorous debate among the bishops and in Parliament. (The very fact that the conservatives were *not* grievously offended evidently persuaded the evangelicals that what Cranmer had produced could not possibly be acceptable.) Unity, in any case, was not achieved. Cranmer's prayers (beautiful compositions by one of the supreme masters of English prose) were embedded in a new Act of Uniformity, but the fact that they were in English rather than Latin ensured a skeptical reception in many places. Stiff penalties for failure to use the new service added resentment to the brew. An uneasy sense that all the old ways were under direct attack by people determined to force a religious revolution was heightened by passage of a statute making it lawful for clergymen to marry.

All the chickens came home to roost in 1549. The protector's brother Thomas, who had learned nothing from his earlier escape from the consequences of his own recklessness, now intensified almost to the point of insanity his efforts to advance himself at Somerset's expense. When his wife, the former Queen Catherine, died shortly after giving birth in September 1548—inevitably it was rumored that he had poisoned her—Seymour turned his attention back to King Edward's half-sister Elizabeth. Meanwhile he was taking a cut of the profits of the pirates that it was his duty as lord high admiral to suppress, conspiring with the vice-treasurer of the royal mint to divert a steady stream of gold and silver into their own pockets, and trying so indiscriminately to buy allies that his activities inevitably became widely known. The council had no choice but to respond. Summoned, Seymour declined to appear until a more "convenient" time, thereby making his arrest inevitable. When six weeks of investigation and the interrogation of numerous witnesses resulted in a bill of attainder charging him with thirty-three counts of high treason, he haughtily refused to defend himself. In March he was beheaded. Somerset had freed himself of his most relentless enemy, but not necessarily of a terribly dangerous one; Seymour had been too undisciplined, his ambition and resentment too wildly unfocused, to pose a lethal threat. It would have been wiser of the protector to put him in prison and keep him there, or perhaps to exile him. By executing his own brother (or perhaps only by not stopping the council from having him killed, we don't really know), this man who had ended Henry VIII's bloodbath gave his critics an excuse to complain that he no less than the old king was capable of killing anyone. Such a perception could not have alleviated the distrust and fear that he had already aroused among the gentry and the nobles.

None of which might have mattered if the kingdom had not suddenly convulsed in a series of spontaneous uprisings. These were widespread and uncoordinated, communication across long distances still being little more advanced than it had been in the time of the Caesars, and most of them subsided or were put down without leaving much record of their exact cause, who led them, or what they were intended to achieve. Wiltshire, Sussex, Surrey, Hants, Berkshire, Kent, Gloucester, Somerset, Suffolk, Warwick, Essex, Hertford, Leicestershire, Worcester, Rutland—these and other counties experienced violent outbreaks of discontent in May 1549. After a period of quiet, trouble then broke out in Oxfordshire, Norfolk, Devon, and Cornwall. In all these places except Oxfordshire, where enough of the government's Italian mercenaries happened to be on hand to help the local authorities restore order and send a dozen ringleaders to the gallows, the threat quickly assumed dangerous proportions.

In Devon in the far west the trouble has been known ever since as the Prayer Book Rebellion. On Whitsunday (the feast of Pentecost, when the priest traditionally wore white vestments), in obedience to the new Act of Uniformity, the vicar of the church at Sampford Courtenay used Cranmer's new Book of Common Prayer instead of following the customary Latin liturgy. This provoked nothing worse than grumbling at first, but discontent somehow turned overnight into hot anger, and on Monday the townsfolk demanded celebration of the old rites. Resentment must have been smoldering throughout the region, because as word of what had happened spread, people from distant places began converging on Sampford Courtenay. Within a few days a ragtag army of ten thousand had formed and was on the march. An experienced soldier named Humphrey Arundel, a member of a landowning family with no liking for the evangelical reforms, made himself its leader. Lord John

Russell, upon arriving at the head of a body of government troops, realized that he was hopelessly outnumbered and did what the Duke of
Norfolk had done at Doncaster when faced with the Pilgrimage of
Grace: he offered to negotiate. The insurgents presented a list of demands, all of which dealt with religious issues. They wanted a restoration of the Latin Mass, Henry VIII's Six Articles, images in church, and
at least two abbeys in every county. Perhaps most remarkably, and
demonstrating that even in the most remote corners of the kingdom
there could be detailed understanding of England's doctrinal struggles
and the personalities involved, they demanded that Reginald Pole be
brought home from exile and given a place on the Privy Council.

Archbishop Cranmer, when these demands reached London, wrote a
lengthy response that expressed contempt for the rebels and their pre-
sumption in addressing such weighty questions. Somerset issued a series
of proclamations. He offered a pardon to every rebel who submitted to
the Crown. He declared that the lands and other possessions of any
rebels who declined to submit could become the property of any loyal
subject who chose to seize them, that anyone responsible for an unlawful assembly was to be put to death, and, rather curiously, that his commissioners were to proceed with the undoing of illegal enclosures while
seeing to it that they themselves were free of guilt. There was no reason
to think that enclosures had been a significant factor in the rising. The
attention that Somerset gave them at this juncture raises questions
about whether he understood what was happening in the west country,
or whether he was sufficiently focused on crushing this challenge to the
council's authority to satisfy men of property. In any event he was lucky.
Instead of advancing eastward into counties where they would almost
certainly have been able to attract recruits, the rebels laid siege to the
city of Exeter, where the Crown's garrison troops held them immobile
for forty days. When a royalist force made up largely of Somerset's German and Italian mercenaries arrived on the scene at last, the rebels were
forced to break off their siege and then were crushed in a series of increasingly lopsided battles. In the end nothing remained but a panicky
mass of fleeing peasants. As many as four thousand men were dead by
the time it was all over, most of them killed in combat but the last executed. A striking feature of the whole episode was the extent to which

the Crown had to use foreign mercenaries to save itself from its own subjects.

Far to the east, in Norfolk, an even bigger rebellion was playing itself out almost within striking distance of London. As if to illustrate the breadth of the problems facing the Crown, this one rose out of complaints completely different from those that had sent the west up in flames. As in Devon, a trivial incident had mushroomed into a general uprising, and this time not ten but twenty thousand men joined. Their demands, like those of the Prayer Book rebels, were essentially conservative, expressive of a yearning to get back to what once had been, but here the focus was economic rather than religious. An extraordinary figure named Robert Kett, a wealthy tanner and landowner, though fifty-seven years old and a grandfather, had not only joined the rebellion but made himself its leader and spokesman. He announced a number of demands: an end to enclosures (a much bigger issue here than in the west country, obviously), a rollback of rents, freedom for bondsmen or serfs (of whom there were few in Norfolk by this time), punishment of corrupt officials, and the replacement of incompetent priests and royal councilors "who confounded things sacred and profane and regarded nothing but the enriching of themselves with the public treasure, that they might riot in it during the public calamity." The last demand was, all too clearly, a challenge to the authority of the council ruling in King Edward's name. When the rebels were offered pardon if they would disperse, Kett replied indignantly that pardons were for criminals, not for subjects loyal to their king. With that, the rebels left themselves with no alternative to a fight to the finish, which is what Kett's Rebellion became.

Somerset, who had preparations for another invasion of Scotland under way at this point, sent William Parr, the late Queen Catherine's brother and now the Marquess of Northampton, to Norfolk with a mixed force of English and Italian troops. Parr, no soldier, made the mistake of leading his men into Norwich, then the largest city in England after London, where the narrow streets made it impossible for them to mass against the rebels. They were bloodily driven out. Somerset meanwhile was increasingly isolating himself, refusing to confer with the other members of the Privy Council and sending out signals that confused rebels and loyalists alike. With one proclamation he condemned destruction of the hedges with which formerly common lands had been enclosed, and with the next he promised pardon to those who committed such acts so long as they expressed sorrow for their deeds. New local risings continued to erupt—in Kent, in Surrey, in Sussex—and increasingly the violence was directed at the property of the wealthy. When Somerset cried out in near-hysteria that the demands of the rebels were "fair and just," his fellow councilors concluded, not unfairly, that he was cracking under pressure.

Norwich remained the epicenter of the crisis, so dangerous by now that Somerset had no choice but to call off his Scottish campaign and summon to center stage the next great figure in the Tudor saga, John Dudley, Earl of Warwick. The reader will recall that at the beginning of the reign of Henry VIII, when the young king and his councilors were eager to dissociate themselves from the unpopularity of Henry VII, the lawyers Edmund Dudley and Richard Empson had been attainted and executed on a ridiculously implausible charge of having plotted to seize control of the government. Their real offense—which probably involved no violation of the law, was largely if not entirely aimed at the acts of bona fide lawbreakers, and certainly was done with Henry VII's knowledge—was to have been their royal master's all-too-visible instruments as he went about the hard business of extracting money from the most prosperous and powerful of his subjects. Edmund Dudley, whose professional and political skills propelled him into the speakership of the House of Commons and a seat on the Royal Council, had accumulated an impressive fortune as reward for his services. He had also boosted his social status by marrying a viscount's daughter. Attainder meant that all the fruits of his success were confiscated by the Crown, so that his widow and their three sons and one daughter, of whom the six-year-old John was the eldest, were ruined.

But just a year after Dudley's execution, his widow entered into an advantageous second marriage with Arthur Plantagenet, an illegitimate son of King Edward IV. A half-brother of Henry VIII's mother, Elizabeth of York, Plantagenet was such an amiable soul that, in spite of being more than twenty years older than the new king, he became one of his closest companions. In short order Edmund Dudley's attainder was posthumously revoked, perhaps a tacit admission that he had never been guilty but more likely an easy way of enriching King Henry's bastard uncle: the part of the Dudley estate that remained in the Crown's possession was awarded not to the dead man's widow or children but to Plantagenet. For reasons unknown to history, the boy John became the ward not of his stepfather but of a soldier and courtier named Edward Guildford. At some point in early adolescence he was admitted to court as a page, a humble first step on the ladder of royal service but one that was naturally much coveted. In due course he made the acquaintance of another young courtier-in-training, Edward Seymour, the future Duke of Somerset.

The lives of the two were intertwined from that point. Both participated in King Henry's invasion of the continent in the early 1520s, and both were knighted in France in 1523. Thereafter Dudley began to advance more rapidly than Seymour in spite of being younger by four years. His success may have been owing at first to the prominence at court of both his stepfather Plantagenet (who by the time of the French war was Viscount Lisle and a member of the council) and his onetime guardian and then father-in-law, Guildford. Later, however, the talent he displayed in martial arts including jousting, one of the king's favorite pastimes, would have brought him to the fore. By 1524 he was an esquire of the body, an honor that Seymour did not achieve until 1531, and in 1534 he became a member of Parliament. He and Seymour were among the first courtiers to affiliate themselves with evangelical reform, becoming associates of Cromwell in doing so. That they were more than casual acquaintances is suggested by the fact that, in 1532 or thereabouts, Dudley signed as guarantor of a loan taken out by Seymour.

The door to wealth and power opened wide for both of them in 1536, but from then on, thanks to his sister Jane's marriage to the king, it was Seymour who took the lead while Dudley followed doggedly in his tracks. When Seymour became an earl and member of the Privy Council, he helped to secure Dudley's appointment as vice-admiral with responsibility for driving pirates from the English Channel. When Seymour took command of King Henry's invasion of Scotland, Dudley assumed the key supporting role of warden-general of the Scottish marches. But Dudley was far more than a mere sycophant riding the crest of his friend's good fortune. In the chronicles of the time he seems to pop up everywhere: as envoy between the king and the Duke of Norfolk during the Pilgrimage of Grace, delivering to Henry the terrible news of Catherine Howard's confession, negotiating treaties, commanding troops. Wherever he was sent, he was effective. In 1543 Dudley (himself a viscount by now, having been given the title vacated by the death of his stepfather) was made lord high admiral and a knight of the garter, and he joined Seymour on the Privy Council. No one could doubt that he had earned these honors. Nor could anyone have been surprised when, after Henry's death, Dudley joined with Seymour in dominating the executors of the king's will, became Earl of Warwick when Seymour made himself Duke of Somerset, and commanded the frontline troops when Somerset again attacked Scotland. In alliance with Cranmer, who looked after their interests where the church was concerned, Somerset and Dudley had control of nearly everything.

But by the summer of 1549, with Kett's rebels in possession of Norwich and disturbances continuing to erupt in many places, it was all in danger of falling apart. Somerset's behavior became more and more erratic, his leadership more and more confused. He appeared to be sinking into a paranoia that made it impossible for him to trust even his oldest allies. In a pair of mistakes either one of which might have been enough to doom him, he distanced himself both from William Paget, the canny master of court politics who had steered him through the first days of the protectorate, and from Dudley. He had refused to restore Dudley to the post of lord high admiral, an assignment Dudley loved and took seriously, after the execution of Thomas Seymour left it vacant. He had forced Dudley to give up Warwick Castle, a demand that made no sense unless he regarded the new Earl of Warwick as too untrustworthy to be left in possession of such a mighty stronghold. Dudley by now was himself an immensely wealthy landowner—that followed more or less automatically from political success in the Tudor kleptocracy—and so had much to lose. Like his whole class, he was alarmed by the rebellions and convinced that Somerset was encouraging and condoning them.

It may have been distrust that caused Somerset to send the inexperienced William Parr rather than Dudley to put down Kett's Rebellion, but whatever the reason it was another of the duke's mistakes. Parr's ignominious expulsion from Norwich left Somerset with no alternative to Dudley unless he were willing to take command himself, which would have destroyed the image that he had built for himself as the special friend of the people. And so Dudley advanced on Norwich with an army of some eight thousand men, a quarter of whom were German cavalry. His performance there confirmed his reputation for courage and resolution and his image as a charismatic commander. Upon arrival he offered the rebels pardon in return for their abandonment of the struggle, and when they refused he attacked, penetrating the city's outer defenses. The city fathers of Norwich, fearful that if the rebels bested Dudley as they had Parr they would go on a rampage of destruction, implored him to take his campaign elsewhere. Instead he gathered his lieutenants and in a moment of high drama kissed his sword, made the sign of the cross, and swore to fight to the death rather than surrender or withdraw. When his subordinates took the same oath, the spines of the townsfolk were stiffened and the fighting resumed. Step by bloody step Dudley's men bludgeoned Kett's out through the city gates and into open country. The rising ended with the last of the rebels surrounded and shouting defiance at a final offer of pardon. They didn't believe the offer to be genuine and said they would rather die fighting than on the gallows. Dudley, in probably the noblest act of his life, rode forward to tell the rebels face-to-face that if they would lay down their arms he would personally guarantee their safety. They decided to believe him, and Dudley was as good as his word. Kett was executed, inevitably, and so were ten other rebel leaders, but that was the end of the killing. When the landowning gentlemen of the neighborhood said they wanted revenge, Dudley asked if they intended to do their own planting after their tenants had been exterminated.

When Dudley returned to London, he was the hero of the governing class, the one man who had proved capable of restoring order. Somerset by contrast, though the rural peasantry continued to revere him, was so discredited in the eyes of the elite, so alienated even from a majority of the Privy Council, that he found it necessary to leave the capital and withdraw with his nephew the king to Hampton Court. There ensued a power struggle of great complexity. After first and briefly allying himself with the religious conservatives, Dudley embarked on a purge of those same conservatives as soon as he no longer needed them, thereby freeing himself of a connection that the young king could never have found acceptable. The turmoil continued for months, with many twists and turns. In October Somerset was deprived of the protectorship and became a prisoner in the Tower. Four months later he secured a pardon by confessing on his knees that he had abused the powers of his office. Still later he was readmitted to the council, and eventually he achieved such an advanced state of rehabilitation that his daughter Anne was married to Dudley's eldest son. Like his late brother, however, Somerset proved incapable of being satisfied. He wanted to be lord protector again, and with that in mind he plotted a marriage between King Edward and another of his daughters, a girl bearing the name of her aunt Jane Seymour. Dudley could not possibly trust him; in practical terms it was becoming difficult even to permit him to remain alive. Dudley arranged to have himself elevated to Duke of Northumberland in October 1551, which put him on an equal footing with Somerset at the apex of English nobility, and a few days later Somerset and his wife and most powerful allies all were arrested. Somerset was charged with having committed treason by planning to capture or murder Dudley, and of having feloniously involved others in his plot. He was tried in the House of Lords and somehow found guilty of the felony but not of treason. The outcome was inevitable in any case: early in 1552 he was beheaded on Tower Hill before a crowd of thousands of his lowborn admirers. The execution was a scene of immense tension, with the onlookers appearing to be on the verge of turning on the authorities.

Thus the king, in early adolescence now, lost a second uncle to the headsman's ax. As with the first of those losses, there is no record of his having been affected emotionally to even the smallest extent. It is not clear that Edward had much capacity for affection, which is understandable in light of how little he appears to have received in the course of his young life and how many of the people to whom he might have been close had gone to their graves. Two of the closest friends of his childhood, the sons of the Duke of Suffolk and the woman he had married after the death of King Henry's sister Mary, had been carried off by the sweating sickness. Another had been sent off to study in France. Of his two half-sisters, he appears to have been closer to Mary, who was old enough to be his mother, but as he matured Edward came to regard even her with a prim and prudish disapproval. Mary insisted on remaining a papist, after all, and therefore, sadly, was damned. Nothing Edward said, nothing he did to pressure her, could deflect Mary from having the old Catholic mass said regularly in her private quarters. That had to be a cause of deep distress to a boy schooled to be very serious about his role as supreme head, and to take nothing so seriously as his duty to show everyone in England the way to the true religion.

John Dudley, now the Duke of Northumberland and rapidly becoming the richest man in England thanks to an appetite for church and Crown lands no less voracious than Somerset's, knew that he needed the king's favor in order to maintain his place. He was adroit at winning that favor and at keeping it. He dared make no claim to the title of lord protector—that had never been held by anyone outside the royal family—but he adopted and made good use of "lord president of the Privy Council." He invited the king to attend council meetings, seeing to it that he was briefed in advance on matters to be discussed and even given words to say at the appropriate times (words that the boy, always conscientious, would memorize for delivery). In so doing he encouraged Edward to believe that he was not merely participating in the governance of the kingdom but beginning to *rule*. At the same time, Dudley embraced the increasingly Calvinistic theology of the king and his tutors. It would be unfair to accuse Dudley of adopting whatever beliefs were most certain to please the king; he had been, as we have seen, a member of the evangelical faction before Edward was born. Still, he was a man of action, and his proper arena was that in which power, not ideas, was in play. It is not impossible that he would have become a conservative if doing so would have helped him to maintain control of king and council.

Be that as it may, King Edward was a sincerely fervent evangelical, and Dudley, by displaying his own fervor in the same cause, found it possible to have things almost entirely his way. And he was never as feckless as Somerset in the exercise of his power. He gave up Boulogne, and though many Englishmen thought the terms he accepted from the French were humiliating, doing so was vastly wiser than continuing a struggle that the kingdom could not afford and could gain nothing from. Peace with France brought peace with Scotland, too, and after a final, desperate devaluation of the coinage (the Crown remained in terrible financial condition), Dudley began taking painful steps to restore it to respectability. The conservatives were required to absorb blow after blow: the venerable Cuthbert Tunstal was losing not only his bishopric but his freedom, the altars were being torn out of every church, and a revised and unmistakably Protestant Book of Common Prayer was made compulsory while attendance at mass became unlawful. But justifications for such acts seemed in good supply. To the victors go the spoils, after all. And there was no reason to think that the conservatives wouldn't have been just as vindictive if given the chance. Religious tolerance remained inconceivable: in sixteenth-century Europe almost no one could imagine a kingdom surviving while its people were separated into camps with incompatible beliefs.

Dudley had achieved everything that an Englishman not of royal blood could ever have imagined achieving. He was rich beyond the dreams of avarice, he was so powerful that no one dared challenge him, and he had five fine and faithful sons to whom to pass on what he was building. And if it all depended on the goodwill of the king, he had every reason to expect that the king, if properly handled, would continue indefinitely to be Dudley's fine and faithful instrument.

It was all perfect. And from the point in the spring of 1552 when the king was briefly bedridden with measles and smallpox, it was all doomed.

CALVIN

WHEN EDWARD VI BECAME KING, MARTIN LUTHER HAD
been dead for thirteen months and the Lutheran part of the Reformation
had largely run its course. After changing the world, the former Friar
Martin had withdrawn into a relatively quiet life as the father of a growing family and a writer of biblical commentaries. In the last decade of his
life he was tortured by constipation, hemorrhoids, and kidney stones,
plagued by the scandal that had erupted when he endorsed bigamy, and
increasingly consumed by a virulent anti-Semitism. (Three days before
his death he preached a sermon urging the expulsion of the Jews from
Germany.) His theology, having conquered half of Germany and all of
Scandinavia, had been overtaken on the cutting edge of the religious
revolution by newer varieties of Protestant belief.

Edward became king, therefore, at the point where a second generation of evangelical thinkers, based in Switzerland rather than Germany,
was making itself heard. Its increasingly dominant member was a
Frenchman living in Switzerland, John Calvin, one of history's most
paradoxical figures. In assuming the leadership of a revolt against the
authority of the Roman church, Calvin came to claim for himself more
power than any Renaissance pope had ever dared to do. He not only declared himself to be something very like the infallible head of a one true
church of his own devising—any lunatic might have done that, and one
or two of the sixteenth century's more interesting lunatics did—but
through willpower, sheer force of intellect, and unshakable integrity he
largely made good on that claim. In the little city of Geneva, a place not
particularly friendly to reform, he constructed a regime that came about
as close as anything in Europe ever had to an enduring totalitarian theoc-
racy. In laying down the rules by which the people of Geneva (and, by
implication, the whole Christian world) were to live, and more important by articulating a rationale for the validity of those rules, he made

himself one of the most influential theologians in history. In places as remote from his home base as Scotland (where his disciples transformed
not only the church but the culture) and England (where his teachings
triggered the Puritan movement), it was Calvin more than Luther who
defined what it was to be Protestant. The reach of his ideas is evident
in the fact that from 1550 to 1650, a century that encompassed the careers of Shakespeare and other writers of gigantic stature, Calvin was England's most published author. This happened although Calvin never set
foot in England, rarely showed more than passing interest in its affairs,
and was reviled by an Anglican church that persecuted his followers and
attempted to suppress his teachings.

Both in background and in temperament, Calvin was profoundly different from Luther. He was trained in the law rather than in theology, and
much of his impact was rooted in a lawyerly impulse to systematize, to
impose order on what can sometimes seem the *dis*order, the emotional
excess, of Luther's attacks first on the abuses of the church and then on
some of its doctrines. Born in 1509 (the family name was Cauvin, Latin-
ized as "Calvinus" when young Jean began putting his ideas in writing),
he was raised by a devoutly Catholic mother but came of age in a France
that was being shaken apart by the disputes that Luther had ignited. He
was drawn to the cause of reform while still a student in Paris, where he
began acquiring the mastery of Latin, Greek, and Hebrew that would
make him one of Europe's most formidable Scripture scholars. The beliefs that he adopted at this early stage were, not surprisingly, almost
identical to what Luther was then preaching. Thus he agreed with
Luther's view that original sin had so damaged the human soul as to
make it impossible for anyone to *merit* salvation and that man was therefore entirely dependent upon a divine grace that cannot be earned. Like
Luther, he repudiated most of the traditional sacraments (all, in fact,
except baptism and the Eucharist) along with the practices (celibacy,
fasting, pilgrimages, and indulgences, for example) that the Catholic
Church had long offered as ways of winning divine favor. Throughout his
public life Calvin displayed a hatred of Rome at least as intense as
Luther's, but he never descended to the kind of childishly scatological
rhetoric with which the German reformer defaced so much of his own
writing. (Thomas More and others, to their own everlasting shame, answered him in kind.)

Theologically, Calvin soon went beyond Luther. He is best known for making explicit something that had remained implicit in Luther: the conclusion that, because fallen man has no free will and can do nothing to win salvation or escape damnation, some are predestined to be saved while others are predestined for hell. The saved are the *elect,* in Calvin's system. Though they can be recognized by their acceptance of divine truth, their love of the Eucharist, and their upright conduct, these are not the *means* by which they achieve salvation but rather a *sign* of election. Calvin's notion of "double predestination"—of some being marked for damnation just as surely as others are fated for salvation—has too often been regarded as the centerpiece of his theology. It is said to have made his God a kind of insanely cruel monster and to explain the severity of the regimen that Calvin imposed upon Geneva. In fact, however, Calvin regarded predestination as logically inescapable but otherwise beyond human understanding and in practical terms not of great importance. It was his followers who, after his death, moved predestination closer to the center of "Calvinist" belief. Calvin's own view was that the idea of predestination should make it possible for believers to set aside their anxieties about earning salvation and put their trust in the mercy of a gentle, compassionate divine father (who was also, Calvin suggested, a loving mother). Calvin was generally disinclined to take a passionate interest in theological questions that consumed many of his contemporaries but seemed to him to have little practical value in addressing the needs of the elect. He finessed one of the most contentious of issues, for example, by declaring that Christ was really present in the Eucharist but only in a "spiritual" sense, and letting it go at that. He regarded the heart as more important than the intellect in establishing a right relationship with God.

What separated Calvin from the Lutherans most radically, at least in terms of practical consequences, was his approach to the governance of the church as well as—church and state being inextricably connected in his system—the civil society. Luther, in renouncing the traditional church, had discarded Catholic belief in a priesthood endowed with special authority and unique sacramental faculties. In its place he offered a "priesthood of all believers," and while acknowledging the church as a legitimately distinct element of society, he emphatically subordinated it (especially after the Peasants' War) to civil authority. For

Calvin, by contrast, the church and its clergy retained a unique authority, with not only the right but the duty to reshape the world in such a way as to make it a fit habitation for the elect. Hence one of the defining characteristics of Calvinism (and the Puritanism to which it gave rise in England): a zealous commitment to making the world a fully realized part of Christ's kingdom. Curiously, people who believed they could do nothing to alter their eternal destinies nevertheless dedicated themselves to making everyone in the world conduct themselves in a holy manner as Calvin defined holiness. This was a matter of duty, and its aim was not to save souls but to protect the elect from the doomed.

Calvin's whole career was an expression of commitment to a Christian reordering of society. He came early to be certain not only that Catholicism was a gross perversion of the gospel—his contempt for the old religion appears at times to border on the pathological—but that he himself, by reading Scripture correctly, had found in it truths that European Christianity had either intentionally suppressed or, more charitably, remained blind to for more than a thousand years. Among his recovered truths were highly specific instructions as to how the church and the community of believers should be organized and managed. It was of course extraordinary, his conviction that virtually all of Christendom had been grievously in error almost from the beginning and that he alone was free of error. On its face it was outlandish. But in the theological confusion of the sixteenth century, Calvin's impregnable self-confidence and the clarity of his ideas brought him an eager audience.

Most of his core ideas were already in place when, in 1536, Calvin happened to make an overnight stop in Geneva and was persuaded to remain there and join the embattled local forces of reform. He quickly showed himself to be the most unhesitating and uncompromising of crusaders, answering disagreement with scorn and demanding that everyone in the city either assent to his beliefs or face excommunication and expulsion. During his first months in Geneva he published the first edition of his *Institutes of the Christian Religion,* which as it evolved would become arguably the most important single work in the history of Protestantism. When after two years he insisted that the city council submit to the authority of the clergy—to *his* authority, in effect—he found that he had overreached. Now it was he who was sent into exile.

Geneva remained a religious cockpit, however, and the most ambitious of its reformers soon were yearning once again for strong leadership. In 1541 Calvin was invited to return. He did so on very nearly his own terms, demanding that the council enact and enforce his Ecclesiastical Ordinances, and from that point until the end of his life twenty-three years later he outmaneuvered one after another of his adversaries until Geneva became the Sparta of Protestant Europe. His rules were not only given the force of law but declared "holy doctrine"—infallible, or something not easily distinguished from it. The regime that he imposed was democratic in the sense that church members chose their pastors, but once chosen, those pastors, working with and through lay elders, were able to rule virtually unchallenged. Eventually Calvin's consistory, an ecclesiastical court presided over by the pastors, was empowered to investigate and discipline anyone in the city. Not only drunkenness, gambling, and sexual promiscuity but dancing, singing outside church, swearing, and failing to attend sermons became crimes. Catholic practice, of course, was absolutely forbidden. Punishments ranged from reprimands and public confession to beatings, banishment, even execution. In a five-year period toward the end of Calvin's career, fifty-eight Genevans were sentenced to death, seventy-six exiled.

Calvin became a major force in England's religious evolution without really trying to do so. Many of the evangelicals who could not accept Henry VIII's quasi-Catholic Church had taken up exile in Geneva, where Calvin's mind and personality powerfully affected their beliefs. When they flooded back into England after Edward VI's accession, they carried a white-hot Calvinist fervor with them. They formed the nucleus of what would become a potent new element in English national life. They sparked a movement that knew what it wanted, knew that it was right, knew that its opposition was damnably wrong in the most literal sense, and was not inclined to compromise.

3

A Revolution and a Coup

Edward Tudor was fifteen and a half years old when, on the second day of April 1552, he suddenly fell ill. His physicians were of course concerned, especially when it became clear that he had not only measles (a dangerous disease into the twentieth century) but smallpox to boot. The men who were ruling in the young king's name had reason to be more worried than the doctors. If Edward died, everything they had achieved, both for themselves and for their faith, would be at risk. If he were followed on the throne by his half-sister Mary, next in line under Henry VIII's final arrangements, they could expect little better than disaster. However, the boy's recovery was swift and soon seemed complete, and in short order everyone was breathing easier.

On the brink of manhood now, Edward was taking an increasingly conspicuous part in the management of the kingdom. Under the indulgent tutelage of John Dudley, Duke of Northumberland and lord president of the Privy Council, he gave every evidence of developing into a formidable monarch. He had the Tudor intelligence, and like his father and sisters he was being given the rigorous training in languages, the classics, and theology that Renaissance Europe deemed appropriate to royalty. From early childhood he had been schooled in a very particular view of the world and his place in it, and he embraced everything he was taught: that his authority came directly from God, so that he was accountable to no living person; that God had given him dominion over the English church no less than over the state; that as God's vicar he had a solemn responsibility to establish true Christianity throughout his realm; and that the only true Christianity was the evangelical faith of his godfather Cranmer and his tutors. Having been raised and educated by passionate anti-Catholics who scorned tradition—even his stepmother Catherine Parr believed that God had chosen her to be Henry's sixth queen so that she could do her part in fending off the dark forces of superstition—he was a firm believer in justification by faith, in predestination, and in other things that his father had never ceased to abominate. Things that Henry had never stopped believing, on the other hand, were now Edward's abominations. And he displayed the eager combativeness of the incipient Puritan—a determination to engage the world and transform it into God's kingdom. Francis van der Delft, the Catholic ambassador of the doggedly Catholic Charles V, reported dryly that "in the court there is no man of learning so ready to argue in support of the new doctrine as the king, according to what his masters tell him and he learns from his preachers."

In fact, however, by 1552 Edward was no one's mere puppet. As early as 1550, barely in adolescence, he had delighted his mentors and horrified the court's remaining conservatives by demanding the removal of any invocation of the saints (veneration of saints having become an obnoxious vestige of the old religion) from the consecration oath taken by new bishops. By that time, too, Edward was objecting to the masses being said in his sister Mary's household, refusing to agree when his advisers suggested that it would be better to turn a blind eye to such practices than to provoke the wrath of her cousin the emperor. The mass was sinful, Edward insisted, and if he tolerated sinfulness he himself would sin. England's second Reformation was thus now fully under way, and it had no advocate more enthusiastic than the young king himself. It was in every respect a revolution from above, driven by a council whose conservative members had been either purged or politically neutered. With the power of the Crown at its back, it was gathering momentum in spite of having feeble support in the population or even the clergy at large. The narrowness of its base is suggested by the fact that the Canterbury and York convocations of the clergy were never asked to approve or even express an opinion about the changes being made. They were not regarded as trustworthy.

The revolution's main driver was Cranmer, whose changing beliefs had by this time carried him beyond the Lutheranism of his earlier years and to the more radical austerities of Swiss, and specifically Calvinist, reform. He achieved perhaps the greatest triumph of his career in 1552, when Parliament passed the Second Act of Uniformity and thereby mandated the use of his reworked (by himself) Prayer Book. If the earlier 1549 edition, issued before the evangelicals were sufficiently entrenched to disregard conservative opposition, had been an equivocal thing, a stopgap that satisfied no one and that exasperated the most ambitious of the reformers, the revision, or rather its adoption by Parliament, signaled the all-but-total victory of what now could be called the English Protestant church. Services cleansed of all vestiges of tradition—prayers for the dead, any mention of saints, the old familiar music and clerical vestments—became compulsory for laity and clergy alike. Harsh penalties were imposed: six months imprisonment for being present at any service not in conformity with the new law, a year for a second offense, life for a third. In other ways, too, Parliament brought to an end the liberality that had marked the beginning of the new regime (a pro forma liberality that in practice had been extended to the evangelicals only). Once again it was made treason to deny not only the royal supremacy but any prescribed article of faith. More positively, the provisions by which Henry VIII had permitted treason convictions on the basis of testimony from a single witness, prevented defendants from facing their accusers, and prescribed the death sentence for any first offense were expunged by Parliament. Henceforth the death penalty could be imposed for a first offense only if the treasonous statements were expressed in "writing, printing, carving or graving." Treason by spoken word was punishable by imprisonment and loss of possessions for first and second offenses, with a third conviction required for execution. Edward's regime, if not exactly a national liberation, continued to be not nearly as bloody as his father's.

The revolution proceeded apace, receiving fresh impetus from the many reformers who had come hurrying from the continent after the death of Henry (who would have had many of them killed for their beliefs). Seven of Henry's bishops were replaced with men of solidly evangelical credentials—men who impressed king and council with their

zeal to make England a fitting home for the elect. The Dudley administration launched yet another assault on what remained of the church's
wealth, confiscating most of the endowments of the dioceses and destroying the last of the guilds and chantries. Such raids served an array
of purposes. The government's financial state remained dizzyingly pre-
carious, and Dudley and his cohorts welcomed opportunities to funnel
fresh revenues into the treasury while skimming off a share for themselves. The most radical of the reformers would have been pleased not
merely to reduce the bishops to penury but to rid the church entirely of
its traditional structures, bishops and dioceses included. These, too,
were regarded as vestiges of the old Roman decadence.

The religious landscape was growing more complicated by the year.
Cranmer's difficulties were compounded by the fact that the uniformity
he hoped to establish at any given time was always based on what he
himself happened to believe at that time, and his beliefs were endlessly
developing. Thus he repeatedly found himself demanding that everyone
believe what he himself had previously denied, and forbidding beliefs
that he had previously held to be compulsory. There were of course no
longer any avowed *Roman* Catholics in positions of importance in the
central government or the national church, and anyone conservative
enough to try to retain the old forms without the old connection to
Rome was rendered voiceless when not purged. It was the radicals,
therefore, who now presented the most serious challenge to consensus.
Their beliefs differed bewilderingly; the innovations with which Martin
Luther had rocked Europe just three decades before could seem conservative if not reactionary when compared with the ideas more recently
imported from Geneva and Zurich. Confusion was inescapable, and discord followed inevitably in its wake. When Cranmer introduced his revised Prayer Book, the fiery Scottish preacher John Knox (trained in
Geneva and a protégé of Dudley, who had given him employment as a
royal chaplain) complained loudly because it did not ban the old practice
of kneeling to receive communion. Though Cranmer was archbishop of
Canterbury and Knox by comparison was scarcely more than a nonen-
tity, there followed a struggle for royal approval during which Edward
himself intervened to postpone the issuance of the new service. Cranmer finally prevailed, at least to the extent that worshippers were in-

structed to kneel, but he was obliged to insert into the Prayer Book a
so-called Black Rubric explaining that the practice was a gesture of
respect, not a worshipping of bread and wine.

It is hardly surprising if many men and women, faced with endless
surprises and reversals and disagreements, witnessing the abandonment
of one aspect after another of the church in which they had been raised,
simply lost interest in religion. That this was happening is suggested by
the Second Act of Uniformity, which deplored the emptiness of pews
and compelled regular attendance at approved services. But it was too
late for Parliament, or any archbishop or king, to restore uniformity on
any basis. England had become a religiously divided nation and would
remain one until, after four more centuries, it became essentially post-
Christian.

John Dudley, soon after Somerset's fall, had made himself a kind of
father figure for Edward, coaching him and encouraging his involvement in governance of church and state. At first Edward was most active
in religious matters—delaying, as we have seen, issuance of the 1552
Prayer Book—and always his aim was the acceleration of evangelical reform. Always he acted in the conviction that he was charged by God to
lead the people to the truth, and always he was applauded for this by
Dudley and Cranmer in spite of the fact that those two worthies were
often at odds with each other. In affairs of state, too, Edward gradually
became not only active but important. By 1553 he was signing the
Crown's financial warrants not only with but in place of the council.
Though it would be saying too much to claim that he was actually *ruling,* certainly he was receiving a thorough preparation for the responsibilities of kingship. His apprenticeship, reinforced by his intelligence and
immense self-assurance and an education probably more rigorous than
that received by any English king before or since, suggested that a remarkable career lay ahead.

The soldier Dudley broadened Edward's daily regimen to include the
kinds of martial exercises in which his own sons were being trained,
skills needed to make him a warrior-king in the ancient tradition. The
boy underwent instruction in horsemanship, jousting, archery, hunting,
and the latest weaponry, and though he had inherited little of his father's
strength and vitality he appears to have responded with enthusiasm. If it
is idle to wonder about what sort of man Edward might have become, it

is nonetheless irresistibly interesting. What he revealed of himself suggests that he would have ruled as flamboyantly as his father: while still little more than a child he showed a passion for gambling, lavish dress, and other extravagances. In true Henrician fashion he spent outlandish sums to acquire some of the costliest gems to be found on the continent even as his government struggled to stave off insolvency. He appears to have been like his father, too, in taking no interest in whatever misfortunes—hunger resulting from failed harvests, outbreaks of plague or the sweat—might be afflicting his subjects. Perhaps his least attractive characteristic was his apparent conviction, which could easily look like priggishness anchored in arrogance, that he possessed not only the authority but the wisdom to manage the lives of his elders. He not only attempted to prevent his sister Mary from hearing mass but admonished her to refrain from dancing, an innocent pleasure that that thwarted and unhappy spinster must have badly needed. When his schoolmate Barnaby Fitzpatrick went off to study in Paris, Edward sent him hectoring letters cautioning him to avoid not only Catholic observances but the company of women. On the other hand, he displayed no thirst for blood; so far as is known, the fact that neither Somerset nor Dudley killed a single conservative for resistance to reform was perfectly acceptable to the king.

As for what the future might bring—for Edward VI it brought almost nothing. What sixteenth-century medical science could not know was that at some point in childhood or early adolescence he had contracted tuberculosis. The infection had been confined inside the healthy tissue of his lungs but not eliminated, and his brief illness of April 1552 amounted to a sentence of death because measles destroys the immune system's ability to keep latent tuberculosis in check. As the year proceeded he continued with his studies, continued to pursue the military exercises that Dudley had introduced, and continued to participate in the work of the council and the formalities and festivities of what remained a fairly splendid Renaissance court. But he was slowly, inexorably, invisibly dying. He had never been an impressive physical specimen (an Italian physician named Hieronymus Cardano, upon meeting him, reported that he was "of a stature somewhat below the middle height, pale-faced with gray eyes . . . rather of a bad habit of body than a sufferer from fixed diseases" and "carried himself like an old man"), and in the course of growing up he had occasionally been seriously ill with diseases including malaria. Overall, however, through most of 1552 he seemed healthy enough and even engaged in jousting for the first time. Eventually, it became evident that something was wrong. By year-end a chronic cough and increasing weakness were making it obvious to all, the king himself included, that something was *seriously* wrong. He continued to deteriorate through the first months of 1533, then experienced a remission that sparked hopes of a recovery, and finally relapsed so severely that in the first week of June both he and his councilors were advised that death was now not only inevitable but likely to come soon.

He makes a melancholy picture: this solitary boy, his father and mother and stepmothers all long dead, separated by religion from the one sister to whom he appears to have had a strong bond of affection, faced with oblivion just as a life of limitless possibility was opening before him. It is difficult to comprehend, today, the extent to which his life as a juvenile king in an almost fantastically formal court had cut him off from normal human interaction. Not even Edward's sisters could speak to him without first kneeling, and when either of them dined "with" him, she had to sit not at the same table but off at a distance, on a low cushion. His food was served by nobles and gentlemen who were obliged to kneel before placing their offerings on the table. All this went far beyond the protocols of even the French court, where serving was done by pages rather than mature men of high rank, and where even the pages had only to bow rather than kneel. Everything reinforced in Edward the sense that he was a being apart, existing on a plane beyond the reach of ordinary humans. Eventually some suitable marriage might have brought him companionship. Though his early betrothals—first to Mary, Queen of Scots, and then to a French princess—had come to nothing, and though a nearly bankrupt English Crown no longer could play as weighty a role in continental affairs as it had during his father's prime, Edward was still as marriageable a young bachelor as any in Europe. Now, however, none of that meant anything. There would be no marriage, no fourth generation of Tudor kings . . . no companion.

Facing the end, the certainty that he could hope for nothing in this world, Edward turned his attention to what would happen after he was gone. In all of England and Wales hardly anyone could have been more passionately devoted to the cause of religious reform, more certain that the Protestant revolution being carried out during his reign was a triumph for divine truth and that a reversal of that revolution would be a disaster worse than war or plague. But under the terms of his father's last will, the throne was to pass next to his sister Mary, who in Edward's presence had proclaimed herself ready to die rather than abandon her Catholic faith. The affection that Edward had always shown for Mary did not keep him from recoiling at the prospect of a Catholic queen. Thus was he moved, as his life began to ebb away, to search for a way to pass the crown to someone other than Mary and also other than his other sister. (Elizabeth, whatever her religious inclinations, was burdened with the same liability as Mary: though Henry's will recognized her as third in line to the throne, she like Mary remained illegitimate under a statute that Parliament had never repealed. Thus if Mary were to be set aside on grounds of bastardy—probably the best available way of denying her the crown—Elizabeth, too, would be disqualified.)

Edward needed an heir of royal blood and impeccable legitimacy. At least as important, because this was the point of everything he was setting out to do, his heir must be solidly Protestant. But the condition of the Tudor family tree in 1553 was such that, to find someone who satisfied all three criteria, he was going to have to stretch the law in awkward ways.

The first problem was the curious fact that, among the descendants of Henry VII then living in England, Edward was the only male. As a result of the early deaths over two generations of several Scottish princes, the only surviving product of his aunt Margaret Tudor's marriage to King James IV of Scotland was the young Mary, Queen of Scots. Henry VIII, perhaps because Margaret's offspring were foreigners and perhaps out of pique with her irregular marital history, had excluded her entire branch of the family from the succession. Had he not done so, Edward would have found Mary unacceptable anyway. She was reputed to be almost as fervent a Catholic as he was an evangelical. Nearly as bad, she was not only living in France but betrothed to the heir to the French throne.

This left the fruit of the love match between Henry VIII's younger sister Mary and Charles Brandon, Duke of Suffolk. Four children had been born of this union, two sons and two daughters, but the boys had both died in childhood. When Mary herself died at age thirty-seven, she was

survived only by the girls Frances and Eleanor, who were married to
Henry Grey, Marquess of Dorset, and Henry Clifford, Earl of Cumber-
land, respectively. Eleanor Clifford was dead by 1553, but she and her sister between them had four living children, the eldest just reaching
maturity. All, as it happened, were female: Frances's daughters Jane,
Catherine, and Mary Grey, and Eleanor's daughter, Margaret Clifford.
(The Grey sisters, incidentally, were granddaughters of one of the sons
that Elizabeth Woodville had before her marriage to Edward IV.)

If Frances or any of her children or Eleanor's one child had been
male, Edward would have had no difficulty in selecting his heir. The absence of a single male among them, however, complicated matters considerably. Throughout the thousand-plus years of post-Roman English
history, there had been only one attempt to place a female claimant on
the throne, and that had led (back in the twelfth century, when King
Henry I died leaving only a daughter) to years of disorder and war.
A pair of documents survives showing the steps by which the dying
Edward groped toward a solution. In the first, a draft in Edward's
own hand, he proposes leaving the throne of England to "the Lady
Fraunces's heirs masles" first (Frances was still in her mid-thirties, possibly still capable of producing a son), then to the male heirs of Frances's
daughters beginning with "the Lady Jane's" because she was the eldest.
The problem was that none of the Grey girls had heirs male or otherwise—Jane was only sixteen, her sisters scarcely more than children. According to this first plan of Edward's, after his death the throne would
have to remain vacant until someone in the Grey family gave birth to a
boy. And what if one of the younger sisters had a son before Jane?
Would the succession remain in abeyance until Jane either bore a son or
grew too old to do so?

It was impossible. Edward in his next draft removed Frances from the
succession—there is no evidence that she objected—and with a few
strokes of his pen outlined an almost outlandishly ambitious new plan.
The deletion of an apostrophe and a single letter turned "Jane's" into
"Jane," and the words "and her" were inserted immediately thereafter.
Now the crown was to pass not to the male heirs *of* Jane Grey but to *"the
Lady Jane and her heirs masles."* (Edward was of course highly literate, but
spelling was a kind of free-form creative art in the sixteenth century.)

Thus did a doomed youth put his mind at rest. The Greys were confirmed evangelicals. In their hands his church, his legacy, would be safe.

But there was a joker in the deck, one that added a bizarre dynastic twist to the king's plan and continues to complicate historians' efforts to understand why the situation unfolded as it did. Shortly before Edward's remission ended and the imminence of death became undeniable, a flurry of grand marriages and betrothals had been arranged by John Dudley. His youngest daughter was wed to the son and heir of the Earl of Huntingdon, who was of royal blood through the Pole family and an ally worth having. The duke's brother Andrew Dudley was betrothed to Margaret Clifford, who was thirty years his junior but, as we have seen, a possible heir to the throne. The two younger Grey sisters were likewise dispensed to the advantage of the Dudleys: Catherine was affianced to the son and heir of the Earl of Pembroke, who owed his title and much of his wealth to his alliance with the Dudleys, Mary to the son of a somewhat lesser notable. Each of these unions served to tighten the duke's connections to important families and factions—sources of support that might become a matter of life or death in case of serious trouble. Even when taken together, however, they were trivial in comparison with the wedding that formed the centerpiece of the celebrations that spilled out into the streets of London from John Dudley's grand residence. On May 25 Lady Jane Grey, heir presumptive according to King Edward's still-secret plan, was married to young Guildford Dudley (he was in his late teens, though his year of birth is not certain), fourth among the duke's five sons.

Even if King Edward had not been dying, the wedding would have been a coup for the Dudleys. Quite apart from her royal blood, Jane as the eldest daughter of a sonless duke was a great dynastic prize. At one time she had been considered a possible bride for the king himself; probably they would have been a good match, being not only of almost exactly the same age but physically attractive, superbly educated, and devotedly evangelical. The Duke of Somerset, during his time as lord protector, had made preliminary arrangements to marry his son to Jane, but that opportunity was lost with the Seymour party's fall from power. John Dudley's success in bringing the girl into his family, combined with the altering of the succession, set the stage for Dudleys—possibly Guildford himself, certainly any son that he and Jane succeeded in producing—to be kings of England. The question of whether the scheme originated with Edward or with the duke remains unresolved. Whatever the case, both were entirely committed to the project and had excellent reasons to be so. For the king it meant that the gospel could be preserved in England for all time—that his short life and shorter reign would have vast and eternal value. For the duke it meant not only deliverance from his many enemies—and the gruff Dudley, for all his courage and ability, was disliked by almost everyone except his own family and his king—but the opportunity to continue ruling England indefinitely through a daughter-in-law whom he undoubtedly expected to be the pliant instrument of his will.

Poor Edward, who could only listen from his deathbed as news was brought of the nuptials of the young woman who under other circumstances might one day have become his bride, was by June in a desperately bad state, weak and racked by fits of coughing, needing stimulants to remain focused. He knew that no scribbled statement of his desire to bypass his sisters in favor of Jane could be depended upon to alter the succession. Something more formal, more official, was needed. On June 12 he revealed his thinking to a group of the court's legal officers, explaining why he regarded it as impossible to allow Mary to succeed him and instructing them to draw up whatever documents they deemed necessary to make Jane incontestably his heir. Two days later, in reporting to the Privy Council as the king had ordered them to do, the lawyers complained that if they followed Edward's instructions they would violate Henry VIII's final Succession Act and thereby commit treason. John Dudley, infuriated at being blocked in this way, arranged for the lawyers (among whom were the solicitor-general and attorney-general) to meet again with an equally dissatisfied king. They told Edward that the succession, having been established by statute, could not be changed except through passage of a new statute. This was a trenchant argument—a measure of the extent to which Parliament's role in the making of law was taking firm root even in the midst of the Tudor autocracy—but entirely unacceptable to Edward, who could have no confidence of living long enough for a Parliament to be summoned and put through the necessary paces. He declared that he wanted the matter settled immediately by execution of a deed that the next Parliament could ratify when it met in September, and he tried to assuage the fears of the lawmen by assuring them that it could not possibly be treason to obey a living king. After a good deal of bullying by various lords and members of the council, Sir Edward Montague, chief justice of the Court of Common Pleas, agreed to comply on two conditions. He wanted a written commission authorizing him to act—a document bearing the imprint of the Great Seal. And he wanted, in advance, a pardon freeing him from any future charge of treason. When this was granted, all the lawyers fell into line.

One last thing could be done, short of parliamentary ratification, to give a patina of legitimacy to Edward's plan. The deed that Montague and the others now hastened to complete for the king's signature could be endorsed by every personage of importance in the kingdom. The collection of signatures, and of the seals of the individuals doing the signing, therefore became a matter of urgency. Generally there was little difficulty: the Privy Council and Crown offices had, over the preceding few years, been packed with men of Dudley's choosing, and there remained few bishops or nobles with reason, doctrinal or financial or otherwise, to want the throne to pass to an adherent of the Roman church. Cranmer proved more difficult than most, complaining that he could not sign without violating the oath he had sworn to Henry VIII. Ultimately, however, he showed himself to be as willing to conform to the will of the son as to that of the father. His signature became the last of the 101 affixed to the formidable document declaring Jane Grey to be Edward's rightful heir.

It came none too soon. The bright and earnest young king, as yearned-for a prince as had ever been born in England, was at the end of his resources. His final days, horrible to behold, must have been far more horrible to undergo. "He has not the strength to stir, and can hardly breathe," the imperial ambassador reported. "His body no longer performs its functions, his nails and hair are falling out, and all his person is scabby." Another courtier reported that the king's body was riddled with "ulcers," probably a reference to bedsores. In any event he was no longer capable of anything more than waiting, preparing, and perhaps hoping for death. The fulfillment of his last great wish was going to depend, and depend entirely, on John Dudley.

Dudley understood that, no matter how many signatures and seals were affixed to a piece of vellum, success was not assured. He controlled the government and all its instruments, but by this point it was a weak government not only financially but militarily, the sorry state of the treasury having made it necessary to disband the mercenary troops, Italian and German mainly, used in suppressing the risings of 1549. Dudley himself was a charmless, graceless figure, resented at court for his rough style and for having risen so high after beginning as the son of an attainted traitor. (In all of England there were currently only three dukes, one of whom had been languishing in prison since before the death of Henry VIII, and Dudley was the first in history without even a trace of blood connection to the royal family.) To the common people he had always seemed a distant and threatening figure, the bad duke who had destroyed their friend the good Duke Somerset and crushed them for seeking redress of their grievances. Nothing if not practical and hardheaded, Dudley is unlikely to have harbored many illusions about the number and quality of his friends.

The central issue, however, proved to be not Dudley's popularity but the strength of Lady Jane's claim versus that of Mary Tudor. Jane was in fact a person of rather lofty character for a sixteen-year-old, dignified, serious about serious matters, to all appearances utterly without personal ambition. But few people outside the court had ever heard of her, and almost no one knew anything about her. It was hard to believe—it was inconceivable, actually—that her sudden emergence as monarch was going to be greeted with widespread enthusiasm. Mary, by contrast, had been born and raised a public figure, a mighty king's eldest daughter and therefore generally recognized as the rightful successor once his only son was gone. She was a woman against whom no bad thing could be said except by those who regarded her religion as intolerable. Great sympathy had been aroused by the humiliations to which she and her mother had been subjected over a quarter of a century. She was a formidable threat to everything Edward had planned, and would have to be dealt with.

Edward's sufferings came to an end on the evening of July 6. He died in the arms of a Dudley son-in-law, Sir Henry Sidney, who later reported that the "sweetness" with which the king had surrendered his spirit "would have converted the fiercest of papists if they had any grace in them of true faith in Christ." Before losing the ability to speak, Sidney said, Edward "made a prayer to God to deliver this nation from that uncharitable religion of popery, which was the chiefest cause for his election of the Lady Jane Grey to succeed before his sister Mary . . . out of pure love to his subjects, that he desired they might live and die in the Lord, as he did." The death was kept secret while Dudley made his arrangements to transfer the crown to his daughter-in-law. The Tower of London and Windsor Castle were put on alert, the Privy Council was assembled in the Tower, lords lieutenant in every part of the kingdom were instructed to be ready to muster their forces, and warships were deployed in the Channel to intercept any vessel attempting to carry Mary away. A Dudley daughter was dispatched to escort Lady Jane (not yet informed of the king's death) from Chelsea (where she had gone to recover from what she believed to have been an attempted poisoning) to Syon House (which had been a great abbey until seized by Henry VIII, briefly became the property of Lord Protector Edward Seymour, and now belonged to the Dudleys). John Dudley himself, at the head of a delegation including the late Queen Catherine Parr's brother and three earls, called on Lady Jane there and informed her on his knees that the king was dead and had named her as his successor. Jane, by her own later account, thereupon fell to the floor and began to weep, protesting that she was unprepared for and unworthy of the crown. In due course she was persuaded to accept God's will and vowed to do her best. The next day, July 10, Jane's elevation was proclaimed throughout London along with a declaration that neither Mary nor Elizabeth could inherit. Three reasons were given: Henry VIII's daughters were bastards under the law, were merely half-sisters to the king, and might, if either became queen, jeopardize England's autonomy by marrying some foreign, possibly Catholic, prince. The first and second arguments were, if they had an impact at all, counterproductive: the denial of Mary's legitimacy was widely offensive, and not to the conservatives only. Jane was escorted to the Tower amid the celebratory firing of cannons and such other fanfare as Dudley and his associates could arrange. Behind the scenes, however, there were early signs of discord: when Dudley advised his daughter-in-law to declare her bridegroom king of England, he was immediately rebuffed. The crown, Jane declared with a firmness that must have taken her father-in-law aback, was "not a plaything for boys and girls." In the great scheme of things it was a minor setback; at worst, it meant that the crowning of a Dudley king might have to be postponed a generation.

The duke had already overreached himself and was lucky to have been refused. People were reacting with sullen surprise to the news that someone called Jane was their new queen. Many would have been outraged to learn that a son of the unpopular upstart Dudley was being foisted off on them as king. In the streets of London the lack of enthusiasm for the new regime was painfully obvious. There were no cheers or demonstrations, no spontaneous lighting of bonfires, none of the effusions of joy with which the citizenry customarily welcomed the advent of a new reign. Still, Dudley's position, and Jane's, seemed unassailable. Dudley controlled the levers of power. He had even received assurances of support from Henry II of France, eager to help if he could to keep a cousin and protégé of Charles V from the English throne. Charles's representatives in London, meanwhile, were reporting glumly that the English capital, government, and treasury were all in Dudley's hands, that Queen Jane had already been officially recognized, and that Mary's chances of reversing this fait accompli were virtually nil.

Mary, however, had ideas of her own. Convinced that she was the rightful queen, willing to believe that it was her destiny to restore the true faith to her homeland, she had no intention of surrendering. She and Elizabeth had been at their country seats as Edward entered his final decline, keeping themselves as informed as they could about his condition. When they received instructions to come to the king at Greenwich, both sensed danger. Elizabeth claimed to be too ill to travel. Mary set out from her residence at Hunsdon, but proceeded so slowly that in two days she covered barely five miles and at the end of the second day was still at Hoddesdon on the outskirts of London. She would have entered the capital the next day, placing herself at the mercy of Dudley and the council, but during the night someone sent a message informing her of the king's death. Within minutes, with members of her household struggling to keep pace, she was galloping off northward, away from London and toward her Kenninghall estate in East Anglia. Since her reconciliation with her father a decade before, she had been the owner of extensive East Anglian properties, and the local population was friendly. Dudley dispatched two of his sons, Henry and Robert, to find Mary and deliver her to London, but when the latter arrived at Hunsdon he found her gone. Word soon reached London that fighting men by the hundreds were rallying to Mary, and that she was receiving substantial financial support as well. When she moved on from Kenninghall, she and her followers were refused admittance to Norwich, a city that had fresh and painful memories of what was likely to happen to those who defied John Dudley. The town of Framlingham, however, threw open its gates.

In short order Mary found herself in command of tens of thousands of armed men. As word spread of what was happening, impressive demonstrations of support spread from London up the Thames valley into Oxfordshire. The fleet deployed to keep her from escaping across the Channel returned to port and declared for her. Still, Dudley continued to have the advantage. When Mary sent a messenger to the council demanding recognition as queen, an order to the lords lieutenant, supposedly from Queen Jane but actually written by Cranmer, instructed them to ignore any appeals from the "bastard doughter to our said dearest cousin and progenitor great unkle Henry the eight of famous memory." When the clergy were told to preach against Mary, none did so more energetically than Nicholas Ridley, evangelical bishop of London. The congregations he addressed listened impassively while word reached the capital of the growing numbers of volunteers gathering around Mary in East Anglia.

Dudley knew that it was essential to confront Mary and disperse her supporters before things got out of hand. His troops, however, were all in or near London, and among his associates there was scarcely a man who was both capable of leading an army into battle and entirely trustworthy. By the same token he had no one he trusted to hold his party together in London if he went off to fight. He tried to send the Duke of Suffolk, Queen Jane's father (not much of a soldier, but unlikely to defect), but she would not allow him to go. In the end Dudley had no choice except to assemble such troops as he could muster—not more than a few thousand probably—and lead them out of the city himself. Before departing he sent word to the nobles to join him as quickly as possible with as many men as they could muster.

Both in East Anglia and in the capital, Dudley's situation quickly fell apart. He proceeded to Cambridge and from there toward Framlingham, but as his troops advanced they encountered increasing demonstrations of the population's hostility. He reached Bury St. Edmunds in a state of thorough demoralization and, finding no support there, decided to turn back. In London, meanwhile, a frightened council had broken up into bickering factions and finally dissolved. On July 19 a number of the leading councilors, among them the earls of Shrewsbury, Bedford, and Arundel and the same Earl of Pembroke to whom Dudley had given Lady Catherine Grey as a daughter-in-law, broke ranks and declared for Mary. Jane's own father pulled the cloth canopy of royalty from above his daughter's head, announced that Mary was queen, and fled. Jane herself, nine days after being proclaimed queen, quietly withdrew to Syon House.

John Dudley's years as the most powerful man in England ended with a whimper. His army having deserted and his cause lost, he stood alone in the market square at Cambridge and tearfully declared Mary Tudor his queen. In a forlorn attempt to demonstrate a joy he cannot have felt, he threw his cap into the air. The next day he was taken to London surrounded by guards who were needed less to keep him from escaping than to protect him from angry crowds.

Two weeks later, accompanied by her sister Elizabeth and Anne of Cleves, Queen Mary I entered London. This time the expressions of joy were loud and long and genuine.

THE MAKING OF MARY

WHEN THE FIRST WOMAN EVER TO RULE ENGLAND TOOK the throne in 1553, she was already a tragic figure. For a quarter of a century she had been immersed in betrayal, loss, and grief. Her life had been blighted first by the egotism of a father who was quite prepared to destroy her, then by a young half-brother who regarded it as his sacred duty to save her from her own deepest beliefs and, when that could not be arranged, to save England from her.

It was all doubly sad because Mary's life had begun so brilliantly. From earliest childhood she had been an ornament of the English court, a pretty little golden-haired princess doted on by her parents and by every noble, churchman, soldier, and diplomat eager for her parents' favor. Her father would carry her about, proudly showing her off. Her mother had raised Mary as she herself had been raised: to become the wife and partner of a monarch. It was impossible to doubt that she would become exactly that. She was betrothed to the eldest son of Francis of France at age two, and to her cousin Charles V at five (when the emperor was twenty-one). Later there were discussions of her possible marriage to her Scottish cousin James V, to other princes of France, to a son of the Duke of Cleves, and to Francesco Sforza, Duke of Milan. One by one these possibilities faded as international alliances came and went, but there seemed no cause for hurry. Quite the contrary: the French ambassador, in reporting on the eleven-year-old Mary, told Francis that though she was "admirable by reason of her great and uncommon mental endowments," she was also "so thin, sparse and small as to render it impossible for her to be married for the next three years."

Meanwhile she continued to prepare for whatever great match lay ahead. She was tutored not only by leading English scholars but by respected humanists from the continent, and she wrote and spoke Latin fluently by age nine. She was equally proficient in French, shared her father's love of music and dance and learned to play several instruments, and under her mother's watchful eye was given a solid grounding in the classics and theology. In the Tudor pattern she was a dutiful child, eager to please, and throughout the first decade of her life she had no reason to think that either of her parents would ever want her to be anything other than a faithful and obedient daughter of Holy Mother Church. In England as in all of Europe's greatest royal houses, conventional Catholic piety was taken for granted as integral to being female and royal.

At age ten Mary was set up with her own court at Ludlow Castle, the very place to which Catherine of Aragon and her first husband had been sent shortly after their marriage—the place where Prince Arthur met his early death. There Mary became a figurehead under whose banner a council of Cardinal Wolsey's appointees managed Wales and the marches that bordered it. This was to be the beginning of her apprenticeship in government. It also made her, in effect if not by official proclamation, the first *Princess* of Wales. It was a signal that, in spite of the signs of favor that her father had recently showered on his illegitimate son Henry Fitzroy, *she* was his heir and rightful successor.

When Mary was recalled to court a year and a half later, however, she found everything changed in alarming ways. Her father and Wolsey, unhappy about the dominance that Charles V now enjoyed on the continent in the aftermath of his victory over the French at Pavia, were considering a treaty under which Mary would become the wife not of Francis I's son but of Francis himself. Queen Catherine could only have been appalled, not only because of her wish for friendship between England and her imperial nephew but also because Francis, a thirty-three-year-old widower with voracious and wide-ranging sexual appetites, was hardly the husband that any loving mother would have chosen for her not-yet-grown child. Francis, in any case, had no interest in waiting for a girl who was still years short of the age at which cohabitation would become permissible under church law. Mary was betrothed to his second son, the Duke of Orleans, instead. Assuming that Mary was informed of any of this, she is unlikely to have taken it seriously; the volatility of her father's relationship with Francis made this latest arrangement as implausible as those that had come before. (In fact, Francis would eventually repudiate his treaty with England and marry Orleans—the future King Henry II—to Pope Clement's niece Catherine de'

Medici, who in the fullness of time would join the ranks of France's most remarkable and ultimately tragic queens.)

It was not the bartering over possible marriages that caused life to turn dark for Mary, but the unmistakable evidence that her parents' union was breaking down. By the spring of 1527, when she returned from Ludlow, the king was not only far advanced in his obsession with Anne Boleyn but raising questions about the validity of his marriage. In July Henry informed Catherine that they had never been married, and from that moment the two of them were at war. Mary regarded her mother as entirely innocent and grievously wronged, but like Catherine she was unable to blame Henry. Anne became the villain, responsible for the unhappy wreck that the royal family had become, and her understandable inclination to see Mary as a rival for Henry's affection, and therefore as a mortal threat, was soon inflamed. As Mary entered adolescence, she found herself spurned by her father. Her mother, who had always been devoted and would remain so through all the misfortunes now descending upon them, was sent away, she and Mary forbidden to see each other. As Henry's rejection of wife and child broadened into an attack on the church that both parents had always taught Mary to revere, the magnitude of the disaster must have become literally incredible in her eyes. Anne for her part became so ferociously hostile, swearing that Mary would be either reduced to servility or given to some lowborn husband, that people loyal to Mary feared for her life. Her health, which had always been good, began to fail under the strain.

In 1533, with the king's marriage to Anne and the birth of their daughter Elizabeth, a separate household was established for the newborn at Hatfield House some seventeen miles from London. Mary's household was shut down, and she was ordered to become a maid of honor to her infant half-sister. She was told also that she herself, being illegitimate, was not a princess and never had been and must stop using the title or expecting others to use it in addressing her. Mary accepted none of this; to do so would have seemed a gross betrayal of her mother. She said disingenuously that she did not understand what princess she was supposed to serve, dryly noting that "Madame de Pembroke" (a reference to the title that Henry had conferred on Anne before their marriage) could have no child of such exalted rank. The situation at Hatfield proved to be intolerable not only for Mary but for Anne, who visited with some fre-

quency. Mary's stubbornness sparked quarrels; most of the temper appears to have been on Anne's side, while Mary maintained a coldly insulting disdain. Things only grew worse when Anne, attempting to make
peace, offered to intercede with the king on Mary's behalf if she would
recognize her as queen. Mary replied that she recognized no queen except her mother. Anne retaliated in pettily vindictive ways, confiscating
Mary's clothing and jewelry. A low point was reached when the household was moving temporarily to another place so that Hatfield could be
cleaned and aired out at the end of winter; Mary refused to go unless
acknowledged as princess. In the end she had to be forcibly stuffed into
a cart and hauled, complaining, away.

Henry held himself aloof from this latest mess of his own making, refusing to see Mary when he visited Hatfield, which he did rarely. One of
the most poignant scenes of the whole Tudor story took place at the conclusion of one of his visits. On the morning of his departure, happening
to look up as he mounted his horse, the king saw Mary alone on a ter-
race at the top of the house. She was on her knees, hands clasped before
her, gazing down at her father in silent supplication. He touched his
hand to his cap in salute, but rode away without saying a word. He was
angrier with Mary than she knew, seething at her refusal to accept her reduced state. Still scarcely more than a child, adoring her father as daughters are naturally inclined to do, she continued to lay all the blame for
her troubles on Anne. Like her mother she clung to the barren hope that
her father would recover his senses and return to his family.

This grotesque battle of wills went on unresolved for two and a half
years; Mary fought back against what she could see only as malicious
humiliation, and Anne was unable to avoid regular confrontations with
an implacable little stepdaughter whose actions—whose very existence—were a challenge to her and her child's place in the world. Their
drama unfolded against a background of historic events: the bishops'
surrender of their ancient rights, the resignation of Thomas More, the
start of Henry's judicial murders. When Parliament's passage of the first
Act of Succession required everyone in the kingdom to take an oath acknowledging Anne as queen and Elizabeth as heir and both Catherine
and Mary refused, Henry let it pass. Possibly he wished, out of some
residuum of affection and respect, to spare them the penalty for high
treason. It is at least as likely that he was simply being sensible. Nothing

in the world would have been more likely to provoke his subjects than the trial or attainder—never mind the execution—of the admired woman most of them still regarded as their queen and her dutiful young daughter. The terms of Mary's confinement were, however, made even more stringent. She was allowed no visitors except, occasionally, Charles V's longtime ambassador Eustace Chapuys. By 1535 she and Chapuys were aware of rumors that the Boleyn party were planning to have her and her mother killed. (There is no evidence that any such thing was planned, but even the ugliest rumors had to be taken seriously now that Henry was killing old friends for refusing to accept his supremacy.) Soon Mary, her nerve failing along with her health, was begging Chapuys to help her escape to the continent. Nothing came of this, in part because Mary became too ill to flee (her physicians reported that she was immobilized by "grief and despair"), in part because the emperor Charles, short of money as usual, had no wish to assume responsibility for providing Mary with the kind of household appropriate to the princess that he himself declared her to be.

The death of Catherine early in 1536 brought fresh grief; even at the end Henry would not allow Mary to visit her mother. The political situation, however, was unaffected by the passing of the old queen (who was all of fifty when she died). It was her daughter, not she, who had a claim to the throne and therefore constituted a challenge to the new queen's security. Everything did change four and a half months later, however, with the nullification of Anne's marriage followed by her beheading; now the child Elizabeth was no less a bastard than Mary. Suddenly everything seemed open to negotiation and rearrangement. With no woman living who could claim to be his wife, Henry was free not only to marry whomever he chose but to do so with the blessings of the church; a healing of the breach with Rome had become entirely possible. The pope expected this to happen, as, probably, did Mary. Henry, however, appears never to have considered compromising the supremacy that he had taken such extreme measures to achieve. He wed Jane Seymour without so much as a nod in Rome's direction and proceeded with the consolidation of his power over the church. Nor did he display any interest in reconciliation with his eldest child.

It was left to Mary to seek an end to their estrangement. She began by approaching Cromwell, now the king's right hand, who replied that nothing would be possible until she showed herself willing to extend to her father the obedience that was his right. Cromwell meant, by this, that Mary must acknowledge that her parents had never been married and that Henry was supreme head of the church. Mary, however, chose to put an easier interpretation on his words, taking them as an invitation to assure her father in general terms that she remained his faithful and loving daughter. She wrote directly to the king, asking him "to consider that I am but a woman and your child, who hath committed her soul only to God, and her body to be ordered in this world as it shall stand with your pleasure." She assured him of her willingness to submit to him in all things "next to God."

Clearly she had little understanding of who her father was at this stage—of how convinced he was that the only way to be faithful to God was to be submissive to him. She must have had no understanding of how little the destruction of Anne Boleyn had done to soften his attitude toward anyone who resisted. Her three words "next to God" acted on Henry like a red cape on a bull. Instead of answering Mary's letter, he sent the Duke of Norfolk and the bishop of Chichester to where she was now being kept, at Hunsdon. They demanded to know whether she accepted the Act of Supremacy and her own illegitimacy. In refusing both points, Mary made herself doubly guilty of high treason. The climactic struggle between father and daughter was joined, throwing Mary into a situation vastly more dangerous than the worst of her earlier experiences.

The king and Cromwell had all the advantages, and they used them to full effect. What Cromwell wanted was not Mary's death, with its incalculable political risks, but her surrender. Therefore, though he removed members of the Privy Council suspected of being sympathetic to her, at the same time he brushed aside the demands of other members that she be brought to a trial that could only end in her conviction. And though some of her oldest and closest friends were arrested and questioned, this was done not in the expectation of learning anything but simply for the purpose of frightening Mary and anyone inclined to support her. Finally, three weeks after her first hopeful letter to the king, she broke, signing the articles of submission that Cromwell had prepared for her. Thereby she repudiated not only the Roman church but, in a real sense, her mother. Anyone inclined to judge her for this act should remember that she was almost totally isolated, threatened not only with her own de-struction but that of her most faithful friends, and barely twenty years old.

It was perhaps King Henry's most grotesque victory, grotesque not only because he achieved it over his own helpless child but because he seems to have crushed, very nearly to have extinguished, her spirit. Cha-puys would claim, in his dispatches, that Mary had yielded without reading the articles of submission, that her motive had been to save not herself but her friends, and that she was prostrate with guilt over having compromised herself so deeply. Other evidence suggests that her surren-der was very real and very nearly complete. A letter of effusive thanks to Cromwell for saving her life gives no hint of being anything but sincere. The same is true of Mary's letters to the emperor Charles and his sister, the regent of the Netherlands; she told them of having been shown by the Holy Spirit that the pope had no authority in England, and that her parents' relationship had been incestuous. It is possible that she wrote such things in the expectation that her correspondence was being inter-cepted by Cromwell; there is no way of being certain.

One thing only indicated that the autonomy of Mary's person had not been utterly destroyed. Ordered to provide the names of those who had advised and supported her in her refusal to submit, she not only de-clined but said she would die before betraying her friends in any such way. At this point Cromwell—or was it Henry?—decided that the game was at an end, that nothing could be gained by further intimidation or new demands. Though not legitimated, Mary was restored to favor. Henry visited her in company with his bride Jane Seymour, invited her to begin spending time at court, and significantly increased her al-lowance. The household at Hatfield House was expanded and reorgan-ized so that Mary's standing was equal to Elizabeth's.

By late 1536—the time of the Pilgrimage of Grace, which she did nothing to encourage or support—Mary was spending a great deal of time in her father's presence. She established an affectionate relationship with Queen Jane, who was close to her in age and of similarly conserva-tive religious leanings. The birth of Prince Edward in October 1537 came as an immense relief to Mary: the existence of a male heir reduced her political importance to an extent that she can only have welcomed after so many years of tension. It must also have encouraged hopes that the king might remove the cloud of illegitimacy from over her head. (In fact Henry, in futile pursuit of an understanding with France, offered at about this time to legitimize Mary in order to make possible her marriage to yet another prince of France's royal house.) Jane's death appears to have been at least as hard a blow for Mary as for Henry, but it did nothing to disturb her status at court. On the contrary, during the two years that the king remained unattached Mary basked in his favor, emerging as the most important female personage in England. His next wife, Anne of Cleves, came and went too quickly to present difficulties. Even during her father's marriage to Catherine Howard, Mary remained a significant presence at court. In Catherine Parr Mary found another friend; the fact that the two women became close in spite of Catherine's evangelical convictions is suggestive of the extent to which Mary was, at this point, unwilling to make an issue of religious differences.

A development of greater importance than Henry's sixth marriage was the new Act of Succession of 1543. It stated that if Edward died without offspring the crown was to go first to Mary and "the heirs of her body" and then, if Mary, too, died without issue, to Elizabeth and her descendants. This act became law without any effort to legitimate either Mary or Elizabeth (the king's marriages to their mothers remained null). It meant—bastardy always having been a barrier to succession—that for the first time in history an English king was claiming the right to *choose* his successors. Though it must have seemed improbable, in 1543, that not one of Henry's three offspring would leave a child to carry on the dynasty, the act made provision for such an eventuality by giving his Grey and Clifford cousins a place in the order of succession. It is ironic, in light of what history held in store, that the descendants of Henry's elder sister Margaret were excluded altogether. It is only through Margaret that today's royal family is related to the Tudors at all.

King Henry's death at the start of 1547 appeared at first to improve Mary's position. Now she was not only first in line to the throne but financially independent. Under the terms of her father's will she inherited property generating an annual income of nearly £4,000, which made her wealthier than anyone else in England aside from the new king and perhaps two or three members of the high nobility. For the first time in her life, and she was entering her thirties now, she did not have to look to the treasury for her support. The fact that much of her property was concentrated in East Anglia, having been taken from the Howards when Henry attainted the Duke of Norfolk and had the Earl of Surrey executed, gave her a base not far from London. She had always had a good relationship with the boy Edward, so the start of his reign appeared to presage good fortune.

The good times in Mary's life were always brief, however, and now as before, the question of religion brought trouble. It began with the Privy Council's determination, under the Duke of Somerset's leadership, to push ahead with innovations that the late king had consistently rejected. A decade had passed since Mary's acceptance of her father's supremacy. Since then she had shown herself to be consistently, almost surprisingly comfortable with the church that Henry had brought into existence—a church that conformed in most respects to Catholic tradition. In this she was no different from other leading conservatives, bishops such as Gardiner, Tunstal, and Bonner, and nobles such as Norfolk until his calamitous fall. If a definite settlement of disputed questions had not been achieved under Henry, a fairly solid truce had. It might have endured for years more, might have hardened into something permanent, if the evangelicals led by the increasingly heterodox Thomas Cranmer had not begun campaigning for further change, and if they had not received the full support of Protector Somerset, the council that he headed, and the boy-king himself. We saw earlier how Cranmer, just months after Henry's death, issued for the use of the entire clergy a book of homilies, sermons, that propounded the archbishop's acceptance of Lutheran dogma including justification by faith alone. This was, according to the Act of Six Articles passed by Parliament at Henry's direction in 1539 and still in effect at the time of his death, heresy pure and simple. Not surprisingly the book met with much resistance and much complaint. Some of the more prominent objectors—Gardiner, Bonner, old Tunstal—soon found themselves in prison and deprived of their offices.

Mary, not only of royal blood and popular with the people but heir presumptive to the throne, presented the reformers with a delicate challenge. Without questioning the royal supremacy—doing so would have made her no less a heretic than the evangelicals—she protested that Cranmer and his faction were violating the law of the land, trampling on the terms of her father's last will and testament, and imposing innovations that could not possibly be acceptable until her brother reached his majority and became capable of leading the church. When Parliament changed the law, nullifying the Six Articles and other obstacles to reform, she again took the position that it had no right to do any such thing during the king's minority. By 1549, when the new reign's first Act of Uniformity replaced the mass with Cranmer's service and ignited the Prayer Book rebellion, Mary protested more vehemently than before and received from the council a letter advising her to be "conformable and obedient to the observation of his Majesty's laws." Her response dripped with contempt. She told the councilors that the Act of Uniformity was "a late law of your own making for the altering of matters of religion, which in my conscience is not worthy to have the name of law."

For much of the next four years she was virtually at war with the government whose head she would become in the event of Edward's death. With the fall of Somerset and the rise of John Dudley, things grew so much worse that Mary once again believed she was going to have to flee to the continent to save her life. Charles V sent three ships to rescue her by dark of night; at the last moment, though frightened and confused, she decided that duty required her to stay in England. She became the most conspicuously defiant champion of the old ways. Ordered to travel to London and present herself to the king and his council, she entered the city at the head of an entourage of some 150 friends and retainers, every one of whom displayed either a rosary or some other forbidden symbol of the old faith. Ordered by Edward to conform, she reduced him to tears by replying that she would die first. Several of the senior officers of her household, upon refusing to try to persuade her to abandon the mass, were thrown into prison. When representatives of the king arrived to inform her that she would no longer be permitted to hear mass (the delegation was headed by Baron Rich, now lord chancellor and a very wealthy man, the same Richard Rich whose perjured testimony had facilitated the killing of Thomas More and John Fisher two decades before), she dismissed them scornfully.

The conflict ended in a standoff. The law against the saying or hearing of mass continued in effect, but no effort was made to enforce it in Mary's case. Eventually she was even able to resume her visits to her brother, spending time with him amicably as long as both avoided the subject of religion. It was clear to everyone, however, and to Edward more than to most, that in all of England there was no enemy of his evangelical establishment more dangerous or determined than his heir. Nothing could be less surprising than Edward's decision, when he knew that his life was ending, to prevent Mary from succeeding him. Or Mary's commitment, once she had stopped Dudley from putting Jane Grey on the throne, to destroy the Edwardian Reformation root and branch.

4

Another New Beginning

From the hour she entered London as queen, Mary Tudor faced a daunting array of challenges. She had to take charge of a government most of whose senior members—both those who were now her prisoners and those still in office—had actively opposed her succession. She had to assume the headship of a church whose primate publicly condemned her as a heretic and had supported Jane Grey to the end. The treasury she had inherited was not only empty but deep in debt, her kingdom too enfeebled by financial mismanagement to play a weighty role in international affairs, her people confused and divided by three decades of religious convulsion.

Of course she had an agenda of her own and her own priorities. She wanted a regime, a religious settlement especially, that accorded with her view of what was true and false, what right and wrong. To accomplish this she was going to have to decide who were her friends and who her enemies, who could be trusted and who could not. She had had almost no training in government, had in no way been prepared to rule. And, being a thirty-seven-year-old virgin whose heir was both the daughter of her mother's great enemy and obviously on the evangelical side of the religious divide, she had good reason to want to produce a child. But she had little time in which to do so—her biological clock was approaching sunset.

When she arrived at the Tower, which in keeping with tradition was to be her residence until her coronation, Mary was welcomed by a rather pathetic little collection of eager well-wishers. One was the old Duke of Norfolk, an octogenarian now, who had remained a prisoner since narrowly escaping execution at the end of Henry VIII's reign. Another was Stephen Gardiner, who had risen high in Henry's service only to lose his seat on the council, then the Bishopric of Winchester, and finally his freedom. Still another was young Edward Courtenay; like his cousin Mary he was a great-grandchild of King Edward IV, and he had literally grown up in the Tower after being locked away at the time of his father's execution fifteen years before. For them and for others, Mary's arrival meant deliverance from what otherwise might have been confinement until death. And for all of them, release meant more than liberty. The bishops deposed during Edward's reign were soon restored to their sees. Gardiner was not only restored but became chancellor. Norfolk was given back much of the Howard family patrimony and his place on the council. Courtenay was made Earl of Devon and, because of his royal blood and his family's conservative credentials, found himself put forward as a possible husband for the queen. If they were not all her friends, strictly speaking, at worst they were the enemies of her enemies. That was not nothing.

Mary was generous even with those who obviously were her enemies—at least with most of them. The whole sprawling Dudley connection—John, Duke of Northumberland, his brother Andrew, all five of his sons, his daughter-in-law Jane Grey and Jane's father the Duke of Suffolk—were in custody along with various of their supporters and allies. Most were put on trial for treason, convicted (the guilt of the accused being, for once, certain beyond possibility of doubt), and attainted. But only the duke and two obscure henchmen were executed. Jane and her husband Guildford Dudley, though under sentence of death, were kept in the Tower in comfortable circumstances, as were Guildford's brothers John, Earl of Warwick, Ambrose, Robert, and Henry. Suffolk was, somehow, released without being charged. Thomas Cranmer, who after initial hesitation had thrown himself fully behind Dudley's attempted coup, was merely confined to Lambeth Palace, the archbishop of Canterbury's London residence. He was permitted to preside at King Edward's funeral ceremony and to use the reformed rites in doing so. Mary declared that she "wished to constrain no man to go to mass" or to "compel or constrain other men's consciences." A proclamation informed her subjects that nothing would be done to alter the Edwardian settlement until a Parliament was assembled to address the question. When that old champion of reform John Dudley faced the crowd that had gathered to witness his execution, he professed himself to be a Catholic who prayed for England's return to the old faith. (He could hardly have meant the *Roman* Catholic faith, but possibly he was hoping to win favor for all the members of his family whom Mary had in custody.) The conservatives must have thought that a reversion to the traditional ways was going to be accomplished without great pain: Dudley's conduct would have encouraged them to believe that the evangelical movement was made up entirely of self-seeking opportunists prepared to abandon their heresies as soon as pressure was applied.

The evangelicals for their part, having had things almost entirely their way since the last months of Henry VIII, remained fiercely committed to expunging every trace of Catholicism from English life. This was true of no one more than of Cranmer, who seemed to grow more radical by the month. By 1553 he had had ready for Parliament's attention his Code of Ecclesiastical Constitutions, a revision of canon law that, if enacted, would have made it heresy to believe not just in papal supremacy but in transubstantiation (described as "repugnant to the plain words of scripture") and *not* to believe in justification by faith alone. Anyone accused of such offenses was to be tried in the church courts, excommunicated upon conviction, and given sixteen days in which to recant or be turned over to the civil authorities for execution. John Dudley, who blamed Cranmer for the frequency with which evangelical preachers were offending the rich and powerful by criticizing their ongoing seizures of church property, had taken his revenge by blocking action on Cranmer's code in the House of Lords. He then discredited the proposal—cleverly gave Parliament a reason to reject it—by allowing it to be published under a demonstrably false claim that it had the approval of the Canterbury Convocation.

In all likelihood Dudley was able to thwart Cranmer only because by this point the young king was on the brink of death. Almost certainly the code would have become law—Dudley might not have dared even to raise objections—if Edward had remained strong enough to give it vigorous support. It accorded perfectly with his revulsion against

Catholic doctrine and his belief that it was his responsibility to transform England into Christ's kingdom on earth. Cranmer's attempt to revise canon law shows that he was no less willing than the most radical reformers on the continent to use the state's power over life and death to stamp out error and spread the gospel. It is impossible to doubt that Edward would have gone along with him.

Cranmer was understandably bitter after Mary became queen. Not only had everything that he still wanted to achieve suddenly become impossible, but the stupendous gains of the past half-dozen years were in imminent danger of being undone. News reached him of one setback after another. Even Elizabeth, in whom the evangelicals had invested so much hope, was reported to be attending mass with her sister the queen, establishing a chapel in her home, even ordering from the continent a chalice, a cross, and other things useful only for engaging in the ceremonies of the papists. Cranmer exploded in rage when informed that a mass had been celebrated in his cathedral church at Canterbury and, worse, that it was said to have been done with his approval. His printed denial dripped with invective, condemning the mass as a concoction of the pope, that arch-persecutor of Christ and true religion. He asked for an opportunity to demonstrate to the queen herself that the mass was blasphemy and that the church as purified during her brother's reign expressed the authentic spirit of Christianity. This got him a summons to appear before the council, followed by commitment to the Tower. Neither he nor anyone else can possibly have been surprised. Cranmer had not only been conspicuous among those proclaiming Jane Grey queen, he had contributed part of his personal security force to the army with which Dudley had set forth from London to confront and capture Mary. Now he was accused also of "spreading abroad seditious bills, and moving tumults to the disquietness of the present state," and his guilt was again obvious.

From the start of Mary's reign, however, the attention of council, Parliament, court, and even the kingdom at large was focused at least as much on the question of the queen's marriage as on religious issues. Mary appears to have had little if any personal interest in taking a husband. There was nothing in her past to suggest that she had ever had strong romantic inclinations, or that she was a particularly sexual creature. In the 1530s, at the nadir of her fortunes, she had expressed the hope of entering the religious life, possibly in Spain. By 1553 she seemed a settled, satisfied, and distinctly middle-aged spinster, an amiable creature who enjoyed music and dance and gambling for small stakes and shared her father's and brother's taste for jewelry and costly dress, but was no more inclined than she had been in youth to engage in flirtations or dalliances. It was a long time since she had had great value on the international marriage market, an equally long time since she had given evidence of wishing for a spouse or children.

But she had been raised and educated to be not a ruler but a consort to some male monarch. And now, contrary to everyone's expectations including her own, she found herself an unmarried female monarch in a world that scarcely knew what to make of such an anomaly. Her situation seemed unnatural to almost everyone—certainly to Mary herself. It seemed contrary to nature that any woman, even a queen, should not be subordinate to some man. The universal question, virtually from the first day of her reign, was not *whether* she should marry but *whom*.

It is understandable if Mary herself, so alone and vulnerable for much of her life, welcomed the thought of a partner with whom to share the unfamiliar burdens of rule. It is no less understandable if she wanted a child—and not for sentimental reasons, but as the one sure way of ensuring that England would not fall back into the hands of the evangelicals after her death. If she could find a partner capable of compensating for her lack of political experience and skill, so much the better. But what was truly essential was that her husband be a religious conservative—certainly a Catholic, preferably a Roman Catholic. That narrowed the field of candidates. One obvious possibility was Mary's cousin Reginald Pole, who as a young man had broken with Henry over the divorce, observed from abroad as the king destroyed one of his brothers and executed another and finally had his mother killed as well, and now was a cardinal of the church (though not an ordained priest and therefore not under a binding vow of celibacy). Pole was so well respected as a person, a scholar, and a reformer-from-within that in 1549, while doing nothing to advance his own candidacy, he had come within two votes of being elected pope. He had only one disadvantage, but it was a decisive one: seventeen years older than Mary, Pole had no intention of marrying her or anyone else. In fact he was opposed to Mary's taking a husband, seeing more clearly than most that whoever she chose, whether English or foreign, was going to present her with serious political problems.

Another possibility was another of the queen's cousins, that same Edward Courtenay, now the Earl of Devon and endowed with estates consistent with his new rank, who had come to manhood as a prisoner in the Tower. Among Courtenay's advantages was the fact that his mother, the widow Gertrude, Marchioness of Exeter (Henry VIII had had her husband killed), happened to be one of Mary's oldest, closest, and most faithful friends. Courtenay was a quarter of a century younger than Pole, a decade younger than the queen. His mother, not surprisingly, thought he would make a splendid consort, and the fact of his royal blood won him the support of most of the experienced politicians on the council, Chancellor Gardiner among them. These men believed, as did virtually everyone in those days, that no woman should attempt to rule without a husband. They believed also that popular opinion would be far more accepting of an English husband than of any foreigner. Gardiner had another, more personal reason for supporting Courtenay. During their years as fellow prisoners they had formed a close relationship, one that apparently caused the bishop to regard the youth as a kind of surrogate son and blinded him to the defects in Courtenay's character.

The list of possible foreign husbands was extensive and included the king of Denmark and the heir to the throne of Portugal. When Mary sought the advice of her cousin the emperor Charles—she had been taught by her mother to trust her Hapsburg kin, and all her life looked to them for guidance and support—he briefly considered offering to marry her himself. Mary made it clear that she would welcome such an offer (the two had, after all, been engaged when Mary was a small child); Charles was a widower (not for the first time), and though she had not seen him in decades he had, at long distance, come to seem not only a protector but a kind of father. But he was Pole's age, and thoroughly world-weary after a lifetime of struggling to hold together his vast but ramshackle and perpetually threatened empire. He had the good sense to rule himself out. But rather than forgo the advantages of a firm and lasting alliance with England, even perhaps of adding England to a Hapsburg patrimony that already included Spain and the Netherlands and much of Germany and Italy and the New World, he offered his son Philip.

Immediately Philip became, with Courtenay, one of the two leading candidates. He also became a bone of contention inside the English court. Favored by most of Mary's female intimates and the men who had been officers of her household in the bad old days before her brother's death (several of those men now sat on the Privy Council despite being political innocents), Philip was opposed by Gardiner and most of the council's other old hands. These seasoned professionals, several of whom had sat on Edward VI's council and been followers of John Dudley right up to the point where the effort to enthrone Jane Grey collapsed, understood the impact of the anti-Spanish propaganda that had begun with Henry VIII and grown steadily more intense as the Reformation proceeded under his son. Many of the people alive in England in 1553 had been taught from childhood that Spain was the handmaiden of the Antichrist. Philip, though a Hapsburg, was a *Spanish* Hapsburg, and many of Mary's subjects were certain to find him hard if not impossible to accept.

Mary was unpersuaded, perhaps in part because she had little confidence in some of the men who warned her of danger. A number of her advisers remained on the council only because they were too influential, too dangerous, to be put aside. Everything in her experience disposed her to want an alliance with the Hapsburgs. When she was shown a portrait of the blond and blue-eyed Philip—no doubt one of the portraits that showed off the legs of which he was so proud—this inclination turned into infatuation.

In fact Philip had much to recommend him, and not just his family connections. At twenty-six he was already a significant figure on the world stage, intelligent and serious-minded and an experienced junior partner in the management of his father's immense (and at times unmanageable) domains. Like his father a widower (his first wife had been a Portuguese cousin), he had a young son and so was obviously fertile. If he was known to dally with women to whom he was not married, he never did so as recklessly as young Courtenay, who had begun to run wild almost as soon as he was released from prison. In any case, such dalliance was neither unexpected in royalty nor easily condemned in a healthy young man whose wife had been dead for eight years and whose chances for remarriage were circumscribed by the political schemes of his father the emperor. The Hapsburgs had for centuries been masters of the advantageous marriage; it was how they had extended their empire into the Netherlands, Spain, and elsewhere. It would hardly have been reasonable to expect the men of the family to be entirely satisfied with wives chosen for reasons of territorial expansion. As for Mary, no daughter of Henry VIII could have been deeply shocked by the thought of discreet sexual adventuring on the part of royal males.

Courtenay, whose good looks and aristocratic bearing had made a favorable initial impression in the days just after his release, was soon showing that fifteen years in prison had left him desperately eager for the pleasures of the flesh. Arrogance and dissolute behavior soon cost him all but his most indulgent supporters, mainly his mother and Gardiner. The queen, who had little difficulty in taking Courtenay's measure, appears never to have seriously considered marrying him. English and Spanish diplomats were put to work on constructing the terms of a Hapsburg marriage, while Mary turned her attention to other concerns. Arrangements got under way for the first Parliament of the new reign, and for a coronation ceremony to be conducted beforehand, so as to avoid any suggestion that Mary's possession of the crown was dependent on parliamentary approval. The coronation, a lavish affair, took place on October 1 with Gardiner presiding in place of Archbishop Cranmer. Mary took an oath that avoided any mention of the reforms of the preceding reign and omitted all the words with which the boy Edward, at his coronation, had laid claim to supremacy over the church. Two days before, in an even more forceful demonstration of her determination to break with the recent past, Mary had gathered the members of her council in the Tower. Lowering herself to her knees, she had spoken earnestly, almost tearfully of the *duties* rather than the powers of monarchs, and of her wish to fulfill those duties to the limits of her strength. The episode suggests the depth of Mary's wish to rule well and wisely, and her lack of confidence in her own abilities. It is impossible to imagine her father, or her brother even at age nine, assuming such a posture or uttering such words.

Philip, meanwhile, was coming to terms with the prospect of taking as his wife a woman eleven years his senior, a woman he was accustomed to calling his aunt. He had been exploring a marriage to yet another Portuguese princess (his mother as well as his first wife had come from the royal house of Portugal, the Hapsburgs being almost suicidally insensitive to the dangers of inbreeding) when Europe was surprised to learn that Mary Tudor had emerged from the turmoil following her brother's death in firm possession of the English throne. It seems improbable that the emperor Charles, in offering his son to Mary, was motivated primarily by the hope of adding England permanently to the family business. He was aware of Mary's age and the chronically troublesome state of her health; the likelihood of her producing healthy children would have seemed less than impressive. Beyond that he already possessed more of Europe and the Americas than he and his son together could properly manage even with the help of various kin, and the England of the 1550s seemed to Charles and Philip alike (not entirely without reason) a poor, half-civilized island of distinctly secondary importance perched off one of Europe's less attractive coasts. But the marriage offered important advantages all the same. It could eliminate the danger of England's entering into an alliance with Spain's archenemy, the king of France. The south coast of England formed the northern edge of the English Channel, the nautical highway that connected Spain to the Hapsburgs' Low Countries possessions and was bounded to the south by France. Charles, after decades of fending off ambitious rivals, after recurrent wars that had cost him much and gained him nothing, after the failure of all his attempts to stamp out the Reformation in Germany, was worn down and heartsick. He was beginning to dream of passing his burdens to his son, of devoting whatever remained of his life to a preparation for death. The English marriage could help to make this possible. In all of Europe there were few economic relationships more important than that between England and the Netherlands, and Hapsburg—meaning Spanish—rule of the Netherlands was far from popular. But if Philip married the queen of England, if he himself became England's king, he could at a single stroke be transformed from an alien oppressor to an asset valuable to the Dutch. The delicate process of passing the crown of Spain (and with it possession of the Netherlands) from Charles to Philip might be vastly simplified. That alone was enough to make the marriage appealing.

Ten days after Mary's coronation Philip's formal proposal of marriage arrived at her court. Within the month, with Parliament in session, Mary informed the council of her decision to accept. The news proved to be as unpopular as Pole and Gardiner had feared: England did not want a foreign king, least of all a Spanish one. Parliament sent a delegation to the queen, expressing its unhappiness with her plans and begging her to reconsider. Her peremptory refusal—her anger at Parliament's presuming to intrude into a matter as personal as matrimony, its effrontery in supposing that she might subordinate the interests of her subjects to the promptings of her heart—soon persuaded an assortment of disaffected and unstable hotheads that only desperate measures could save England from becoming an appendage of the Hapsburg empire. Mary had made the first great mistake, indeed the seminal blunder, of her reign. She had put herself at odds not only with some portion of England's ruling elite but with many of her people.

A marriage treaty still needed to be hammered out, one that would settle the specific terms of the union. Mary had sufficient acumen to assign the negotiations to Stephen Gardiner, who, as the highest-placed opponent of the match, could be depended upon not only to drive a hard bargain but, once he had satisfied himself, to have maximum credibility in bringing other skeptics around. Parliament meanwhile, perhaps chastened by the queen's anger, proved cooperative in other matters. By repealing Henry VIII's Succession Act of 1534 it restored the validity of the marriage of Mary's parents, thereby making her once again legitimate. The most recent and aggressive definitions of treason were likewise repealed, so that treason became once again what it had been in the fifteenth century: an overt action, not just something *said*. All nine Edwardian reform statutes, Cranmer's acts of uniformity and the legalization of clerical marriage included, were swept away. Essentially the church was returned to what it had been at the time of Henry VIII's death, and in some respects to what it had been under Henry VII. Praemunire crimes were abolished, along with felonies that had not been violations of the law until Henry VIII made them so.

Ambitious as all this was, Mary and Gardiner were proceeding with caution. They had separated the question of Mary's legitimacy from the religious issues, specifically from the issue of supremacy. Nothing had been done to bring the supremacy under discussion and thereby to alarm at least the more moderate reformers. (About the radicals nothing could be done. They of course had been alarmed and offended since it first became plain that Mary had won the throne.)

Nor was anything done or said to indicate that the new regime was so much as thinking about the one subject even more explosive than the marriage: the church land that had been seized by Henry and his cohorts in the 1530s, had since then been given to favorites or sold and broken up and sold again, and now was in the hands of noble and gentry families in every corner of the kingdom. Gardiner had warned Mary not only that there was no possibility of returning this property to the church, but that any move in that direction would spark a reaction so violent as to wreck any possibility of progress on other fronts. The emperor Charles and his son, who had come to regard it as one of their purposes in life to heal the schism in England if they could not do so in Germany, agreed so completely that they successfully pressured Pope Julius II to assent as well. They were opposed, however, by Cardinal Pole, whom the pope had ordered to England as his legate and was now in the Low Countries awaiting permission to cross the Channel. Pole, after decades of exile from his home country, had no understanding of how alien the notion of papal supremacy now was to many Englishmen, or of how the dispersion of the church lands had given rise to a whole new class that would go to war before surrendering the foundation of its wealth and influence. He found himself stalled just a short voyage from home. The Hapsburgs wanted him kept away until Philip was safely married to the queen—Charles wrongly feared that if given the opportunity Pole might claim the bride for himself—and Gardiner wanted no trouble over the land question. Parliament, both of its houses dominated by exactly the kinds of men who had prospered mightily from the dispersion of the church land, was relieved to find that Mary was doing nothing about the subject. It remained distrustful, however, and would continue to be so.

Before year-end Gardiner was able to disclose the contents of a completed marriage treaty. It was, from the English perspective, a thoroughly favorable arrangement: Gardiner had been able to use the Spanish ambassadors' understanding of English public opinion to extract extraordinary concessions. If Mary and Philip had a son, the treaty stated, he would be heir not only to England but to Philip's possessions in Germany, Burgundy, and the Netherlands. Philip's son Charles, then eight years old, was acknowledged as heir to Spain and the Hapsburg holdings in Italy and the New World, but if he died without issue that entire empire would go to the English heir as well. If on the other hand

Mary died without issue, Philip was to have no claim to the English crown or, for that matter, to anything in England. Mary and any children that she might bear were not to leave England without permission of Parliament, thereby ensuring that the children would be English in their upbringing. Though Philip was to be styled king of England he was to assist Mary in ruling, not rule himself. Nothing was to be done to alter the laws or customs of England, and England was not to be involved in the Hapsburgs' wars.

Opponents of the marriage could hardly have hoped for more, but nevertheless news of the agreement was received without enthusiasm. People grumbled that words on paper meant nothing, because the Spanish could not be trusted, and that if Mary did have a son he would grow up to rule not England but a far-flung assortment of domains of which England would be only a part. There was grumbling on the continent, understandably, where some thought too high a price was being paid for a union of little real value to anyone except the English and perhaps the Dutch. Philip himself, when he learned the details of what his father's representatives had promised, was aghast. To him the agreement seemed insulting. He secretly signed a document repudiating the treaty on grounds that he had not been consulted about its terms and therefore could not be bound by them. Thus what should have been seen as a diplomatic victory for England became instead a shaky foundation upon which to erect a lasting understanding.

Disclosure of the treaty's terms, which remained subject to approval by Parliament, did nothing to stop secret plans for simultaneous rebellions in several parts of England. These plans—it is not clear where they originated—had been in preparation since shortly after the queen's refusal to be deflected from the marriage. The aim of the plotters also remains unclear and was probably a confused mixture. They certainly wanted to stop the wedding, probably hoped to depose Mary (though a proposal that she should be assassinated had been rejected), and possibly intended to replace her by marrying Elizabeth to Courtenay and crowning them together. The risings were scheduled for March 1554 and were to take place simultaneously in four places: Devon in the west, Hereford and Leicestershire to the north, and Kent near London. The hope, evidently, was that a government that had no standing army would find it impossible to deal with so many irruptions at the same time. But by January Gardiner had learned that trouble of some kind was brewing. He had his protégé and onetime prison-mate Courtenay brought in for questioning. Whatever Courtenay knew he quickly revealed, and when the plotters saw that their secret had been disclosed they decided to act without further delay. Everywhere but in Kent the results were disastrous—or pathetic. In Devon the ringleaders ran for their lives as soon as they saw that no one was willing to rise with them, and the attempt in Hereford fizzled almost as quickly. In Leicester Jane Grey's father the Duke of Suffolk, the only nobleman among the plotters, foolishly put himself at the head of a rebellion that likewise came to nothing. On the run, he tried to hide in a hollow tree but was found out by a sharp-nosed dog and taken to the Tower in chains.

In Kent, however, it was a different story. There the rising was led by a cabal of disaffected country gentlemen with substantial military experience, a history of association with King Edward's regime, and hopes of gaining much if Mary's government could be overturned. Prominent among these men was Sir Thomas Wyatt, son of a famous poet and courtier of the same name. He had been involved in the plotting as early as November and was able, when the rising went off prematurely, to quickly assemble several thousand fighting men. That was a force quite big enough to challenge the queen—it soon swelled to fifteen or even twenty thousand—and with it Wyatt began advancing on London. He was met at Rochester by troops mustered in London and commanded by the aged Duke of Norfolk, who found himself first outnumbered and then neutralized by the defection of a substantial portion of his army.

It was a genuine emergency. The capital was virtually undefended, the queen in real danger of losing the crown that she had won scarcely half a year before. The imperial ambassador offered to request troops from the continent, while many of Mary's councilors urged her to flee. Once again she was saved by her own courage. She refused the offer of foreign military support and refused also to leave London. Instead she put her faith in her subjects, and her fate in their hands. She went to the Guildhall, one of London's great gathering places, and in an impromptu speech addressed a gathering of citizens assembled by the lord mayor. She denounced Wyatt and his fellow conspirators, accusing them of wanting not only to prevent her marriage but to usurp the authority of the Crown and use it for their own narrow purposes. Scepter in hand, she declared her confidence that her subjects would never allow the rebels to prevail.

"As for this marriage," she said, "ye shall understand that I enterprised not the doing thereof without the advice of all our Privy Council. Nor am I, I assure ye, so bent to my own will, or so affectionate, that for my own pleasure I would choose where I lust, or needs must have a husband. I have hitherto lived a maid; and doubt nothing, but with God's grace I am able to live so still. Certainly, did I think that this marriage were to the hurt of you my subjects, or the impeachment of my royal estate, I would never consent thereunto. And I promise you, on the word of a queen, that if it shall not appear to the Lords and Commons in Parliament to be for the benefit of the whole realm, I will never marry while I live. Wherefore stand fast against these rebels, your enemies and mine. Fear them not, for I assure ye I fear them nothing at all." It was as splendid a moment as any in the history of English royalty. Mary departed to shouts of approval, and within hours more than twenty thousand men had volunteered to defend her and the city. By the next morning Wyatt, because he had failed to attack while the city lay open to him, was doomed to defeat. His followers, faced with the defiance of the queen's defenders, began to melt away. He proceeded nevertheless, penetrated to St. James's Palace and beyond, and again caused a panic that only Mary's resolution prevented from turning into a headlong flight of the entire court. Finally, on the morning of February 7, what remained of the rebellion fell apart. Wyatt threw down his sword and surrendered. It had been a near thing, but when it was over Mary found her position strengthened. The fact that Wyatt's early success had not caused the rebellion to spread, and her fresh demonstration of courage, were enough to put heart into the queen's friends and discourage further plotting. For the second time in half a year Mary had been tested, as had the loyalty of the kingdom, and neither had been found wanting.

As always in such matters, the rebellion left a residue that had to be cleared away. Wyatt of course was executed for treason, along with a number of the other ringleaders. The Duke of Suffolk, having again betrayed Mary in spite of the leniency that she had extended to him after the fall of John Dudley, also went to his death. Far less inevitably, his daughter Jane and Jane's husband Guildford Dudley were executed as well. They had had nothing to do with the rebellion, but it was not unreasonable for the authorities to fear that if the pair remained alive they would serve as a rallying point for the discontented. In all some 480 men were convicted of treason, but fewer than a hundred died. The others were pardoned, in most cases without so much as being fined. Mary's government took far less vengeance than that of Edward VI had done five years earlier in dealing with risings that never challenged his right to the crown.

Restrained as they were in meting out punishment, however, the queen and her chancellor made a mistake that would prove to have poisonous consequences. Faced with the confused aims and conflicting grievances of the rebel leaders, they chose to conclude that the rebellion had erupted not chiefly in opposition to the Spanish marriage (such a conclusion would have been uncomfortable in light of Mary's determination to proceed) but in the hope of restoring the evangelical church. Their willingness—possibly it was eagerness—to believe that Protestantism had given rise to treason made it easy to go a step further and conclude that Protestantism *was* treason, to equate religious dissent with sedition. This could help to explain the execution of Jane Grey and her husband: if evangelicals were irreconcilable enemies of Mary's regime, they were likely to try again to put Jane on the throne. Such thinking would lead Mary and her associates to acts that echoed the outrages committed by Henry VIII and foreshadowed further atrocities in the next reign. It was profoundly misguided, there being no conclusive evidence that the objectives of Wyatt and his cohorts were mainly religious at all. Not only when put on trial but before and during the revolt, many of them had professed to be Catholic.

Elizabeth and Courtenay presented a particularly difficult problem. Courtenay certainly had been aware of the conspiracy before it became known to the government; after telling Gardiner everything, he had declared his support for the queen and even participated—though in a characteristically ineffectual and even cowardly fashion—in the battle with the rebels. Equally certainly, Wyatt had written of his plans to Elizabeth, but if she replied she did so orally or her letters were destroyed. After the collapse of the rebellion she along with Courtenay was confined in the Tower, but relentless questioning failed to draw anything incriminating out of her and evidence of her involvement remained circumstantial and thin. The imperial ambassador argued for her execution, warning that her very existence made her a danger to the queen, a focus not only for evangelical subversion but for a French king so desperate to prevent the union of England and Spain that he was encouraging sedition wherever he could find it. It certainly lay within the power of the Crown to have Elizabeth done away with, but Mary and Gardiner refused. Ultimately Elizabeth was sent to the royal estate at Woodstock, where she prudently did everything possible to satisfy her sister that she was a sincere and observant Catholic. Courtenay, too, was released. He was sent traveling on the continent, undoubtedly in the hope that at such a distance he would be less able to make a nuisance of himself. The French ambassador, though he had encouraged the rebellion and even promised that his king would support it with troops, was likewise set free after brief confinement.

Mary had won. She was free to enter upon what would prove to be the golden part of her reign, probably the best months she had experienced since childhood. That it would end so soon and so badly is the saddest part of her story.

SCHOOLING AND THE SCHOOLS

ONE OF THE FEW ENDURING MYTHS ABOUT THE SHORT, sad, and largely forgotten reign of Edward VI is that it brought a new birth of education to Britain, an explosion in the number, availability, and quality of schools. The myth finds support in the fact that a number of England's oldest and most prestigious private schools proudly bear Edward's name and claim to have been founded with money provided by the Crown.

The truth, as usual with Tudor myths, is neither so simple nor nearly so edifying. A great many of the so-called Edward VI schools were not started or endowed but *re*-endowed during their namesake's time on the throne. Many in fact were merely the survivors of the pillaging of church and community property that made the Tudor era not a boon to education but rather the interruption of a long, slow process of educational expansion. That process had begun before Edward's father was born (St. Paul's School, which would set the standard for grammar schools across England, began in the same year Henry VIII became king), and it would not recover its momentum until years after the boy-king himself was dead.

Throughout the Tudor era education remained what it had long been in England: a thing available, at least beyond a rudimentary level, to only a tiny part of the population. It had begun, of course, as an enterprise of the church; instruction had always been one of the functions of the monasteries and the parish clergy. In 1179 the Lateran Council in Rome had ordered every bishop to establish an institution to train clergy for his diocesan chapter, and the resulting "cathedral schools" had joined the monasteries as places where young clerics could become literate and be prepared for university. Outside the church there was, for centuries, almost no such thing as an educational establishment and no need or demand for one. The elite families were obliged to do little more, in occupational terms, than manage their lands. To the extent that their male offspring aspired to anything beyond more wealth and more power, it was usually to become warrior-knights of the kind idealized in tales of medieval chivalry. The nobility sent their sons to each other's castles to be trained in the martial arts, to learn to comport themselves in a manner appropriate to their status, and to make the kinds of connections that could pay dividends later in life. Hence the desire to find places in the homes of the most important people possible, and the supreme value, at the court of the young Henry VIII, of being good at jousting and other aristocratic games. Though education was gradually coming to seem relevant, the barely literate could still flourish in high society.

For the great mass of people, at the end of the Tudor period no less than at the beginning, education beyond some basic reading and perhaps writing instruction from the local parish priest was simply not an option. The only available careers, at the bottom of the social pyramid, were agricultural labor and domestic service, and that was literally as far as opportunities went. For families of greater but still modest means, the best road to prosperity often led through apprenticeships. Such a family could, upon payment of a bond, enter a son (or even, in relatively rare cases, a daughter) into an indenture contract that provided a years-long course of training in the household of a skilled specialist in some craft or trade. Apprentices were usually between ten and fourteen years old at the start of their training, which lasted about seven years during which they received food and lodging but little or no pay and were pledged to remain unmarried and avoid drunkenness, gambling, and other forms of misbehavior. ("Fornication within the house of his said Master hee shall not commit," an apparently representative indenture reads, "matrimony with any woman dureinge the said tearme hee shall not contract.") Upon completing his apprenticeship and a further year or so as a journeyman working for pay, the new carpenter, tailor, cordmaker, tanner, butcher, barber, baker, or whatever would become free to join a guild and set up shop as a master of his specialty. The guilds regulated competition (limiting the number of shops in a particular area and the amount of work that any member could undertake, for example), monitored quality and maintained standards, provided assistance to the sick or unemployed, and supported local charities. Their aim was a stable, almost static marketplace in which every competent participant was protected and no individual was allowed to get too far ahead of the rest.

Before becoming old enough to enter an apprenticeship, a child might (or just as possibly might not) spend a few years in a petty school or "dame school," basically a kind of day-care facility, usually operated in the home of some literate member of the community, where some degree of instruction in the basics of religion as well as reading (but usually not writing) English was available. Girls attended such schools, but this was as far as they could go with education outside the home. Sons of the most prosperous and ambitious families could proceed to grammar schools rather than into apprenticeships, and that was where education turned serious. The entry age for grammar school was seven, generally, and those who completed the full course remained for about seven years. Their lives, during those years, appear to have been positively hellish. Grammar school pupils, like all children through the Middle Ages and the Renaissance, were regarded as miniature adults and therefore capable of adult behavior, and all but the most exceptional schoolmasters subjected them to iron-hard discipline. The school day started at six in the morning—seven during the dark months of winter—and continued until about five P.M. The heart of the curriculum was instruction in Latin, supplemented with religion and arithmetic and sometimes a smattering of Greek, and though the older pupils were supposedly exposed to such classic authors as Ovid, Cicero, Virgil, and Horace, most of their time was devoted (books being expensive and therefore scarce except in the most generously funded establishments) to memorization and recital by rote. Unsatisfactory performance was met with lashings with birch canes or similar instruments. This was the routine year-round, the only breaks occurring at Christmas and Easter and lasting just two and a half weeks.

Latin was emphasized so heavily because it was the language of the universities and therefore synonymous with academic achievement, and because it was what the teachers knew. Because in most schools all age groups were together in a single large room (most had only a single master plus, sometimes, an assistant or "usher"), all the chanted recitations must have created a constant racket. Even the exercises in English would present special challenges for today's students. The alphabet in use in England in the sixteenth century had only twenty-four letters: *u* and *v* were the same letter (the first was used in the middle of a word, the second at the beginning), as were *i* and *j* (*j* being used as the capital form of *i*). Though other letters were used exactly as we use them today, in the handwritten form of four and a half centuries ago they would be indecipherable to the modern reader. A long-since-forgotten symbol that was almost but not exactly the letter *y* represented the same sound as *th* (as in "ye olde chandlery" or whatever). Roman numerals were much more commonly used then than now, and the last in a series of Roman *i*'s was written as a *j*: thus "King Henry *viij*." Spelling was freely improvised and would remain so until someone presumed to publish a guide to the subject in 1558.

From about the mid-fourteenth century on, families of means showed increasing willingness not only to subject their sons to the grammar school regimen but to make significant financial sacrifices in order to do so. Their reasons were perfectly rational: in a developing economy where subsistence farming was no longer an inescapable fate for nearly everyone, opportunities were opening up in commerce, government, and other fields but were available only to the educated. And though the use of English for official purposes was no longer as unusual as it once had been, being properly educated still meant being at least somewhat proficient in Latin. Grammar schools were therefore portals to advancement, increasingly in demand and increasingly common, and some were even operated under secular auspices with lay rather than clerical teachers. Seventeen such schools are known to have been in operation in the county of Gloucestershire at the time of the dissolution of the monasteries, and there is no reason to think that an untypical number. London, where there had been only three in 1440, would have fifteen by 1660, each able to accommodate a hundred pupils on average. This two-hundred-year emergence of a national educational system was not accelerated but temporarily reversed by the two decades that began with Henry VIII's attack on the monasteries and ended with the death of his son. Where schools were allowed to survive, they did so less often as a result of increased support from the Crown than because patrons of particular institutions had enough wealth or influence, either at court or in their own home districts, to save them from destruction.

The universities began a profound process of change during those same decades, in large measure because the most privileged families started wanting their sons to become "gentlemen" according to the emerging fashion. Gentlemen were still expected to have basic military skills—swords and daggers continued to be essential elements of their attire and were not always left sheathed—but under the new code it was no longer enough to be able to fight and hunt and hawk. No doubt in part because of the example set by the Tudors in providing even their daughters with superb educations, any young man hoping to make his mark at court knew that he was going to need more than a passing acquaintance with Latin if not other ancient languages and with subjects ranging from rhetoric to theology, from philosophy to astronomy. Boys from the best families continued almost without exception to be educated by private tutors rather than at grammar schools, but in increasing numbers they were entering Oxford or Cambridge at the customary age of fourteen or fifteen. In the fifteenth century Oxford's Magdalen College became the first to open its doors to the sons of "noble and powerful personages" even if they were not preparing for careers in the church—so long as their fathers paid well for the privilege. By the middle of the sixteenth century a few years at Oxford and Cambridge were a familiar rite of passage for the well-born young. Problems arose, inevitably, as the quasi-monastic serenity of the universities was invaded by rich young aristocrats whose interest in the life of the mind was easily overwhelmed by the opportunities for mischief that their new freedom put in their way. Some of the fun-seekers went, no doubt wisely, to London's Inns of Court instead, the inner sanctum of the English legal profession. There they could find an education recognized as fully equal to that available at the universities, along with the advantages of being situated in the capital with all of its bawdy temptations.

5

And Another Early End

Within weeks of the collapse of the Wyatt Rebellion, Parliament approved the treaty that laid out the terms under which Mary was to become the wife of Philip of the House of Hapsburg. On July 19 the bridegroom arrived. Aware of the extent to which the marriage was disliked by Mary's subjects high and low, he conducted himself with care. He made a great display of bringing with him chests supposedly loaded with treasure, was ostentatiously generous with Mary's council and court, and let it be known that the costs of supporting his princely household would be paid out of his coffers and not the queen's. Though he spoke no English he used his considerable charm, brought to a high polish in some of the most elegant courts in Europe, to ingratiate himself with England's elite. "His way with the lords is so winning," one of the Spanish grandees who had accompanied him to England reported in words that may have been a better reflection of his hopes than of reality, "that they themselves say they have never had a king to whom they so quickly grew attached."

At the same time Philip was making a dazzling impression upon his wife-to-be. But how much of his bonhomie was a facade? And what might it have cost him to appear more delighted with his situation than he possibly could have been? He had been compelled by duty to move to a damp and chilly northern island, not many of whose inhabitants were at all happy to see him, and now he was obliged to conduct himself impeccably night and day while making preparations to marry an older cousin. He had left behind on the continent an aging father who was sinking into a morbid depression, perhaps even the mental illness that had caused Philip's grandmother, Catherine of Aragon's sister Joanna the Mad, to be kept in confinement most of her long life. He had put the Channel between himself and the various nerve centers of the sprawling Hapsburg family business, an empire that was beset with enemies, stumbling endlessly from crisis to crisis, and desperately in need of careful management. England must have felt like exile to Philip, like a distraction from more important matters. Even his displays of generosity—his lavishing of gifts on English courtiers and his pointed refusal to use a penny of Mary's funds for his own purposes—were a painful pretense. In fact Philip was the financially hard-pressed junior partner in an insolvent international enterprise, and every gold coin that he bestowed on England was needed elsewhere. "If the English find out how hard up we are," one of his retainers wrote, "I doubt whether we shall escape with our lives."

Philip did his duty, however, and six days after his arrival he and Mary were wed in a grand public ceremony in which both were robed in cloth of gold. There was no coronation for Philip—Parliament refused to consent to that—but henceforth he was to be addressed as king. The marriage treaty granted him that dignity, and to remove any doubts about his entitlement to it, his father had had him declared king not only of Naples but, rather absurdly, of Jerusalem as well. And in fact he soon found himself functioning as something very like a king. From the start of their life together, Mary gratefully relied on Philip for guidance, support, and even leadership. Members of the council, even those opposed to a foreign marriage, found their dislike for the interloper overridden by their preference for dealing with a male rather than a female monarch. It seemed more *natural*.

With the wedding celebrated and the marriage presumably consummated, the Crown no longer had any need to keep Reginald Pole out of England. At the urging of the Hapsburgs, Pope Julius signed a bull relinquishing all claim to the English church's alienated lands, at the same time instructing Pole, in his capacity as legate, to issue a general dispensation to all the current holders of those lands. Pole also absolved of schism a number of the conservative bishops who had accepted the royal supremacy under Henry VIII but lost their posts under Edward VI, so that they could now be restored to the good graces of their Catholic queen. Late in November he set foot on his native ground for the first time in two decades and was escorted from Dover to a barge waiting at Gravesend by eighteen hundred mounted men including court officials, bishops, and representatives of the nobility. These worthies presented him with an act of Parliament that repealed the attainder passed against him in the time of Henry VIII. His arrival at Westminster was made a great occasion, one that in pomp and solemnity almost rivaled Mary's coronation and wedding. The cardinal was met by Chancellor Gardiner upon disembarking from his barge, by Philip at the gate of the palace, and finally, at the top of the stairs, by the queen. The four of them then set about accomplishing what Mary and Philip had already declared to be the purpose for which the new Parliament had been summoned: reconciliation with Rome.

Pole was at least as burdened as Mary by the religious struggles of the past quarter century, most of his family having been obliterated by Henry VIII, and he brought to his new duties a weighty array of assets and liabilities. On the positive side he was a man of high moral character, blameless in his personal life, a leader in ecclesiastical reform. He had long been a major figure at the papal court, serving (among many other assignments) as one of the pope's representatives at the first meeting of the reformist Council of Trent in 1545. He probably would have been elected pope in 1549 had he condescended to show any real interest in the office. (He took the lofty view that no one should become pope who actively wished to do so.) Instead he declined an opportunity to be chosen by acclamation, and when the matter came to a vote he fell short by the thinnest of margins. He was committed to correcting the abuses of the Renaissance church generally and in England in particular, and in his pursuit of change he emphasized education for the laity and high standards of conduct and learning for the clergy at all levels.

He would have been a superb leader of the national church in more settled times, but in some ways he was ill suited to the England of the 1550s. He no longer understood his homeland (not appreciating, for example, the extent to which Protestantism had taken root in London), and he misjudged his cousin the queen. Not having been on hand to observe Mary as she faced down Dudley's attempted coup and then

Wyatt's Rebellion, he underestimated her strength and courage. He looked not to Mary but to her husband for support, counsel, and leadership. In so doing he made it easier for skeptics to regard him less as an Englishman than as part of Philip's Spanish faction. The effects would be profoundly negative where Pole's (and Mary's) aspirations were concerned: many in England and Rome alike would come to think that opposition to Philip, and to Spain, required opposition to Pole as well. Nor would the Catholic cause be helped, in the long term, by the mild-mannered Pole's increasing determination to find and root out heresy as he and his church defined it. In this he was no different from an overwhelming majority of his contemporaries, his evangelical adversaries included, but he would have been more effective if he *had* differed.

During Mary's reign as in the time of her father and brother, much of the population retained its attachment to the old church and was prepared to welcome its return. Thus Mary and her husband and advisers had little difficulty in seeing to it that the House of Commons was dominated by members who supported their agenda. The Parliament that convened in August 1554, two months before Pole's return, showed no hesitation in cooperating with the new regime—and with the cardinal, too, once he was on the scene. In a great flurry of activity that began at the end of November and continued into 1555, Parliament turned back the calendar to the days when Henry VIII was still a favorite of the pope's. Its two houses (and the convocation of the clergy as well) asked the Crown to petition Pole for a restoration of the ancient connection to Rome. Yet again great care was taken, first by Parliament in its entreaty and then by the queen and Pole in their response, to make clear that there could be no question of restoring the church's lost property; obviously this remained an issue of the most extreme sensitivity. Thereafter a committee representing both houses drafted, and the Lords and Commons approved, a kind of omnibus bill reversing every piece of legislation passed since the end of the 1520s for the purpose of destroying the authority of the pope in England. At the same time Parliament restored heresy laws that dated back to the reigns of Richard II, Henry IV, and Henry V and had been nullified by the Edwardian reformers. This would be momentous in its consequences. It opened the way to an attack on Cranmer and other evangelicals that would end by blackening Mary's name forever.

It was all quite astonishing. The schism, the Reformation, had been reversed with almost no resistance and no shedding of blood. The old faith had been restored, and because people on all sides of the question regarded this as either a profoundly joyous or a profoundly deplorable development, it is worthwhile to recall what, exactly, it entailed. It meant that the bishop of Rome, the pope, once again had the authority to correct heresy; implicit in this was the acknowledgment that the pope (or the papal administrative machinery), rather than the queen, had the right to decide what constituted heresy and who was or was not a heretic. It meant also that the pope had the authority not to choose England's bishops, but to confirm the Crown's choices and veto nominees it deemed unacceptable. It meant that the pope could dispense clergymen from the prohibitions against nonresidence and multiple benefices, set aside the canon law's proscription of certain kinds of marriage, and hear appeals of the decisions of the English ecclesiastical courts. Even when taken together, these powers do not add up to a great deal unless one subscribes to the distinctly modern idea that *no one* has the right to impose religious uniformity. Certainly the pope's authority infringed very little on the prerogatives of any monarch who did not claim, as Henry VIII and Edward VI did, to be the highest arbiter of divine truth. Nor did it have much to do with the everyday lives of ordinary people. For Mary, however, the restoration of the old ways was the greatest achievement imaginable. It appeared to justify all her sufferings and losses, to have made everything worthwhile. That her husband and the churchmen he had brought with him from Spain had participated actively in making it happen added to the sweetness of what she had accomplished.

The culmination came that same autumn with the discovery, confirmed by her physicians, that Mary was pregnant. This was announced to the people and publicly celebrated, and when the queen first felt the child move in her womb she ordered Te Deums to be sung in thanksgiving. Every dream she could ever have had for herself or for England had come to pass. She sat on the throne; she had a husband whom she admired, trusted, and loved; the faith that she had struggled so long to maintain was once again the faith of her countrymen; and now—climactic miracle—there was going to be an heir. Surely God had saved her for this transcendent destiny, and surely it was incumbent on Mary to behave magnanimously in response to so much divine bounty. Already in October John Dudley's widow, after months of begging, cajoling, and bribing anyone who would listen to her and had access to Mary and Philip, had won the release from the Tower of her four surviving sons (one of whom died soon after being freed). Mary even allowed herself, or so it was said, to be dissuaded by Philip from sending Elizabeth to a convent in Spain. The queen continued to look skeptically on her sister's demonstrations of fidelity to the old religion, and time would show that she was right to do so even if she was acting less on the basis of hard evidence than in response to intuition. Philip, on the other hand, had good reason to want Elizabeth to remain in England and succeed to the throne if Mary died without issue. The most obvious alternative to Elizabeth was the other Mary, the young queen of the Scots, who soon would be marrying the heir to the French throne. The thought that a queen of Scotland *and* France might also inherit the throne of England was at least as intolerable from the Hapsburg perspective as Mary's choice of Philip had been to the French.

The period of her pregnancy was the pinnacle of Mary Tudor's life. It did not last long, and the drumbeat of discord, frustration, disappointment, and loss soon resumed. The first thing that went wrong was that the evangelicals proved far more persistent than the conservatives had ever supposed they would dare to be. Protestant preachers who had not fled to the continent when Mary became queen not only publicly condemned transubstantiation, free will, the restored Latin liturgy, and the sacraments but mocked the Crown and challenged the legitimacy of everything it was doing. There were physical assaults on conservative clergy, and pamphlets attacking Mary and her husband and their church poured into England from Europe, often with the assistance of the king of France. Though the dissenters were a diverse lot, divided among themselves on sometimes arcane points of doctrine and practice, to the queen and council they had the appearance of a monolithic threat. Some of the priests who had come with Philip from Spain, including the friar who was now Mary's confessor, urged the necessity of suppressing these heretics and stopping the spread of their sedition.

Action was made possible by Parliament's restoration of the heresy statutes, and targets were available in the form of those evangelicals who had been conspicuous in supporting Jane Grey and preaching against the return to traditional orthodoxy. Several such figures were already in custody, and in January 1555 six of them were brought before a court of bishops with Stephen Gardiner presiding. One of the six recanted, another asked for time to consider his position, and after a day of debate on the all-too-familiar old issues (the mass, justification by faith, and the rest) the remaining four were declared excommunicated. In accordance with traditional practice they were then handed over to the civil authorities for disposition—which meant for killing. The first to die was a preacher named Rogers, who was burned on February 4 and thus became the first of the Protestant martyrs to lose his life to Marian persecution. Within days it was the turn of John Hooper, who had been made bishop first of Gloucester and then of Worcester in the last few years of Edward's reign and was so Calvinist in his opinions (condemning, for example, the wearing of traditional clerical vestments) that he was often at odds even with Cranmer. All four died heroically, scorning invitations to save themselves by abjuring their beliefs. When another six were brought before the court, found guilty of heresy, and excommunicated, they, too, showed themselves to be unafraid to die.

And so began that sustained policy of killing that is the only thing for which Queen Mary I is generally remembered today—the long series of ugly events that earned for her the ineradicable title Bloody Mary. Exactly how it happened, and who exactly was responsible for starting and continuing it, remains one of the mysteries of the Tudor Age. What is clear is that it was controversial even within the court and council. It has been depicted as a transplanting of the Spanish Inquisition, but in fact it differed from Spanish practice in crucial respects and some of the most prominent Spanish churchmen in Philip's household regarded it with horror. On the day after the second group of prisoners was convicted and passed on to the government, Philip's confessor Alfonso de Castro, at a mass attended by the queen and king and other dignitaries, condemned the execution of heretics as contrary to the teachings of Christ and far less likely than patient instruction to keep heretics from attracting followers or suffering damnation. His words (would he have dared to utter them in such a setting without Philip's knowledge and approval?) led to a suspension of trials and executions alike. But little more than a month later it was discovered that yet another rebellion was being plotted, this time in East Anglia. The capture of another ring of would-be rebels added to the court's sense of danger and made it easy to dismiss restraint as a contemptible sign of weakness. Magistrates across the kingdom were instructed to be on the alert for heresy, and to hand un-repentant suspects over to their local bishops for examination. The trials and executions resumed.

It was long and widely believed that Gardiner was a driving force, even *the* driving force, behind the burnings. In fact little evidence sup-ports this notion, and much puts it in doubt. After presiding at the first trial and thereby involving himself in the condemnation of Rogers, Hooper, and their associates, Gardiner handed the direction of the court's activities over to Edmund Bonner, the restored bishop of Lon-don, and took no further part in them. He came to see the executions as unproductive if not inherently wrong. Another figure sometimes sin-gled out as the villain of the story, Cardinal Pole, was indeed fixated on the dangers of heresy, but that he regarded wholesale killing—or any killing—as the answer to those dangers is quite another matter. There is food for doubt in the fact that, when Pole became archbishop of Canter-bury, the burnings came to an abrupt and permanent halt in that juris-diction.

Bonner of London has always been seen as an especially eager killer, but his guilt is no longer so clear as it once seemed. After the resumption of the trials and burnings, the queen's aged treasurer William Paulet complained to the council that the bishops were not displaying enough zeal in taking action against those suspects brought to their attention. At his urging the council reprimanded Bonner specifically, directing him to be more diligent. Under pressure of this kind not only Bonner but other bishops swallowed whatever reluctance they may have felt to take action against those courageous or cranky enough to stand firmly for their de-partures from orthodoxy. Ultimately the blame must be left at the feet of the queen, who cannot be excused from a charge of fanaticism in spite of being neither cruel nor vengeful (she was quite the opposite) in other areas of her life and reign. Disappointingly little is known of her role in the campaign of persecution, and even less is known of what she thought of it all. The results in any case were famously repulsive and naturally destructive of Mary's reputation, her legacy, and the cause that she had put at the center of her life. Something on the order of three hundred individuals were executed before it all ended, an overwhelming majority in the area of southeastern England centered on London. Most were obscure commoners, tradesmen, and craftsmen, incapable of posing a threat to church or state or even the leadership of their home communities.

How aware most people were of the killings, or how deeply or even if they were horrified, is unknown. The burnings were a vile spectacle in any case, and as they went on month after month they fed the evangelicals' hatred of the regime. It became easy to depict Mary's church as synonymous with oppression—worse, with oppression from abroad—and difficult to defend it or the queen herself. A darkness descended upon the reign, one that must have been connected in some deep way to the sufferings of Mary's life—the hatred that she must, at some level, have felt for her father—and would continue to the end. To the extent that Mary thought she was serving Rome, she would soon find herself repaid in strange coin indeed.

At the start of 1555, however, all that lay in the future. For the time being, with her husband at her side and the birth of their child approaching, Mary felt free to think expansively, to pursue new goals in fields not yet explored. She decided to try her hand at peacemaking. The Crown no longer possessed the resources that had permitted Henry VIII and then Somerset to make war on the continent and join in European games of power, but the games went on, wasting lives and treasure as profligately as ever. Perhaps not surprisingly the earnest Mary, devoid of dreams of conquest or personal glory, began to hope that she might be able to bring the adversaries together and help them arrive at a lasting concord. The result was a conference at Gravelines, on France's Channel coast, where neither France nor Spain proved willing to compromise its territorial claims. The meetings cost England a good deal of money and ended with nothing accomplished. Mary had experienced her first failure as queen.

Worse soon followed. Just weeks after the formal reunion with Rome, the death of Pope Julius set in motion a sequence of events that would magnify to an almost preposterous extent the price that Mary paid for having chosen a Hapsburg spouse. Julius had been a throwback to the most notorious pontiffs of the Renaissance, wallowing in luxury, enriching his relatives, and elevating to the College of Cardinals the adolescent whom he had almost certainly made his lover. The excesses of his reign hardened the determination of reformers to bring such scandals to an end. After a period of confusion, during which a reformist pope was elected but died after three weeks in office and Reginald Pole was twice more a leading candidate despite being far away in England and uninterested, the octogenarian Cardinal Giovanni Pietro Caraffa took office as Paul IV. For the emperor Charles and his son Philip, this was a serious setback. The Caraffas were among the leading families of Naples, one of the most important of the Hapsburg possessions in Italy (the emperor, remember, had made his son king of Naples in preparation for the latter's marriage to Mary), and this part of his background dominated the new pope's view of international affairs. Like most Neapolitans he hated the Hapsburgs—a long tour of duty as nuncio in Spain had done nothing to improve his opinion—and though he had no ambition to become pope, he was provoked into accepting election by the efforts of the imperial agents in Rome to defeat him. His supporters saw in him a severely self-denying ascetic, a man whose way of life could not have contrasted more sharply with that of Julius III. One of his most conspicuous characteristics, admired by some cardinals but troubling to others, was a burning hostility to anything that smacked, to him, of heresy, and an inclination to condemn as heresy any idea not clearly rooted in the scholastic philosophy of the Middle Ages. It was possible to see him as either a selflessly holy or a disturbingly hard man. Whether out of holiness or hardness, he was unwilling to compromise or curry favor even with his colleagues at the papal court.

The improbable election of such an impolitic man reflected the cardinals' sense of how desperately necessary it now was to put the church back on the path of reform. In any case it meant trouble for the Hapsburgs and their position in Italy, and Philip and his father knew it. It meant trouble for Pole, too, though in the beginning that must have been less obvious. Both Pole and Caraffa had been prominent in Rome for many years, and both had been active in trying to work out a consistent line of response to the teachings of the Lutherans and evangelicals. In the course of all this, however, the two had become something other than friends. Caraffa, in fact, had come to suspect that the amicable Pole was so willing to arrive at a friendly resolution of such questions as justification by faith as to be flirting with heresy himself. His distrust was compounded, inevitably, by the fact that Pole was now associated with the despised Philip in England. If there was a tinge of fanaticism in Paul's character, however, he was no maniac. Shortly after his election he issued a general condemnation of the confiscation of church property. But he understood that his position could have unwelcome consequences in England. Therefore he neutralized it by issuing a bull declaring that the religious houses suppressed by Henry VIII no longer existed even in a legalistic sense, that they were and would remain legally distinct from any new houses established under Mary, and that such new houses therefore had no claim to what had been taken from the old. In this way he reinforced Mary's position on the land question, the position that Pole, too, had been brought around to accepting. On the surface, all remained well between England and Rome. Though the pope was seeking to ally himself with France against the Hapsburgs, he was, for a while, able to keep his efforts concealed.

For a while, therefore, the worst of Mary's problems had almost nothing to do with pope or church. They were painful problems all the same, and they carried with them painful consequences. By June, after increasingly embarrassing postponements of the date on which her child was likely to be born, it had become clear that she was not expecting at all. There is no way of knowing what her supposed pregnancy was all about—whether she miscarried, or had been swollen by a tumor, or had allowed a desperate longing for an heir to deceive herself and her eager-to-please physicians. Whatever the case, Mary's hopes fell with a smash, and gone with them was the possibility that some son of Philip's might make England a Hapsburg kingdom. Philip began to chafe at being kept in England, and he had compelling reasons to depart. His father was in increasingly fragile health and more eager than ever to rid himself of his burdens. The Hapsburg dynasty now had no future in England, the Spaniards continued to be regarded as interlopers, and because Philip was continuing to pay all the expenses of his household the whole enterprise was becoming not only pointless but seriously wasteful. Mary, however, was almost pathetically devoted to Philip, as eager to depend on him as she once had been to have his father's guidance. When in September he left England, she sank into sorrow. The harvest had failed, turning 1555 into a year of hardship across England and of outright famine in some districts.

Once on the continent, Philip found himself sinking into his family's quagmire of problems. He had been regent of Spain (strictly speaking, of the still-distinct kingdoms of Aragon and Castile) since before his move to England, and now his father made him regent of the Netherlands as well. To Mary's appeals that he return to England, he replied that he could do so only if formally crowned as king—something that (as he undoubtedly understood) Parliament would never allow. When Parliament met in the month after Philip's departure, it showed itself to be less ready than in the past to conform to the Crown's agenda. The session was marked by almost childish conflicts; at one point Commons was locked inside its chambers because of its refusal to approve one of the queen's bills, and at another it locked itself in to avoid having to take action it didn't want to take. At the heart of the squabbling was money. Mary made her first request for a tax levy since becoming queen and was granted only part of what she asked. She had more success in restoring some of the former revenues of the church, winning agreement mainly because the money in question was the approximately £60,000 per year that the government still received from lands seized by Henry VIII and not subsequently sold or given away. In a sense, therefore, the restoration would cost the gentry and the nobility nothing. Even so, Mary was able to win agreement only by arguing that, having repudiated the supremacy, she could not in good conscience keep money that had been diverted to the Crown on the basis of that supremacy. Mary and Gardiner wanted to introduce legislation barring Elizabeth from the succession—they continued to believe her complicit in Wyatt's Rebellion and possibly other plots as well, and had reason to believe that her sympathies lay with the reformed religion—but were held back by the fear that such a move would be not only doomed to failure but dangerous. Enough ill feeling had been aroused by the October executions of former evangelical bishops Hugh Latimer and Nicholas Ridley to make it obvious that there were limits to how far the government could safely go. Questions of religion aside, Elizabeth was the daughter of a king who had placed her in the line of succession. Her claim to the throne, therefore, was widely seen as incontestable.

November brought a weighty loss. Gardiner, having exhausted himself in the effort to extract from a recalcitrant Parliament the resources needed to keep a virtually bankrupt government afloat and allow a threadbare church to recover some of its strength, fell ill and in a short time died. With his death there passed from the scene, and from the royal service, a man whose experience reached far back into the reign of Henry VIII and whose political skills, if not those of a Wolsey or a Cromwell, were unmatched by any living councilor. There was no one to replace him—no one, at least, in whom the queen was prepared to put her trust. Increasingly, in dealing both with Parliament and with foreign governments, she looked for advice only to that little circle of political neophytes that had formed the nucleus of her household before her brother's death. And it, too, was being diminished by mortality. An ever more solitary queen assumed Gardiner's burdens herself and soldiered on, hoping that her husband would return and begging him to do so. Reginald Pole had so completely won Philip's confidence while the two were together in England that Philip regarded him as a kind of unofficial regent and expected him to look out for the interests of the Crown, and Mary, too, had high confidence in the cardinal. But Pole's position was still that of legate, and he was so occupied with the needs of a gravely damaged church that when the queen attempted to make him chancellor, both he himself and the pope objected—no doubt for very different reasons. His emphasis, not surprisingly in a man who from the beginning of his career had wanted only a life of scholarship, was on raising the quality of the clergy through education while also improving the education of the laity. He also explored reconciliation with the evangelicals, if not on the most generous terms; "heretics" were welcomed back into the church so long as they repudiated all the ecclesiastical legislation enacted between 1529 and the death of Edward VI, and married priests could retain their posts only if they put away their wives.

During his years in exile Pole had consistently pointed to the grim consequences of clerical misconduct, accusing the clergy of much responsibility for the disruptions that became the Reformation. He now brought those same ideas to bear upon England by convening, in the closing weeks of 1555, a synod of the clergy at Westminster. This gathering, by the time of its adjournment in February, approved an agenda called the Twelve Decrees aimed at rebuilding the church. Every diocese was to establish a seminary for the training of parish clergy, and the laity, too, were to be made more knowledgeable through the dissemination of a new prayer book (one very different from Cranmer's, of course), new catechisms and books of homilies, and an English translation of the

Bible. Bishops were to be held responsible for maintaining high standards of clerical conduct and for seeing to it that income and expenditures were carefully managed. The criteria that Pole set for the selection of bishops were, if anything, unrealistically high under the prevailing circumstances. The candidates that he chose were of impressive moral character and in many cases had the kinds of exceptional scholarly credentials that he found appealing. But candidates of this kind were not abundant after a generation of turmoil, and vacancies were not filled quickly. Undoubtedly Pole's ideas could have had a major impact if fate had granted him the time required for their implementation. But throughout the kingdom the church was so lacking in resources that only York was able to get a seminary up and running.

And that was not the worst of it. Far away in Rome the new pope was stewing. Determined to drive the Hapsburgs out of Naples, he had continued to pursue an understanding with Henry II of France. Ordinarily Henry would have welcomed the pope's overtures, and in fact he agreed at one point to enter into an alliance that was for the time being to remain secret. But when Philip offered a five-year truce, the French king, his treasury as empty as Mary's and Philip's, grabbed at it eagerly. An exasperated pope was left to fend for himself, and to seethe with anger over reports of Cardinal Pole's putative willingness to come to an accommodation with the heretics of England. Europe was entering one of those periods when the complexities of its politics matched its instability. Charles V abdicated the crowns of Aragon and Castile in Philip's favor, at about the same time reluctantly allowing his brother Ferdinand to succeed him as Holy Roman emperor because the princes of Germany rejected Philip as unacceptably Spanish. Philip, free for the moment of war with France but experienced enough to expect Henry II to resume hostilities as soon as he found the means to do so, returned to Spain to attend to his long-neglected duties there. Meanwhile he had to manage at very long distance his possessions in the Netherlands, Italy, and America. To compound his difficulties he was in conflict now with his uncle Ferdinand, who as new emperor had both possessions and ambitions in Italy. It is hardly surprising if England, and his wife the English queen, seemed of less than the highest importance.

Mary's perspective was of course entirely different. With Gardiner gone, dissenters were becoming increasingly bold in deploring the Spanish marriage, the reunion with Rome, and Mary's whole regime. They accused the queen of being more Spanish than English in her loyalties and of scheming to deliver England permanently into the hands of the Hapsburgs even if she and Philip failed to produce a child. In March the authorities uncovered a plot—originally encouraged by Henry of France, though he lost interest when discovery might have jeopardized his treaty with Philip—to overthrow Mary and put Elizabeth on the throne. Though a number of the conspirators were captured and executed, their leaders (including Sir Henry Dudley, a freebooting soldier and distant cousin of John Dudley, the late and unlamented Duke of Northumberland) remained at large in France. Efforts to trace the plot down to its roots ended in frustration. Elizabeth, who may or may not have been a party to it, was extricated from danger when Philip sent orders that she was not to be questioned or investigated. As in the aftermath of Wyatt's Rebellion, he was acting less as the uncrowned king of England than in the interests of the Spanish Crown. Again his concern was that if Elizabeth perished—and Mary would surely have been satisfied to see her die *if* she could be proved guilty of treason—the next in line to the throne would be Mary, Queen of Scots.

During the investigation of the so-called Henry Dudley conspiracy, with the court feeling itself under threat both from subversives at home and exiles abroad, Thomas Cranmer was burned for heresy. His execution was the most notorious event of Mary's reign, one that cast no credit on any of the people involved, Cranmer included. From the time when his compeers Latimer and Ridley went bravely to their deaths, Cranmer had begun denying the evangelical beliefs that he had devoted himself to imposing upon all of England. He repeatedly renounced the idea of royal supremacy and took upon himself responsibility for all the religious troubles that England had undergone since his consecration as archbishop of Canterbury. He went so far as to beg the pope for forgiveness, declaring that he deserved not only death but eternal punishment. In doing so he repudiated his own entire career and gave his enemies a propaganda victory of tremendous potential value. But Mary and her advisers snatched from the jaws of that victory an even greater defeat. Instead of being satisfied with Cranmer's surrender and allowing him to fade away into obscurity, they pushed ahead with plans for his execution. When the hour of his death arrived, seeing that he no longer had anything to gain or lose, Cranmer declared that all his recantations had been lies told in the hope of saving his life and that in fact he recanted nothing. Famously, when the fire was lit, he is supposed to have held his right hand in the flames—can anyone who has ever scorched a finger with a kitchen match believe this story?—while telling onlookers that it must be punished first because it had written the lies. Be that as it may, the drama of his last moments established Cranmer as chief among those martyred in the English Protestant cause. Others were being burned at this time, but few were known to the public. Many of the evangelical clergy had fled abroad—first to Lutheran Germany, where they were unwelcome because of their departures from Lutheran theology, and then to Switzerland, where they were embraced. Those members of the gentry who could not contain their hatred for Philip and Spain went mainly to France, where they received royal support except during those intervals when Henry II found it advantageous to suspend his hostility to the Hapsburgs and therefore to Mary.

The most recent of those intervals came to its inevitable end in July 1556. Paul IV was still hoping to draw France into his ancestral feud with the Hapsburgs, and now at last he found Henry ready to be drawn. An alliance was agreed under the terms of which, once the Spanish had been expelled from Italy, one of Henry's sons would become king of Naples (evidently the pope was willing to accept foreign rule of his home city so long as it was not *Hapsburg* domination) and another would become Duke of Milan. Philip retaliated by ordering his viceroy the Duke of Alba to invade the Papal States. When the pope found himself without the means to defend Rome, he offered, unhappily, to make peace. That might have been the end of the trouble, but then Henry II sent an army under the Duke of Guise into Italy with orders to support the pope, and all the adversaries found themselves at sword's point yet again. Predictably, the pope was enraged with Philip—so enraged that he excommunicated him, declaring him a "son of iniquity" and ordering the eviction of every Spaniard in Rome and the withdrawal of every papal legate from the territories of the Hapsburgs. Having been installed as archbishop of Canterbury just days after Cranmer's death (he had finally been ordained), Pole was not required to leave England. This fresh rupture, however, gravely compromised his ability to proceed with reform. His work of rejuvenating the church, the Westminster synod included, came shuddering to a halt.

Mary was caught in the middle. She appears to have had little difficulty deciding that, at least in this matter, her loyalty was owed to her spouse. Her inclinations were reinforced in January 1557 when Henry of France opened a new front in his conflict with Philip by attacking the Flemish city of Douai, a Hapsburg possession. Mary had previously warned the French against an action of this kind, reminding them that Douai had been covered by a 1543 mutual defense treaty between Henry VIII and Charles V and asserting that the treaty remained in effect. The French king, who like his father Francis loved to fish in England's as well as Spain's most troubled waters, was predictably unimpressed. As far as he was concerned, Mary's connection to the Hapsburgs meant that she and her kingdom were France's enemies. It was the pope's willingness to challenge Hapsburg rule in Italy that had caused him to rush troops to Italy, and it was because those troops were now stymied that he had turned his attention to Flanders, where he could open a new front against the Hapsburgs.

Philip, his resources stretched thin, desperately needed English help, and as Mary's consort he thought himself entitled to it. In March he crossed the Channel, received a rapturous welcome from his adoring wife, and set about trying to secure the use of English ships, naval bases, and troops. Mary was fully on his side but prudently looked to her council to make the necessary commitment. This presented Philip with a challenge of the first order: most members of the council wanted nothing to do with his war, largely if not entirely because the treasury was so deplorably short of funds. In opposing Philip, they could point to the part of the marriage treaty stating that England was not to be drawn into Spain's conflicts. Even Pole, despite the trusting relationship that he had formed with Philip, was opposed to helping him against the pope. All his life Pole had demonstrated, and repeatedly proved his willingness to suffer for, a keen sense of obligation to Rome. He was not prepared to change now, but neither did he wish to be disloyal to Mary or her husband. And so he withdrew from politics, declining to attend council meetings or even to meet with Philip. He received scant thanks. On April 29 the pope issued an order for Pole to return to Rome for unexplained reasons that were universally understood to involve accusations of heresy. The absurd process was now under way by which, in the space of not many months, Pope Paul would make himself the implacable enemy of the very people who had restored the Catholic Church in England.

Philip might never have received English help if not for an act of pure folly. Among the young rakehells and soldiers of fortune who had gone into exile in France after Mary won the crown was her twenty-four-year-old relative Thomas Stafford, who had inherited royal blood through both his father and his mother, regarded himself as entitled to the Dukedom of Buckingham (which had belonged to his family until his grandfather was executed by Henry VIII), and was an ardent Protestant in spite of being a nephew of Cardinal Pole. Lured by fantastic visions of glory, and drawing on mysterious sources of support that probably included Henry of France, Stafford came ashore at Scarborough in the north of England on April 25 at the head of a mixed force of English, French, and Scottish followers who numbered at least thirty but no more than a hundred. Taking possession of a poorly defended and half-ruined castle, he issued a proclamation calling upon the people of England to join him in deposing Mary and establishing a protectorate. So far as is known, he failed to attract a single recruit. Stafford was in custody within four days of his landing, and before the end of May he was, to little public notice, executed for treason. At court his adventure was interpreted as the latest French outrage. It brought the council around to supporting Philip and the queen.

As preparations got under way for assembling an army and transporting it to the continent, efforts were made to dissuade the pope from recalling Pole. The English ambassador in Rome begged the pope to reconsider, Mary and Philip sent appeals of their own, and at last even the diffident Pole wrote to say that the feeble state of the church in England required the presence of *someone* authorized to represent Rome. All of it availed nothing or less than nothing. It appears, rather, to have thrown Pope Paul into a fresh rage. He placed one of Pole's oldest friends and fellow reformers, Cardinal Giovanni Morone, under arrest on a variety of heresy charges of the kind that probably would have been brought against Pole himself had he been in Rome. Like Pole, Morone had lost the trust of the archconservatives with his willingness to deal with the Lutheran reformers on respectful terms and acknowledge that not all blame for the breakup of the church lay on the Protestant side. The pope made malicious use of Pole's letter by replacing him as legate with Friar William Peto, the same Observant Franciscan who decades before had denounced Henry VIII to his face for seeking to discard Catherine of Aragon. Peto was now back at his old monastery at Greenwich—Mary herself had restored it—and was serving as confessor to the queen. The situation deteriorated into a ridiculous tangle. Pole, loyal as always, would have traveled to Rome as ordered but was forbidden to do so by Mary, who insisted that he was entitled to defend himself in England. Peto, eighty years old and in bad health, protested that he was neither able nor willing to serve. The nuncio bringing official notification of Peto's appointment was intercepted at Calais and prevented from crossing the Channel, and his mission was soon rendered pointless by Peto's death. The pope wanted to declare that Philip was no longer legitimately king of anything but was dissuaded by cooler heads. He contented himself with refusing to transact any business with the English church. Mary's (and Pole's) nominations for vacant bishoprics were ignored, and the number of vacancies mounted.

After three consecutive crop failures and widespread hunger, a weakened population was being ravaged by an influenza epidemic that would in a few years claim hundreds of thousands of lives. Nevertheless an army of seven thousand men was somehow pulled together, and by July it was on the continent ready to join Philip's thirty thousand Spanish, German, and Flemish troops in the war with France. Philip, too, was back on the continent, but neither he nor the English army was on the scene when, in September, the main Hapsburg force inflicted a devastating defeat on the French at St. Quentin. Fully half of the French army was killed or taken prisoner, and upon receiving the news, the pope abandoned his hopes for Italy and signaled his willingness to make peace. Henry II then ordered the army that he had sent to the pope's assistance to return home and asked its commander, the Duke of Guise, to find some way to avenge the shame of St. Quentin. When around the turn of the year Mary announced that she was once again pregnant, no one including her husband paid serious attention. Philip sent congratulations, but they were little more than a formality. It was, after all, nearly six months since he had last seen her.

January 1558 brought the crowning calamity of Mary's reign: the loss of Calais, the last of England's once-vast holdings on the European mainland. The Duke of Guise, having received reports of the sorry state of Calais's defenses from French ambassadors passing through the town after their expulsion from England, knew that no one would expect a midwinter assault. He positioned his army in such a way as to appear to be preparing a move against St. Quentin, wheeled it around for a surprise advance on Calais, and extracted a surrender from its garrison so quickly that neither Philip nor the English had any chance of responding. Though the loss would prove to be of no strategic importance—the English figured out in time that holding Calais had produced no benefits commensurate with the costs—it came as a shock to England's nascent national pride and a humiliation for Mary. Philip, inevitably but unfairly, was blamed. He had warned the council in advance of Guise's offensive and offered to provide Spanish troops for the defense—an offer that was rejected because of groundless suspicions that Philip wanted Calais for himself. Afterward, when he offered to match whatever number of troops England made available to retake Calais, he was again rebuffed. A sense of things coming to an end, a miasma of something like death, was beginning to hang over Mary and her court. A Parliament was called but quickly prorogued after showing itself unwilling to help the government with its financial problems, and by May the queen was no longer talking of an expected child.

Mary was ill that month, and again in August, and yet again in October. In September Charles V died, removing whatever small hope Mary might still have had of Philip's return to England. Finally, knowing that Reginald Pole, too, was seriously ill, resigned to her own impending death and to the certainty that she would be succeeded by her half-sister, she sent a maid of honor to Elizabeth with a letter in which she asked for three things. First, that upon becoming queen she, Elizabeth, would deal generously with the members of Mary's household. Second, that she would repay the debts that the Crown had incurred under Mary's Privy Seal. And third, that she would continue to support the church in the form that Mary had reestablished. Elizabeth had only recently repeated her assurances that she was a believing Roman Catholic, politely complaining of the queen's difficulty in accepting her word on that score. There was no opportunity for her to do so again. On the morning of November 18, Mary quietly expired while hearing mass from her bed. Pole died hours later. The English Counter-Reformation was dead too.

Mary at the end was worn out and thoroughly defeated. She seemed somehow to have lived for a long time, and her reign, too, seemed to have lasted too long and to have grown sterile. It is startling to realize that at the time of her death she was all of forty-two years old, and had ruled for only five years.

PART TWO

Survivor

1558–1603

6

Yet Another New Beginning

It is an hour or two past midnight on March 24, 1603. In the deepest recesses of Richmond Palace the fireplaces are ablaze, the light from shoals of candles dancing in the drafty air. In the shadows at the rear of the palace's innermost chamber Queen Elizabeth lies in bed, her face turned to the wall. Her physicians have made it known that she is dying. Everyone with access to the court has come to bear witness to a momentous event.

Despite the hour the atmosphere is electric: the death of the monarch is certain to bring enormous changes—good things for some, disappointment for others. People bundled up in hats and furs whisper together in little clusters, disperse, gather again in new combinations: the grieving and the hopeful, the worried and the merely curious. Among them is Sir Robert Carey, the queen's cousin, the ambitious grandson of Anne Boleyn's sister Mary. Like the others he keeps his face stern and his voice low, but he is excited and impatient and struggling not to show it. A fast fresh horse awaits him outside, and he has arranged to have other horses posted all along the four-hundred-mile route from Richmond to Edinburgh. He is determined to give himself a leg up with the next regime by being the first to inform the king of Scotland that Elizabeth is dead at last, and that England is now his.

Tudor medicine being the tangle of butchery and superstition and sterile tradition that it is, not even the doctors have any real idea of why the queen is dying. A bronchial infection that has turned into pneumonia, perhaps. Possibly streptococcus, or the failure of some vital organ. Whatever the root cause, it appears to have been aggravated by depression; one thing even her physicians can see is that Elizabeth has been seriously depressed for months. It is possible that she has been poisoned—that she has, inadvertently, poisoned herself. For forty years, ever since smallpox nearly took her life and ravaged her fine fair skin, she has refused to leave her privy chamber without first having her face, neck, and breast caked with the most prized cosmetic of her day, a mixture of white lead and vinegar known as ceruse or spirits of Saturn. Even painters who use brushes to apply white lead not to their own skin but to walls often fall victim to poisoning. That Elizabeth has remained vigorous to such an age while living under a thick coat of such a toxic concoction is little less than astonishing.

By the standards of the day her age is ripe indeed. Ninety-four years have passed since her father Henry VIII became king, 118 since her grandfather won the crown at Bosworth Field. Elizabeth herself, next to Henry VII the Tudor who overcame the longest odds in coming to the throne, has reigned for four and a half decades. This is nearly twice as long as the first Henry Tudor, nearly a decade longer than the second, nine times as long as either her brother or her sister. Her next birthday would be her seventieth.

Longevity in fact is the dying queen's supreme achievement, and that is fitting. Longevity, survival, is all she ever really aspired to. There is no reason to believe that at any point she had high dreams for her kingdom, her people, or herself. Like her father she has always been a master of political theater, creating a jewel-encrusted image with which to awe the whole world and concealing herself behind it. But even in fabricating the persona of Gloriana, the strong, wise, and good Virgin Queen, even in projecting that persona in every direction near and far, she has been driven by defensive impulses—by the determination to make herself *seem* strong, invulnerable, indispensable. Always the aim was to preserve her life and her rule and the status quo. If it is possible to argue that she never accomplished much else, she has unquestionably accomplished that. Therefore she has succeeded in everything that mattered to her— no small achievement for any ruler. In the process, simply by staying in power as the earth made forty-five trips around the sun and forces beyond anyone's control swept over her kingdom, she has also presided over much of England's evolution into a modern nation-state. This is the ultimate irony of her story, because there rarely was a monarch who wanted change less.

One wants to know, as Elizabeth draws her last breaths, what she has been thinking during these strange final days. Her decline began with a refusal to speak, to eat, even to sit down until at last she was too weak not to. Then, seated on cushions with a finger in her mouth, she passed days and nights gazing blankly at the floor or something beyond the floor, locked in a stony solitude. Only when she had lost all power to resist or even complain was she finally put to bed. Has she been asking herself if it was worthwhile, the long drama that is now drawing to a close? Does she wish she had played her part differently? Does it seem enough, looking back, that she has survived this long? Does the price she paid seem acceptable—or to have been necessary?

All we will ever know is what the people attending her take the trouble to record. That is not much, and it has no certain meaning, but it does not suggest a spirit at peace. When begged to get some sleep by the faithful old Earl of Nottingham, longtime commander of her navy and husband of another of her Boleyn cousins, Elizabeth answers that if he saw what she sees when she closes her eyes he would suggest no such thing.

She is a pathetic spectacle, all the more so because throughout her reign she has been vain to the point of childishness. Almost inevitably for someone who has lived this long at a time when dentistry is still little more than a sideline for barbers, she has lost a good many of her teeth and those remaining are mostly black. For forty years she has been concealing the loss of hair suffered when smallpox nearly carried her away, but now, with the end obviously at hand, it is pointless to worry about whether the latest wig fits properly or if it is even in place. As for hygiene, suffice it to recall that bathing is considered unhealthful in the sixteenth century, that it is scarcely practical even for royalty during the dark chill months of an English winter innocent of central heating, and that winter was not over when the queen began refusing to have herself attended to even in accordance with the minimal standards of the time.

If her last moments taste of bitterness, nothing could be more understandable. From 1603 she looks back on eighteen years of uninterrupted foreign war, and on an interminable domestic bloodletting rooted first in the revolution begun by her father and then in the decisions that she herself took in attempting to manage her father's (and her brother's, and her sister's) legacy. Her wars have accomplished little, almost nothing on the whole, and they have laid up much trouble for her successors. Unlike her father's wars they were undertaken not in pursuit of glory but because she believed they would enhance her security, but like her father's they have been financial catastrophes. At a time when the Crown's ordinary revenues still total little more than £200,000 annually, England since 1585 has spent some £2 million to keep a war of rebellion going in the Netherlands, even more to suppress rebellion in Ireland, and untold hundreds of thousands in France and on the high seas. The question of whether all this trouble was avoidable has no simple answer, but there can be little doubt that much and perhaps most of it need never have happened. Even the most glorious event of the reign, the defeat of the Armada in 1588 (a victory owed as much to the weather as to England's doughty sea dogs), drained the treasury of £160,000 and would never have been necessary if Elizabeth had not persisted in goading her onetime protector and brother-in-law King Philip of Spain until finally his forbearance was exhausted.

The effects on the people of England have been very real and painful. Nearly two decades of war have seriously disrupted trade, especially with the crucial Low Countries markets, and thereby given rise to serious unemployment. Ferocious inflation has combined with falling wages to drive living standards to their lowest level since the mid-1300s. This has led to food riots and crimes of desperation, and then to an almost vicious crackdown by frightened local authorities: in 1598 one hundred and twenty-five sentences of death were pronounced by courts of assize in the London area, nearly double the number of just two years earlier. Repeated crop failures have made everything worse. Anyone disposed to believe that nations prosper or suffer according to whether their rulers enjoy divine favor—and such ideas remain common at the dawn of the seventeenth century—would find it easy to argue that heaven has turned its back on Elizabeth Tudor. She is in every way a spent force, and her people are ready to be quit of her.

To a remarkable extent—one all the more striking in light of how deeply the two sisters always differed, and the determination of the younger to set herself apart from the elder—Elizabeth's reign has followed much the same trajectory as Mary's. Both, upon becoming queen, were welcomed enthusiastically by most of their subjects, England being quite as weary of Mary and her Spanish connection in 1558 as it had been of Edward's evangelical regime in 1553. Both went on to enjoy a middle period of popularity and success (Mary's was measured in months, Elizabeth's in decades), and both ended in exhaustion and disillusion (the dark times having lasted well over ten years in Elizabeth's case). If Mary was fated to become a largely forgotten figure, remembered as "bloody" when she was remembered at all, and if Elizabeth by contrast came to be celebrated as one of history's heroines, the difference is largely traceable to factors unconnected to the character of their reigns. No historian today could dispute that Mary was a capable and conscientious queen, or argue that her government killed or tortured or imprisoned as many people as Elizabeth's. She devoted herself to what she perceived (rightly or wrongly) to be the interests of her subjects, and she might have achieved her objectives if she had reigned even half as long as Elizabeth. The process of winnowing the facts has taken four centuries, but it is clear by now that Mary was the more ambitious of the sisters—that she aspired to much more than her own survival, certainly—and that the reason for her failure may be nothing more mysterious (or shameful) than the fact that at the time of her death she was twenty-eight years younger than Elizabeth would be at hers.

This is not to say, of course, that Elizabeth accomplished nothing. She achieved two very big things that had eluded her father, brother, and sister: a settlement of the question of what England's established church should be and do and believe, and a degree of internal stability not seen in a very long time. From the end of the 1560s until the end of Elizabeth's life, and then for decades beyond that, not a single armed rebellion of even marginal seriousness occurred in England or Wales. Such a protracted period of peace had not been seen since before the Wars of the Roses, and if Elizabeth and her ministers don't deserve credit for that then no one in history should be given credit for anything. Likewise, by 1603 everyone understood what acceptance of the Church of England entailed, and most of the population was conforming. Where persecution was concerned, Elizabeth had differed from her brother and sister only in (much like her father) striking out in two directions simultaneously, both at the shrinking part of the population that still clung to the old religion and at the growing part that demanded rejection of every vestige of the pre-Reformation church. If she continued to meet resistance from both directions, after the first decade of her reign it posed no serious threat.

Still, both the settlement and the stability were bought at a price that Elizabeth herself was careful to avoid paying. Just below the surface of the uniformity her government imposed, England continued to be troubled by the religious conflicts that her father had first put in motion. The actions she took in managing those conflicts are unintelligible unless seen as part of Elizabeth's obsessive focus on her own survival. She declined to address virtually any question of religion that could be passed along to posterity, and to avoid trouble in the near term she ignored growing pressure for adjustments of the religious arrangements put in place at the start of her reign. The bill would come due two generations on, with an explosion that not only permanently weakened the monarchy but actually, for a time, obliterated it. If that was at least partly Elizabeth's doing, however, she took pains to keep it from being her problem.

The England whose queen Elizabeth became late in 1558 was probably not yet halfway along the road from being one of the most devotedly Catholic nations in all of Christendom to one of the most ferociously anti-Catholic. Though of course we have no data on popular religious sentiment as of the start of her reign, much if not most of the population unquestionably continued to be attached to traditional forms of worship, though not to the notion of papal supremacy. Protestantism of the severely Calvinist variety that the evangelicals had attempted to establish during Edward's reign, by contrast, remained a minority movement even in London and those other places (Cambridge University and various seaports, most notably) where it had struck the deepest roots. Despite the setbacks of the Marian interlude, the evangelical movement remained fervently militant and continued to attract adherents who felt impelled to propound their beliefs in writing and in the pulpit. It was becoming economically formidable as well, finding fertile recruiting ground among the mercantile families of London and other commercial centers as well as those that had risen to the top of the rural gentry thanks to the dispersal of church and Crown lands. Inevitably, the wealth of these rising classes was translating itself into political power.

The regime that Elizabeth inherited was Roman Catholic neverthe-less, with the Marian state and church tightly intertwined. In a reversion to long-standing practice, Mary had chosen as her chancellors first Bishop Stephen Gardiner and then, after Gardiner died and Cardinal Pole begged off, Archbishop Nicholas Heath of York. Maintaining the status quo might seem to have been the path of least resistance for Eliz-abeth, especially as Mary's arrangements were in no way objectionable to a majority of her subjects. Elizabeth herself had, albeit without great success, tried continually to convince her sister that she was a faithful daughter of Holy Mother Church. In fact, though, the choices facing Elizabeth when she became queen were not at all simple. Quite aside from her own convictions, she had compelling reasons, from the day of Mary's death, to undertake the fourth religious revolution (or counter-revolution) to be visited upon England in the space of three decades. Practically all of her active political support lay on the Protestant side, and she had been careful to maintain contact with the evangelical community all through the years when many of its members were pre-tending, for the sake of their positions and possibly their lives, to be or-thodox Catholics. She had gone to great lengths, always being as surreptitious as she could, to encourage the Protestants to see her as one of their own, which she undoubtedly was. The Protestants were given good reason to expect that as queen she was going to overturn the Catholic establishment; if she had ignored this hope the Protestants would have been justified in feeling betrayed, and Elizabeth might have found herself without any dependable base of support. To the Catholics, she had always been the bastard child of a schismatic king's heretic concubine. Queen Mary herself suspected that Elizabeth was the illegitimate daughter not of Henry VIII but of Mark Smeaton, the court musician who had been among those executed on charges of adultery with Anne Boleyn. Certainly both England's Catholics and Rome would have accepted Elizabeth as queen if she had left the Marian church in place—most of her Catholic subjects did so even after she set out to ex-terminate their church—but it is not difficult to understand why a wary new queen, taught in a hard school to be cautious about trusting any-one, had no interest in putting her fate in the hands of the Catholics.

What she *did* have in mind, at least at the opening of her reign, is not entirely clear. So many potent forces were in play, and in conflict, that it

has always been difficult to sort out how much of what happened accorded with Elizabeth's own wishes and how much was imposed on her
by circumstance. Essential as it was that she not fail the Protestants who
had made her their champion and their hope, she also had to avoid alien-
ating the still-powerful (and still-popular) Catholic party so completely
as to provoke it into defiance. An exquisitely delicate balancing act was
required, something similar to the one performed by the evangelicals
just after the death of Henry VIII, and for an inexperienced monarch not
yet twenty-five years old this was an imposing challenge. Elizabeth nav-
igated her way through it with the skill of a master (there is no sure way
of knowing, really, how much of "her" policy was actually the work of
her canny secretary William Cecil and her other friends on the council),
dashing no hopes while keeping everyone uncertain. In the beginning
she placated the conservatives by punctiliously observing the established Catholic formalities, not interfering with the saying of mass even
at court until a new Parliament could be summoned. Elizabeth herself
attended Christmas mass at the end of 1558, some three weeks before
her coronation, though when the celebrant followed an ancient practice
that the Protestants had long condemned and elevated the consecrated
communion host above his head, she exited the church in a theatrical
flourish of indignation. She also refused to be escorted, in traditional
fashion, by the Benedictine monks whom Mary had restored to residence at Westminster Abbey. In such ways she made it plain that she
shared the evangelicals' revulsion at papist "idolatry" and their scorn for
monasticism. No one could doubt where her sympathies lay, but she
shrouded her political intentions behind a cloud of ambiguity and left
the conservatives with reason not to despair.

The coronation took place on January 15, 1559. Elizabeth spent
£16,000 of Crown money on it, a stupendous amount, and the city fathers of London were induced to contribute similarly impressive sums.
She was crowned by Owen Oglethorpe, a junior bishop from the distant
and unimportant Diocese of Carlisle. He was the newest of Mary's bishops, and though definitely a conservative, he had throughout his career
shown a tendency to bend when put under pressure. Elizabeth chose
him to do the honors at least in part because Pole of Canterbury was
dead and Heath of York claimed to be too unwell to attend, but she may

also have been demonstrating her disdain for the whole Marian hierarchy and what it represented.

Weeks before the coronation, in an unmistakable sign of the direction of her thinking, Elizabeth had overhauled the Privy Council. Here she was dealing with real power, not symbolism, and everything she did must have been gratifying to the evangelical camp. Within hours, literally, of learning of Mary's death, the new queen was summoning the council to meet and reshaping it by adding new members and removing more than she added. In short order it shrank from thirty members to nineteen: ten Henrician conservatives (men who accepted the royal supremacy but otherwise were inclined to traditional orthodoxy), nine evangelicals of an Edwardian-Calvinist stamp, no Roman Catholics, and remarkably, no clergy from any faction. The Protestants could take particular satisfaction in the appointment of Cecil as principal secretary, the position from which Thomas Cromwell had taken control of Henry VIII's government many years before, and of Nicholas Bacon to replace Archbishop Heath as chancellor. Cecil and Bacon, married to sisters, were members of families that had been Tudor loyalists since the start of the dynasty (or even earlier: Cecil's grandfather, when scarcely more than a boy, had joined the future Henry VII on his march to Bosworth Field). Both were ardent evangelicals whose careers had been in eclipse throughout the Marian years, though Cecil even more than Elizabeth had gone to almost ridiculous lengths to pretend to be a faithful Catholic, showily fingering rosary beads whenever he thought someone with access to the queen might be watching. Both would make plain that they regarded persecution of Catholics—even the torture of Catholics—a necessary means of purging the kingdom of superstition, sedition, and division.

The Protestants could have found no reason to object to the favors that Elizabeth began showering on her few living relatives, mainly the remnants of her mother's family, the Boleyns. Among the first to benefit was her cousin Henry Carey, son of Anne Boleyn's sister Mary and her husband, William Carey. (Actually Henry may have been Elizabeth's half-brother; the uncertain date of his birth makes it possible, though not probable, that he had been conceived when Mary Boleyn was Henry VIII's mistress.) He was raised to the peerage as Baron Hunsdon and granted lands that, by generating some £4,000 annually, vaulted him into the ranks of the richest men in England. This was an extraordinary gesture on Elizabeth's part; throughout her life she would remain deeply reluctant to create new peerages, and the wealth bestowed on Carey was badly needed by her government. Carey's older sister Catherine (more likely than her brother to have been King Henry's child) was made a lady of the queen's bedchamber, a high honor that Elizabeth would bestow on only about two dozen women in the course of her long reign. Catherine's husband, Francis Knollys, upon returning from exile on the continent, was given a comparable honor: a seat on the Privy Council. Still another Boleyn cousin, Sir Richard Sackville, also joined the council. Though Knollys and Sackville were not ennobled, both would use the queen's favor to put their families on courses that would lead to the former's son becoming a baron and the latter's an earl. With appointments like these the queen was able to surround herself with people who were entirely dependent on her for their positions, had impeccable Protestant credentials but no plausible claim to the throne, and so could be counted upon to remain absolutely loyal.

One other of the queen's first appointments must be noted here: the selection of the dashing young Robert Dudley as master of horse. Though he was not put on the council—not yet—Dudley's new position was highly visible and rather glamorous, and his selection was clear and early evidence of the unique place he held in Elizabeth's affections. He was the younger of the only two surviving sons of the John Dudley who as Duke of Northumberland had destroyed himself by attempting to put Jane Grey on the throne, and so he was also the grandson of the Edmund Dudley who lost his head at the start of Henry VIII's reign. Thus for the third time in as many generations a young member of this irrepressible clan won a place close to the throne, and for the second time it was happening in spite of the previous generation's failure and deep disgrace.

Dudley, like almost everyone singled out for preferment, was allied with the evangelical camp. With his four brothers he had spent the first months of Mary's reign as a prisoner in the Tower. (Elizabeth was confined there at the same time, though there is no evidence of their having been in contact.) After his release he had withdrawn to a life of obscurity on his father-in-law's estates in East Anglia. His sudden emergence as a highly visible member of the new regime formed part of a pattern that must have seemed to ensure a swift and thorough triumph for the Protestant cause. But then January 25 arrived, Elizabeth's first Parliament assembled at Westminster with the convocation of the clergy in session as well, and it became obvious that the way ahead was not in fact going to be easy.

The new House of Commons, many of its members chosen as usual for their willingness to accept the guidance of the Crown, showed itself from the start to be a potent engine of religious reform. Under Cecil's direction, and in collaboration with Protestant divines newly returned from the continent, it raised questions about whether the late Queen Mary's religious legislation could be considered valid in light of her repudiation of the royal supremacy. It began pushing for a restoration of all the powers that Henry VIII had taken for himself, and of King Edward's Protestant church. But it met with resistance from a surprising number of directions. A struggle developed in which the Crown, the bishops and clergy, the Protestants of the Commons, and conservative and reform factions in the House of Lords all tried to advance their own agendas. Over a period of months the terms of the conflict remained in flux, with the advantage appearing to shift from party to party. Elizabeth and Cecil, as they threaded their way through endless complexities, had to face the possibility that moving too emphatically in an anti-Roman position could bring papal condemnation down upon their heads, and with it the danger of a Spanish-French crusade. Likewise the queen's Catholic subjects, if pushed too hard, might be driven—might even be led by disgruntled conservative nobles—into armed rebellion. Elizabeth's relations with Parliament at this early stage are best understood not in terms of any attempt on her part to achieve some specific set of religious objectives but rather as one aspect of her broader struggle to maintain a balance between two contending parties: a fearful conservative majority that the queen and her ministers neither liked nor trusted, and an energized Protestant minority bent on domination. The government's goal, if only for the time being, was to win acceptance of a purposely ambiguous status quo.

The Privy Council opened the legislative bidding early in February by introducing bills with an aggressively Protestant slant: if enacted they would officially recognize the queen as supreme head, require all members of the clergy to swear an oath acknowledging her supremacy, and abolish Catholic worship in favor of the Edwardian Prayer Book. Commons not only approved these proposals but toughened them, but the Lords (with a conservative core consisting mainly of the Marian bishops) deleted restoration of the Prayer Book and merely authorized Elizabeth to take the title of supreme head *if* she chose to do so. Archbishop Heath objected even to this, taking the line (which even few women would have challenged in the sixteenth century) that the very idea of a female being head of the church was preposterous. Convocation, meanwhile, was putting itself at odds with queen, council, and Commons by voting to uphold a fully orthodox set of Catholic beliefs, including the bishop of Rome's supremacy. While all this was transpiring, word arrived that England's emissaries to a peace conference at Cateau-Cambrésis in France had succeeded in ending Mary's and Philip's war on the continent. This was important news. It stopped up a painful drain on the royal treasury. At least as significantly, by demonstrating the willingness of France and Spain to enter into a treaty with England, it eased concerns that both countries might refuse to acknowledge Elizabeth's legitimacy as queen. International recognition of the new regime, by immediately lessening the danger of a Catholic crusade, strengthened Elizabeth's domestic situation. She took the opportunity to pause and reconsider her options, adjourning Parliament with nothing resolved.

Her willingness to do as much for the Protestants as she could without putting herself at risk became obvious. What was called an official "discussion" was arranged, ostensibly to give representatives of the conservative and evangelical camps an opportunity to air their views on the future of the church, and any doubts about which side the government favored were put to rest when the leading spokesmen for the Catholic side, the bishops of Winchester and Lincoln, were immediately afterward thrown into prison. This had the considerable advantage, from the Protestant perspective, of removing two staunchly conservative votes from a closely divided House of Lords as the climax of the legislative dispute drew near. When Parliament reconvened on April 3, both houses took up a revision of a supremacy bill that recognized the queen as supreme *governor* rather than *head* of the church, once again separated England from Rome, and re-repealed the heresy laws that Mary's Parliaments had restored. This bill encountered serious opposition in the Lords and might have been defeated there if the old bugbear having to do with possible restitution of church lands had not been resurrected to alarm the lay majority one last time. A uniformity bill outlawing the mass in favor of a somewhat watered-down version of the Edwardian Prayer Book (verbal abuse of the pope was deleted from the worship service) passed even more narrowly after being opposed not only by all the bishops but by eleven lay lords including, rather embarrassingly for the Crown, two members of the Privy Council. Thus yet another new English church was born. It was unmistakably a Protestant church, possibly more emphatically Protestant than Elizabeth herself thought prudent. The new legislation had been softened to avoid extinguishing the last hopes of the Catholics, however, and so it served the queen's chief purpose: it avoided a crisis. Before going further, the government was going to have to weaken the Catholics.

One way to undermine the Catholic party was to eliminate the Marian bishops, and the legislation of 1559 made that possible. Thanks to the breakdown in relations between Mary and Philip and Pope Paul IV, ten of the kingdom's twenty-seven bishoprics were now vacant. A remarkable number of the remaining bishops were aged and infirm, and with Pole dead and Heath of York wanting to avoid conflict the hierarchy was essentially leaderless. Moreover several of its members—including Cuthbert Tunstal of Durham, who had been bullied into submission by Henry VIII early in the divorce dispute and was now in his mid-eighties—had lived through all the turmoil of the past thirty years and survived by bending under pressure. Elizabeth, not unreasonably, expected that some and possibly all of these men would do the sensible thing and once again repudiate the connection with Rome. She found, however, that almost to a man they were unwilling to make Cranmers of themselves by changing their allegiance yet again. Only Anthony Kitchen of Llandaff in Wales took the uniformity oath. Every one of the others, even those who in the past had shown themselves willing to go wherever the winds of fortune blew, stood fast. One resigned, two died in the months following the passage of the new Uniformity Act, and by the end of the year all the others had been expelled from their offices and either imprisoned or placed under house arrest. This time, however, there would be no executions. Elizabeth was not burdened with her father's terrible need for capitulation or his willingness to kill anyone who failed to capitulate abjectly. Determined to put her regime in the sharpest possible contrast to her sister's, she understood that a resumption of executions would have been entirely counterproductive.

Having decapitated the Marian church, the queen found herself at liberty to fill twenty-six bishoprics with men of her own choosing. This proved to be no simple matter. The most impressive candidates, the men who had departed for the continent rather than conform during Mary's reign and thereby achieved heroic stature in the eyes of the English Protestant community, had during their years of exile broken up into quarreling factions. The most important factions were the one centered at Frankfurt under Richard Cox, who had been tutor to Prince Edward before Henry VIII's death and chancellor of Oxford University afterward, and the one at Geneva under the Scotsman John Knox, who had declined a bishopric when Edward was king. Though they had become enemies while in exile, both Cox and Knox were rich in the kinds of credentials that should have brought success under the Elizabethan settlement.

Unfortunately for himself and his followers, however, during the closing months of Mary's reign Knox had written and published a document with an eye-catchingly dramatic title: *The First Blast of the Trumpet Against the Monstrous Regiment of Women*. This was, in essence, a vitriolic attack on three Catholic rulers: Queen Mary of England; the Frenchwoman Marie of Guise, who was ruling Scotland in the name of her daughter Mary Stuart; and Margaret of Hapsburg, Philip of Spain's half-sister and his regent in the Netherlands. Knox's tract excoriated the three for everything he found loathsome about their regimes—their "regiments," in the diction of the time. He had, however, couched his argument in such broad terms that it easily could be understood as (because in fact it was) a condemnation of rule by women as contrary to nature and therefore "monstrous." Elizabeth, who in a fantastically bad stroke of timing for Knox became queen just months after its publication, interpreted it in exactly this way. Not only Knox but those associated with him, even that most seminal of Protestant theologians John Calvin, became personae non gratae in England precisely at the moment when their version of Christianity was once again finding acceptance there. Luckily for Knox, a political-religious coup soon gave the Scots evangelicals control of the government and church in Edinburgh, enabling him to return home and proceed to the next stage of his momentous career as a crusading Puritan and anti-Catholic polemicist. From there he would try without success to persuade Elizabeth that *The First Blast* had never had anything to do with someone as obviously favored by God as she was. Cox meanwhile returned to England, secured for himself the lucrative see of Ely, and resumed his interrupted campaign to purge Oxford of conservative theology; he had the satisfaction of seeing one member after another of his old Frankfurt circle appointed to positions of importance. If not as radical as the Genevan Calvinists, the Coxians, too, were strongly inclined to the austerity that would soon be given the name Puritan. They were just as disposed to look on the old church with horror and only somewhat more willing to enter into alliances of convenience with Protestants less uncompromising than themselves.

The stage seemed set for the triumph of Cox's party. Elizabeth, however, showed herself to be unwilling to let that happen. Whatever her innermost motives—fear of the consequences of going too far, perhaps, or a personal theology capacious enough to make room for her father's kind of conservatism—she was soon obstructing her own new bishops. The nominee for Canterbury, Matthew Parker, was the choice not of the queen herself but of Secretary Cecil and Chancellor Bacon, and he was not one of the evangelical heroes returning from exile, having spent the Marian years staying as inconspicuous as possible at home. He had only the narrowest base of support, therefore, and even before his consecration (an honor, it must be acknowledged, that he tried to escape) he found himself at odds with Crown and Parliament. The point of conflict was a piece of legislation called the Act of Exchange, an attempt to allow the government to enrich itself at church expense (yet again) by taking possession of property belonging to the many vacant bishoprics and promising revenues from tithes in return. The Protestant clergy had as much reason as their Catholic predecessors to object to this latest plundering of their resources, and Parker, to the queen's indignation and the discomfiture of Cecil and Bacon, put himself at the head of the objectors. There ensued a long series of conflicts between Crown and church, and increasingly between different groups of Protestants, that made a misery of Parker's tenure as archbishop and a confusion of the council's efforts to manage the church. The queen went to sometimes outlandish lengths to extract money from the dioceses while staying within the letter of the law. She allowed the Diocese of Ely to remain without a bishop for nineteen years after Cox's death. Bristol remained vacant for fourteen years, Chichester for seven. There were arcane but bitter conflicts over such questions as what churchmen should be required or permitted or forbidden to wear in the performance of their ceremonial duties.

As angrily as they could contend among themselves, the Protestants rarely had difficulty in uniting to expunge from the kingdom their despised common enemy: the Catholic Church and those of their countrymen who persisted in its beliefs and practices. Here again, however, with what must have been baffling frequency, they found themselves unable to get the expected level of cooperation from the queen. Out of the eight thousand priests in England, no more than three hundred were removed from their positions between 1560 and 1566 for failing to confirm to the Act of Uniformity. This number, certainly a small fraction of the conservative clergy, can reasonably be taken as a measure less of concord than of Elizabeth's unwillingness to press the issue. In 1561, after the recently elected Pope Pius IV called the Council of Trent back into session after a years-long adjournment and invited England to send representatives, an alarmed Cecil, horrified by the thought of intercourse between Canterbury and Rome, ginned up enough supposed evidence of Catholic sedition to persuade Elizabeth not only to spurn the invitation but to intensify the harassment of practicing Catholics. The persecution was relaxed as soon as the danger of English participation in the council was past, and two years later, when an increasingly aggressive Parliament made it a capital offense to refuse twice to take the supremacy oath, the queen quietly ordered Parker to see to it that no one was asked a second time. When convocation adopted the Thirty-Nine Articles as a definition of current English orthodoxy, she saw to it that the language was kept general enough that Catholics would not have to repudiate either it or their beliefs. Repeatedly over the first decade of her reign she vetoed legislation intended to increase the difficulties of being Catholic while functioning more or less normally as a member of the English nation.

Nothing in this should be taken as suggesting that Elizabeth was in some way a crypto-Catholic, or that she entertained any thought of establishing a new kind of country in which fundamentally different belief systems would be permitted to coexist. She was not only Protestant but militantly Protestant, and no more capable than her contemporaries of imagining that any nation could tolerate multiple faiths without weakening itself fatally. But her highest objective remained her own security, not the pursuit of any agenda religious or otherwise. For more than ten years she remained content just to inconvenience her Catholic subjects, trying to make them gradually decline in numbers and finally—or so it was hoped—disappear. She was likewise content to keep in place a national church whose doctrines and practices were thoroughly acceptable to very few people except herself, a Protestant church from which increasing numbers of her most passionately Protestant subjects felt utterly alienated.

THE COUNCIL OF TRENT

THE RELIGIOUS AGENDA WITH WHICH ELIZABETH BEGAN her reign, her hope of slowly extinguishing the old church by a process of neglect that was far from benign but also stopped short of lethal persecution, was complicated by an improbable development: the emergence of the Roman Catholic Church, even before Elizabeth became queen, as the most ambitiously reformist element in the whole expanding universe of Christian sects. The energy with which Rome began to address the problems, failures, and doctrinal questions that lay at the root of the Reformation had become a challenge for Protestants of all stripes even before Henry VIII's death. As the resulting changes made themselves felt in England, they decreased the likelihood that Elizabeth's government was going to be able to win over its Catholic subjects simply by making their attachment to Rome an embarrassment and an inconvenience.

What made the difference was the Council of Trent, itself one of the most remarkable developments in the history of Christianity. Its results, for better or worse, were nothing less than momentous. That it happened at all, considering the obstacles that stood in its path from beginning to end, struck many of its participants as little short of miraculous.

Councils had been a central element in the development of Christianity almost from its origins, a way of settling disputed questions by referring them to conclaves of church leaders from every part of the believing world. The eighteen councils that had been convened before Trent, more than one per century on average, had played an essential role in deciding what was required for church membership, which texts were and were not authoritative, what was doctrine and what heresy. Though conflicts had arisen over whether councils or popes had primacy, and though the part played by councils in causing schism in the fourteenth century had caused them to be viewed with deep skepticism thereafter, the fundamental idea of councils as a means by which God could reveal himself to the faithful continued to exert a strong pull. Luther himself, at the start of his rebellion, had demanded that a council be called to pass judgment on what he was teaching. Though scarcely a year later he was declaring that councils had no power to decide questions of faith, by then some of his followers and some defenders of the old orthodoxy were looking to a council as possibly the only hope of preserving unity.

For two decades and more, as the reform movement sprouted more and more branches under the leadership of Zwingli, Martin Bucer, Calvin, and others, multiplying the ways in which tradition was being rejected, Rome failed to respond in anything resembling a systematic fashion. Even within the old church, there was more than a little doctrinal ambiguity—uncertainty about questions that the theologians had never attempted to answer definitively because they had never before seen a compelling need to do so. By the time Henry VIII embarked upon making himself head of his own church, it was generally the Catholics more than their enemies who thought a council desirable and even necessary. They were driven, at the start, by three impulses: to effect a reconciliation by which Christian Europe could be made whole once again, to clarify disputed doctrines, and to address the abuses that even the most conservative churchmen were no longer able to ignore. When it became clear that there could be no reconciliation, that rebellion was hardening into an array of alternative churches that were never going to be defeated or won over, the other two reasons came to seem more urgent than ever. The Roman church was not going to be able to defend itself until it became definitive about what it stood for, and it was not going to be able to command respect until it dealt with (which meant acknowledging) its own failings. The papacy having become so controversial, only a council could confer sufficient legitimacy on whatever the church decided to do. But every specific proposal for the holding of a council was met by objections from one quarter or another.

The political difficulties long seemed insurmountable. In 1523, at the Diet of Nuremberg, the rulers of Germany's newly Lutheran states issued a demand for a "free Christian council"—insisting also that it be held in Germany. Rome rejected the idea on the grounds that such a council would be national rather than ecumenical and therefore could not represent the entire church. Charles V not only supported Rome's position but forbade the holding of a council anywhere within his domains. By 1530, however, conditions had changed and both sides seemed ready: Charles and Pope Clement VII were agreed that a council should be called, and the Lutheran princes were repeating their demand for one. But when the pope sent invitations, it became obvious that although everyone professed to like the *idea* of a council, there was insufficient agreement on practicalities for any real progress to be made. The Germans found Clement's conditions insulting—understandably so, as he had insisted that the Protestants return to the old communion pending the results of the proposed council—and rejected his summons in scornful terms. Henry of England responded equivocally, neither agreeing to participate nor refusing outright. Francis I did likewise, complaining that his bishops could not possibly travel in safety while his country and the empire were at war but actually fearing that a council, if somehow successful in healing Germany's divisions, would make the emperor stronger. The situation drifted until 1534, when Clement died and Alessandro Farnese became Pope Paul III.

The new pope declared almost immediately that he, too, wanted a council—that he regarded a council as the only way of dealing with the crisis facing the church—but at first he seemed just as blocked as his predecessor. Paul was a paradoxical figure, one who gave the Protestants many reasons to remember what they had long found despicable about Rome. In many ways he was a classic Renaissance pontiff—a member of the high Roman aristocracy, extravagant in his spending, scandalously devoted to the advancement of the children whom he had produced early in his career and those children's children (among whom were two grandsons elevated to the College of Cardinals while still in their teens). He was also a ferocious hunter of heretics, the founder, in fact, of the Roman Inquisition. But with all this he was absolutely convinced of the need to reform the church. When in 1536 he called for all patriarchs, archbishops, bishops, and abbots to gather at Mantua the following year, the negative responses of the Lutherans, the king of France, and others— even the Duke of Mantua objected—did not deter him. His proposal, like those of Clement VII, became entangled in the conflict between France and the Holy Roman Empire, England's defection, and the fears of many cardinals that a council could only lead to further trouble. But he continued to push, and the emperor continued to support his efforts in general terms while often disagreeing on the details. After a good many more years of frustration and intrigue, a council finally opened in December 1545 in the city of Trent, an Alpine site that is now Italian but at the time lay within the borders of the Hapsburg empire.

It was, in the beginning, an unimpressive affair. Presided over not by the pope but by three cardinals serving as his legates (one of them was Reginald Pole), its opening session was attended by only one additional cardinal (who was also the bishop of Trent), four archbishops, twenty-one bishops, five heads of religious orders, forty-two theologians, and nine canon law scholars. This was scarcely enough for the council to claim to be representative of the church as a whole; France, England, and virtually all of Protestant Europe had declined to take part. Those present required three sessions and a good deal of acrimonious debate to get past preliminary questions of procedure. Finally in March 1546, having decided who would be allowed to vote (the religious orders were given a single vote each) and that questions of reform and of doctrine would be addressed simultaneously, they were ready to turn their attention to substantive issues. Over the next year, in the course of seven more sessions separated by intermissions during which the theologians and lawyers prepared reports on the matters to be considered next, the number of participants gradually increased and the amount of business completed went far beyond what anyone could have expected at the start.

The initial focus, naturally, was on those points where the German and Swiss Protestants had mounted their most damaging attacks on the old doctrines. Luther's assertion of justification by faith was debated on fully one hundred occasions, at the end of which council members approved an immensely detailed decree (it included sixteen chapters) to the effect that justification (salvation) is achieved not regardless of the individual's actions or beliefs but when man actively cooperates with divine grace. Thus free will was affirmed and predestination condemned. This set the pattern by which the council would proceed from then on, rejecting beliefs that made Protestant theology distinctly Protestant, upholding doctrines that the Protestants had repudiated, and drawing upon Scripture, tradition, and the writings of the church fathers to explain why. In its first months the council also affirmed—with sometimes laboriously detailed explanations—that both the Bible and tradition are sources of revelation; that all seven of the original sacraments are valid; and that the so-called Latin Vulgate version of the Bible (largely developed by Saint Jerome in the fourth century from Greek and Hebrew sources) is an authoritative text. The council's first major action with regard to practice and discipline was to declare that bishops must reside in their sees, thereby ending the "pluralities" long enjoyed by (for example) Cardinal Wolsey.

Perhaps because it was coming to grips with issues of the greatest sensitivity and highest importance, the council continued to grow in size and in credibility. By its ninth session the number of voting participants had more than doubled to include nine archbishops and forty-nine bishops along with the heads, or generals, of an increased number of orders. At the same time, however, the political divisions that had originally made it impossible to convene a council remained a formidable obstacle. After two years the pope found it necessary to shift the meetings to Bologna, where progress slowed to a crawl and finally stopped altogether with his death in 1549.

The council entered its second major period in 1551 under Pope Julius III, who as a cardinal had been its first president. This phase lasted only one year, during which the members met in six sessions. In that time they issued a comprehensive decree of eight chapters on the Eucharist or communion, once again affirming and systematizing traditional doctrine including the real presence. By now the council was giving substantial attention to the correction of abuses, issuing far-reaching rules on clerical discipline and the powers and responsibilities of bishops. This work was barely completed when, in 1552, the Protestant Maurice of Saxony launched a military attack on Charles V that made Trent so unsafe that once again the proceedings had to be adjourned. They remained in abeyance not only until Julius's death in 1555 but through the subsequent reign of Paul IV, who used his office to push an ambitious program of administrative reforms but (possibly because of his hatred of the Hapsburgs, very nearly the only royal supporters of the council) had absolutely no interest in seeing work resume at Trent or elsewhere.

The next pope, Pius IV, announced his intention to reconvene the council almost as soon as he was elected but quickly ran up against complications old and new. Many German states repeated their refusal

5. Edward VI as Prince of Wales.

2. Warrant of Queen Jane.

3. Lady Jane Grey (1537–54), eldest grand-daughter of Henry VIII's younger sister Mary.

Opposite: 4. Edward VI, from a window in the chapel at Sudeley Castle.

1. Lady Jane Grey, depicted in stained glass at Sudeley Castle.

Above: 7. Hugh Latimer preaching before Edward VI from the 'preaching place' Henry VIII had built in the palace garden at Whitehall.

Left: 8. The first page of a letter from Edward VI to his bishops January 1550.

Opposite: 9. Title-page to the first edition of the *Book of Common Prayer*, 1549. The scene above the title shows Edward VI sitting in council.

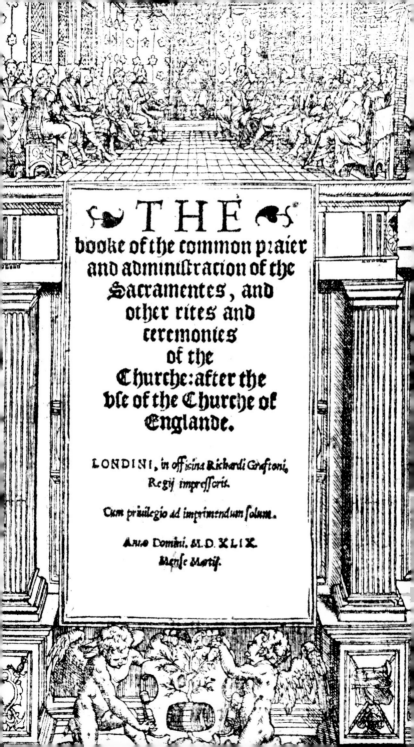

THE

booke of the common praier
and administration of the
Sacramentes, and
other rites and
ceremonies
of the
Churche: after the
vse of the Churche of
Englande.

LONDINI, in officina Richardi Graftoni,
Regij impressoris.

Cum priuilegio ad imprimendum solum.

Anno Domini. M.D.XLIX.
Mense Martij.

My devise for the Succession

To the L' Janes heires masles, To the L' Katerins heires
masles, To the L' Maries heires masles. To
the heires masles of the daughters which
she shal haue hereafter. Then to the L' Marga-
rets heires masles. For lakke of such issue.
To theires masles of the L' Janes daughters
To theires masles of the Katerins daughters
and so forth til you come to the L' Marga-
rets daughters heires masles.

2. If after my death theire masle be entred into
is yere old then he to haue the hole rule
and gouernance therof.

3. But if he be under 18, then his mother to
be gouernres til he entre 18 yere old
But to do nothing without thauctise of 6
parcel of a counsel to be pointed by my
last will to the nomore of 20.

4. If the mother die befor theire entre into
the realme to be gouerned by the cousel
Prouided that after be 14 yere al
grat matters of importaunce be to him.

5. If i died thoth issue, and ther were none
then the L' Fraunces to be gouerneres
for lakke for her eldes daughters
and for lakke of them the L' margat to

12. Princess Mary, daughter of Henry VIII and Catherine of Aragon.

Opposite top: 10. Edward VI's 'devise for the succession' of June 1553.

Opposite bottom: 11. Edward Seymour, Lord Protector of Edward VI.

Above: 13. Greenwich Palace where Mary was born on 18 February 1516.

Left: 14. Detail from *The Family of Henry VIII* c.1545. There is a clear dynastic message in the positioning of Mary on the fringes of the painting.

15. At the age of ten Mary was set up with her own court at Ludlow Castle, the very place to which Catherine of Aragon and her first husband (Henry VIII's brother Arthur) had been sent shortly after their marriage and the palace Prince Arthur met his early death.

16. Queen Mary's instructions to Lord Russell, Lord Privy Seal, and signed 'Marye the quene'.

MARIA : REG

17, 18 & 19. Portraits of Mary I as queen.

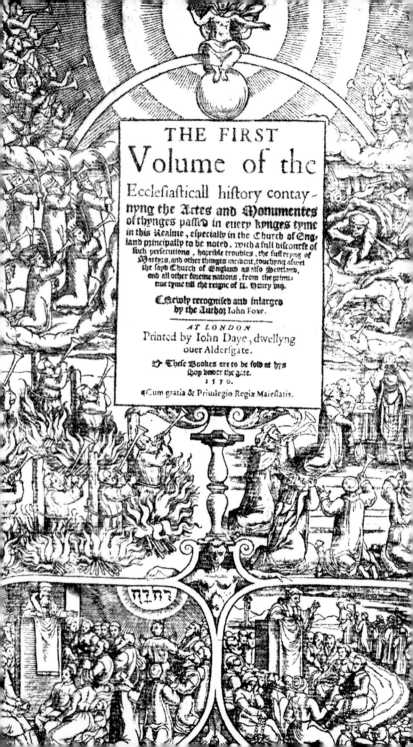

THE FIRST
Volume of the

Ecclesiasticall history contay-
nyng the Actes and Monumentes
of thynges passed in euery kynges tyme
in this Realme, especially in the Church of England principally to be noted, with a full discourse of
such persecutions, horrible troubles, the sufferyng of
Martyrs, and other thynges incident, touchyng aswel
the sayd Church of England as also Scotland,
and all other foreine nations, from the primi-
tiue tyme till the reigne of K. Henry viij.

Newly recognised and inlarged
by the Author Iohn Foxe.

AT LONDON
Printed by Iohn Daye, dwellyng
ouer Aldersgate.

☞ These Bookes are to be sold at hys
shop vnder the gate.
1570.

¶ Cum gratia & Priuilegio Regiæ Maiestatis.

21. The burning of Bishop John Hooper at Gloucester, 9 February 1555 from Foxe's *Book of Martyrs*.

22. The burning of Hugh Latimer and Nicholas Ridley at Oxford 16 October 1555 from Foxe's *Book of Martyrs*.

Opposite: 20. Title page from the 1570 edition of John Foxe's *Acts and Monuments* (usually known as his 'Book of Martyrs'), famous for its detailed accounts of the Protestant victims of Mary's reign.

Above: 23. Edmund Bonner (Bishop of London, 1539–59) as Protestants saw him thanks to Foxe's *Book of Martyrs.* Here he is shown tormenting a captive Protestant by applying a candle to his hand. As around sixty out of nearly 300 Protestant martyrs under Queen Mary were burned in London.

Left: 24. Philip II of Spain, engraving by F. Hogenberg, 1555. Mary married Philip in 1554.

25. Calais, from a sixteenth-century chart. The crowning calamity of Mary's reign was the loss of Calais to France in 1558.

Above: 26. Hatfield House in Hertfordshire, Elizabeth I's childhood home.

Left: 27. 'The Lady Elizabeth', an anonymous portrait of about 1548.

28. Detail from *The Family of Henry VIII c*.1545. The earliest surviving portrait of Elizabeth, showing her aged about twelve.

cto /piritus

72 Igitur da mihi domine prudenti-
am celestem. vt discam. querere, et
inuenire te, et amare te super oīa.

73 Da mihi gratiam abducere ⅌
me ab illis qui me adulantur. et
patienter illos ferre qui me adu-
vexant

74 Quando tentatio, et tribulatio ꝯ
veniunt, digneris succurrere mihi
domine. vt omnia vertentur mihi
in spirituale solatium et semper
feram patienter. ac dicam: bene-
dictum sit nomen tuum.

fragilite laquelle tu congnois le
mieulx

Ayes mercy de moy. et me   74
delyure de tout peche et iniqui-
te accellefin que ie ne soye acca-
ble d'iceux

Il m'est souuentesfois fort gri-   75
ef. et cela quasi me consond. de
ce que ie suis sy instable sy feeble et fragile, pour resister aux
motions iniques: lesquelles, cõ-
bien qu'elles ne me causent de
consentir. ce nonobstant me sõt
leurs assaulx tresgriefz.

29. Prayers written out by Elizabeth (then aged thirteen) in a little volume she presented to her father, Henry VIII, as a New Year's gift for 1546.

Above & left: 30 a. & b. The Tower of London *c.*1550 and Traitors' Gate through which Elizabeth passed on her way to prison in 1554.

Below Left: 31. The Entrance of Queen Elizabeth. Queen Elizabeth's accession (or 'entrance') came to be celebrated as a religious festival.

The Entrance of Q. Elizabeth.

Opposite: 32. Although in Mary's reign Elizabeth had affected the simplest and plainest fashions in dress (in order to distinguish herself from her overdressed sister and to allude to the Protestant aesthetic of plain simplicity), once she became queen Elizabeth re-invented herself with the aid of spectacularly ornate dresses such as this.

33. Sketch for a portrait of Elizabeth I.

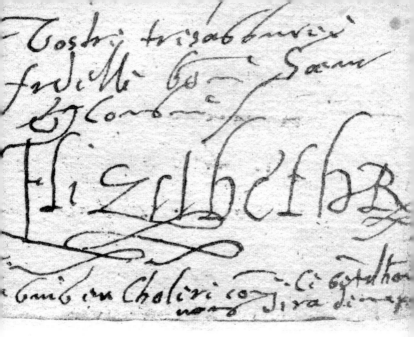

34. Signature of Elizabeth I.

35. Great Seal of Elizabeth I.

36. Robert Dudley was a favourite of the queen's from the start of the reign, and was given the prestigious Court position of Master of the Horse. In the early 1560s Elizabeth was widely reckoned to be in love with him, even though he was already married.

Opposite: 37. Elizabeth I at prayer is the frontispiece to *Christian Prayers* (1569).

38. Elizabeth I and the Three Goddesses, 1569.

Left: 39. Elizabeth's falcon downs a heron. Illustration from George Turberville, *The Book of Faulconrie or Hauking* (1575), p.81.

Opposite: 40. Francis, Duke of Alençon, came closer than anyone else to securing Elizabeth's hand in marriage. He first visited Elizabeth's court in 1576 and to everyone's surprise, Elizabeth appeared completely smitten with him.

41. 'A Hieroglyphic of Britain', which John Dee himself designed as the frontispiece to his *General and Rare Memorials Pertayning to the Perfect Arte of Navigation* (1577). John Dee (1527–1608), alchemist, geographer, mathematician and astrologer to the queen, wrote the *Arte of Navigation* as a manifesto for Elizabethan naval imperialism.

42. Sir Walter Ralegh and his son. Ralegh became the latest in the long line of the queen's favourites in the early 1580s.

43. Robert Devereux (1565-1601), the second Earl of Essex. Pushed forward at Elizabeth's Court by his stepfather, the Earl of Leicester, in the justified hope that he might displace Ralegh as the queen's foremost favourite. Neither his talents nor his means quite matched his ambitions, however, and after losing royal favour he gambled and lost everything in a desperate attempted coup. He was executed in 1601.

44. Mary Queen of Scots, a prisoner throughout the two decades preceding her execution at age forty-four in 1586.

45. In 1586, the Derbyshire gentleman Anthony Babington was the central figure in a plot to liberate Mary Queen of Scots and assassinate Elizabeth.

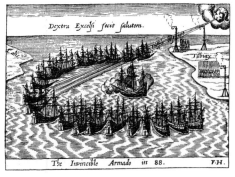

47. Sir Francis Drake.

46. The Spanish Armada off the French coast, 1588.

Top: 49. The 'Procession Picture' from Elizabeth's last years.

Right: 50. Engraved portrait of Elizabeth I by William Rogers c.1595.

Opposite: 48. The 'Ermine Portrait', from 1585, show Elizabeth aged about 52.

51. The 'Ditchley Portrait' (*c*.1590, but not showing the queen's nearly 60 years).

52. Elizabeth I in old age.

53. Funeral of Elizabeth.

to participate and their condemnation of what had been done thus far; the new Holy Roman emperor Ferdinand I demanded that an entirely new council be assembled in some city other than Trent; the French continued to complain and to stay away; and there was no possibility of involving Elizabeth's new regime. When Pius went ahead anyway and the council's members gathered in Trent early in 1562, the problems persisted. Bishops from France arrived for the first time that November, but their presence was very much a mixed blessing: they tried, though without success, to get the council to reconsider its earlier prohibition of pluralities. Despite much turmoil and intrigue, the nine sessions of this last of Trent's three periods led to a grand culmination. New decrees laid out rules of conduct for religious men and women of all types and at all levels from cardinals to lay brothers, and it was agreed that every diocese must establish seminaries for the education of its priests. Church doctrine was set forth in detail on subjects ranging from matrimony to the veneration of saints, from purgatory to the necessity of an ordained priesthood. The council even dealt, finally, with the issue that had triggered the Lutheran explosion: indulgences. To the scorn of Protestants, it affirmed the pope's authority to issue indulgences but ruled that they must never be sold or made conditional on the giving of alms. The council's last decrees were approved by 215 participants, among whom were six cardinals, three patriarchs (leaders of non-Roman rites that accepted the pope as head of the universal church), twenty-five archbishops, 167 bishops, seven abbots, seven generals of orders, and nineteen absent dignitaries voting by proxy. They closed the council on a note of jubilation, confident that their church had been put on a new course. Through their work that church had repudiated the Reformation conclusively, had explained its doctrines more systematically and comprehensively than ever before, and had made a repetition of the lapses and abuses of recent history all but impossible. Pius IV confirmed the council's decisions in the year of life that remained to him, put sanctions in place to enforce compliance, and introduced further reforms of his own that would be carried still further by his successors.

From start to finish the council had taken eighteen years and spanned the reigns of five popes. Its members had spent more than four years actively engaged in their deliberations, with much work ongoing between the twenty-five formal sessions. Those who rejected the very idea of a universal church headed by the bishop of Rome naturally dismissed the results as flawed and exclusive at best, as yet another abomination perpetrated by the Whore of Babylon at worst. Even some within the Catholic community saw the council as an overreaction, one that went too far in giving conclusive answers to difficult questions and made the church too rigidly triumphalist in its claim to be the sole source of religious truth and salvation.

What cannot be doubted is that the council contributed mightily to stopping the unraveling of what remained of Catholic Europe. From the point at which its work was concluded, Protestantism made few geographic gains of any significance. In the four and a half centuries since then, except with limited and short-lived exceptions, the kind of internal disorder that had made the council necessary never recurred. There has never been another pope whom any reasonable person could accuse of moral corruption in the mode of the Renaissance papacy. Almost certainly, Trent made the transformation of England into a thoroughly Protestant nation a more difficult challenge, a bloodier process, than it otherwise would have been.

7

The Succession, Again

Religion was not the only great question pressing in on the new queen. Another, just as thorny in its very different way, cried out for an answer almost from the first day of Elizabeth's reign. It was a question that, like the future of the church, was resurfacing with undiminished force every time one Tudor monarch died and was succeeded by another. It was the matter of the succession.

At the start of Elizabeth's reign, as for a long time thereafter, the solution appeared to be matrimony. In the main line of Tudor descent, now that Henry VIII's only son and elder daughter were in their tombs, no one remained but this one young woman. There were cousins of royal blood, the few living descendants of Henry VIII's two sisters. But the most senior of these cousins had been born in Scotland and absorbed into the French royal family and was a Roman Catholic, making her suspect in the eyes of many Englishmen and absolutely unacceptable to the evangelicals. The others were the Protestant younger sisters of the late Lady Jane Grey and therefore objectionable, although no more so than Elizabeth herself, to the Catholics. The Tudor family tree remained a worrisomely thin organism, and if Elizabeth were to die childless the result was sure to be confusion and could be civil war. If on the other hand Elizabeth married and had children—at least one son, preferably, to end this awkward business of female rulers—the problem would disappear.

That the queen would follow her sister's example and take a husband seemed inevitable. To the extent that Mary's decision had become a source of trouble, the problem lay in her choice of the Spanish Philip. His status as ruler of Spain and the Netherlands and so much else made him an alien in the eyes of many of his wife's subjects, and not the evangelicals alone. But if Mary had not married Philip, those same subjects would have expected her to marry *someone*. The five years between Mary's accession and Elizabeth's did nothing to alter the universal conviction that it was unnatural for any woman not to be subordinate to some man (even nuns were "brides of Christ"), or for a queen to rule alone. Elizabeth herself, though she never forgave John Knox for his attack on *The Monstrous Regiment of Women*, never challenged this belief. She took the position, rather, that though her reign was a departure from the natural order of things, God had permitted it as a necessary means of restoring the gospel in England and preserving the kingdom's autonomy.

When Elizabeth took the throne she was an attractive young woman, with the fair skin and red-blond hair of the Tudors, her mother's dark eyes and slim body, and more than a dash of the Boleyn sexual magnetism. The men who dominated her first Privy Council thought themselves to have been blessed by God with a Protestant monarch, and naturally they hoped that she would become the progenitor of a long line of rulers of her religious persuasion. All this focused them on finding a marital answer to the succession question. For Elizabeth, the prospect of marriage was nothing new. As a king's daughter and the sister of a king and a queen, she had occasionally been in play on the market for royal brides, though in her case even more than in Mary's, illegitimacy had had a dampening effect on her value. We have seen Philip II, from the time of his arrival in England, protecting Elizabeth as a counterweight to Mary, Queen of Scots. He tried at one point, during his time in England, to marry her to his kinsman Emmanuel Philibert, Duke of Savoy. Elizabeth herself could see no advantage in such a match: the duke was little better than a displaced person of high distinction, having lost his ancestral lands to France, and he labored under the additional disadvantages of being Catholic and related to the Hapsburgs. Her lack of enthusiasm contributed to keeping the negotiations from getting serious, and shortly after she became queen Philip offered to marry her himself. She gave him no answer while consolidating her position—getting a new administration up and running, making preparations for her first Parliament. Rather than pressing the issue, Philip betrothed himself to a continental Elisabeth, a fourteen-year-old daughter of the king of France.

In February 1559, just two weeks after Elizabeth's coronation, a select committee of the House of Commons (it was "select" in the sense of being essentially a creature of the Privy Council) presented her with a formal request that she marry without undue delay. That such a step was taken so early in the reign is a good measure of how important the issue seemed to senior members of the new government. Elizabeth's not-unfriendly response to this intrusion into an otherwise intensely personal matter demonstrates that she, too, understood the question to be one in which her council, the Parliament, and indeed the nation had a legitimate stake. New candidates for her hand, meanwhile, were soon sending emissaries (and rich gifts) to explore the queen's availability. Among the suitors were King Erik XIV of Sweden and two young princes of the House of Hapsburg, sons of the emperor Ferdinand I and cousins of Philip of Spain. Efforts were made to arrange for one of the Hapsburg candidates, the archduke Charles, to travel to England, but when Elizabeth would not commit to the betrothal in advance of his visit the project collapsed. The fact that any Hapsburg would be a Catholic was a difficulty but obviously not an insuperable one. What mattered was finding a husband who could save England from being threatened, as seemed possible at this juncture, by an alliance of France and Scotland, or even *Spain* and France and Scotland.

Events with momentous consequences for England were meanwhile taking place in France. King Henry II arranged a lavish celebration both of the Treaty of Cateau-Cambrésis—under which France, Spain, England, and Scotland all were pledging to bring their war-making to an end—and of his daughter's marriage to Philip II. Henry participated in the jousting that was part of the festivities and suffered a slow, painful death (lingering in agony for ten days) after a sliver from an opponent's lance entered his eye and exited through his ear. He was succeeded by his eldest son, who took the throne as Francis II. The change proved to have far-reaching consequences in spite—or because, really—of the fact that Francis II was a frail and feeble fifteen-year-old and utterly incapable of taking charge. His accession meant that his bride of less than a year, Mary Stuart, the queen of Scotland and Catholic heir presumptive to the crown of England, was queen of France as well. Mary, now seventeen years old, had been raised in France while her mother, Marie of the House of Guise, one of France's most powerful families, remained in Scotland as regent. The bond between France and Scotland grew all the closer as young King Francis fell under the domination of his bride's uncles, the Duke of Guise and his brother Charles of Lorraine, a cardinal. Both countries were effectively under Guise control.

The contract under which the child Mary Stuart had been betrothed to Francis specified that if the couple had a son he would inherit France and Scotland as a single unified kingdom. For England this was an intolerable prospect, one that lifted the girl Mary to a position of stupendous geopolitical importance. But for Philip the situation was even more ominous: if Mary went on to succeed her cousin Elizabeth—such a development was far from impossible, considering the high mortality of the time and the fact that the queen of Scots was the younger of the two by almost a decade—he would be in grave danger. His Spanish base would be separated from his possessions in the Netherlands by a wall of hostile kingdoms extending from the islands north of Scotland to France's Mediterranean coast. The English Channel, the nautical highway connecting Spain and the Netherlands, would become a gauntlet lined on both sides by the seaports of his rivals. From Elizabeth's perspective, Philip's worries had a brilliantly positive aspect: they meant that Spain, with its vast European and global empire, needed the friendship of England at a moment when she, too, was urgently in need of friends. As long as Mary Stuart remained queen of France, there could be no possibility of a French-Spanish crusade to pull Elizabeth from her throne. As in Mary Tudor's reign, the existence of Mary Stuart gave Philip all the reason any king could have needed to want Elizabeth to survive.

The French-Scottish union would remain conditional, however, until Mary gave her husband a son. And no such thing was in the cards. Francis II, so unlike the vital and virile grandfather whose name he bore, lost his tenuous grip on life after only a year on the throne, almost certainly without having consummated his marriage. His death broke the power of the Guises over the government of France, and when his ten-year-old brother took the throne as Charles IX, control passed into the hands of their mother, Catherine de' Medici. The tall and rather beautiful Mary Stuart found herself an entirely superfluous second dowager queen, no longer wanted at a court that had been her home since childhood but was now dominated by the enemies of her Guise relatives.

Mary had little choice, really, except to return to the one place where she really was queen. But Scotland, too, had recently been convulsed by radical change and was no longer the kind of kingdom that her mother had struggled for years to preserve for her. Marie of Guise, not long after becoming regent, had found herself embroiled in a civil war with a party of Scottish noblemen, the "lords of the congregation," who were determined to install a Protestant government and establish a Protestant national church. Under the leadership of radical reformers such as John Knox, who had returned from the continent by ship after being denied permission to travel overland across England, evangelicalism had become popular and potent in Scotland's lowlands. Its adherents seethed with hatred for a Roman church that, long used as a source of spoils by the Scottish elite (King James V, Mary's father, had secured lucrative bishoprics for several of his illegitimate sons while they were still boys), had descended to levels of corruption never approached in England. Outnumbered and lacking in resources, despised for her foreign origins in spite of being honest, courageous, and by no means a mere agent of her French kinsmen, Marie of Guise had fought a protracted defensive action that might have been successful if not for two strokes of profoundly bad luck. Her health began to decline precipitously—she was dying, probably of heart disease, though still in her early forties—and England abruptly intervened on the side of the Protestant lords.

England's involvement was entirely the doing of William Cecil, Elizabeth's secretary and de facto minister-in-chief. He saw early what his royal mistress had difficulty seeing at all: that Scotland's internal divisions offered an unprecedented opportunity to drive out the French, establish Protestantism in the only kingdom with which England shared a border, and so turn an ancient enemy into a pacific neighbor if not an actively grateful friend. This was an enormous risk for Cecil, one in which failure could have meant ruin, because he had to labor to get the queen's assent (threatening to resign at one point) and in doing so took on full responsibility for the intervention's success. Elizabeth thought the chances of success small and the costs likely to be painful. But the death of Marie of Guise in June 1560 doomed the Catholic cause in Scotland and cleared Cecil's path. The result was a new Treaty of Edinburgh, a triumph for the Scottish rebels, for Knox and his newborn Church of Scotland, and not least for England. When the young widow Mary returned from France in 1561, it was to a Scotland profoundly different from the one in which she had been born nineteen years earlier. It was under the control of people who reviled her religion and her French associations, had no intention of allowing her to be more than a figurehead, and made her no more welcome than she had been in France in the eight months since her husband's death. She faced a challenge beyond anything Elizabeth had experienced in England.

Elizabeth, meanwhile, was growing steadily more adept at dancing around the subject of marriage when discussion could not be avoided altogether. One need not be Sigmund Freud to find reasons for her lack of interest. She was, after all, the daughter of a queen whose marriage had brought her to the block, the stepdaughter of another queen executed by a wrathful husband and of two queens who died as a result of giving birth, and the sister of a queen who had accepted it as her destiny to marry and paid a high price for doing so. She had seen her own reputation dangerously compromised when, still a mere girl, she became resident in the home of the newly married Catherine Parr and was subjected by Catherine's husband to advances that were obliquely sexual at least. She had good reason to see matrimony as a dubious portal to fulfillment, or to safety.

And there was another factor at play. Not surprisingly for a healthy and unmarried woman of twenty-five whose position exposed her to the flattering attentions of some of the cleverest, most privileged, and best-educated men in Europe, Elizabeth was in love. Her choice of objects would provide one of the most sustained and dramatic narrative threads in the long story of her reign and an eventful chapter in the saga of that most astonishing of Tudor-era families, the Dudleys. She had fixed her affection, her passion, on her master of horse, Robert Dudley—"Rob" to her—a son of the late and not-much-lamented Duke of Northumberland. The simple animal attraction was understandable: Dudley was handsome and young and distinctly virile, with a fine education, the kind of sophistication and polish that only an upbringing at court could produce, and experience as a fighting man. (As a youth he was with his father at the crushing of Kett's Rebellion, and in 1557 he participated in the siege of St. Quentin, where his brother Henry was killed in his presence.) He and the last of his brothers, the three-years-older Ambrose, were accepted as leaders by the circle of soldiery that had originally coalesced around their father. They would have impressed any monarch, male or female, as living symbols of military potency.

Having grown to manhood during the years when his father was rising to become the most powerful man in England, Robert Dudley was intimately familiar with the royal household and not intimidated by any of it. He would eventually claim, not implausibly, to have known Elizabeth before she was eight years old, and he appears to have been the sort of boy who would have effortlessly impressed almost any younger girl (he was older than Elizabeth by about a year), however exalted her parentage. It is likely that, along with Elizabeth, he became a beneficiary of the scholarly establishment put in place for the education of the boy-king Edward VI. At any rate he emerged with the attainments—proficiency in French, Italian, and Latin, for example—that were among the fruits of royal life for the third generation of Tudors. He became a gentleman of Edward's privy chamber, an honor that any ambitious young Englishman would have hungered for, and from an early age was accustomed to the company of the richest, most powerful people in the kingdom. He even, before his father's fall, sat as a very young member of Parliament.

Beyond all this, and quite aside from the possibility that early in life the two had formed a bond of which we have been left no record, Elizabeth had reason to regard Dudley as a kindred spirit. Although the Duke of Northumberland died professing himself a Catholic, all his offspring embraced evangelical Protestantism. The male Dudleys who had not been executed were still being held in the Tower when Wyatt's Rebellion led to Elizabeth's confinement there. The experience, which for Elizabeth and Robert alike included the very real possibility of execution, gave them a profoundly memorable experience in common. Both were ultimately saved by the intercession of Philip after his arrival from Spain, Elizabeth as a safeguard against Mary Stuart, Dudley and his brothers because of their stature among England's warrior elite and Philip's wish for influential friends. Both remained deep in the political wilderness, however, as long as Queen Mary remained alive. The properties bestowed on her in her father's will had made Elizabeth rich, and during Mary's reign she was an inherently important personage as heir presumptive, but her life was quiet except for those moments of near-terror occasioned by official suspicion that she was involved in plots against the queen. Dudley, his conviction for treason set aside thanks to Philip's intervention, settled into the peaceful existence of a country gentleman.

Mary Tudor's death was a deliverance for the Dudleys almost as much as for Elizabeth. Ambrose and Robert were given military appointments that made them figures of some importance at court, the former as master of ordnance and the latter as master of horse. They received other signs of favor; in Robert's case these included knighthood in the exclusive Order of the Garter, the lieutenantship of Windsor Castle and, to fatten his purse, a license to export wool without paying duty. (Later he would receive a more important license to import sweet wines.) Their sister Mary, the wife of the courtier Sir Henry Sidney, became a lady of the queen's privy chamber, her husband president of the council responsible for governing the territories bordering Wales.

It became obvious at court that Elizabeth had a singularly strong liking for Robert's company and was conspicuously unwilling for him to be absent. Inevitably, quite possibly without anything improper transpiring between them, a whiff of scandal began to emanate from their relationship and give rise to backstairs talk. There can have been no gossip of a possible marriage, however, because for almost two years after Elizabeth became queen such a thing was literally impossible. It would have been problematic for the queen to marry even the noblest of her subjects; such a union would have seemed demeaning to the Crown and would have carried with it the danger of dividing court and country into the husband's allies and rivals. For Elizabeth to marry a member of the Dudley clan would have provoked resentment among the more ancient noble families. But that was not the worst of it. The fatal fact was that Dudley was married. In 1550, in what would appear to have been a love match because it brought no political and little financial advantage to the bridegroom or his family, John Dudley had allowed Robert to marry a girl named Amy Robsart, only child of a respectable but unimportant East Anglian landowner. It was on his father-in-law's properties that

Robert had passed the years after his release from the Tower, living happily enough with Amy so far as is known but having no children. When the Dudleys were restored to royal favor, Amy was not brought to court with them. Her health may not have been good, and Robert undoubtedly understood that the queen would not have welcomed reminders that he had a wife. Dudley did visit Amy for a while, but with decreasing frequency and finally not at all.

But then came an earthquake. On the evening of September 8, 1560, Amy Robsart Dudley was found dead in her country home in Berkshire. An investigation followed, to the extent that such a thing was possible in the sixteenth century, but the result was a meaningless ruling of "death by misadventure." Amy's neck may or may not have been broken. She may or may not have had breast cancer. The possibility of suicide was raised, but her servants insisted that she never would have taken her own life. Naturally a suspicion of murder arose, and inevitably that suspicion focused on the husband. But Dudley had incontrovertibly been at Windsor on the day of Amy's death, having just returned from accompanying the queen on one of the "progresses" by which, every summer, she displayed herself to her subjects. The death was, and has remained, an impenetrable mystery. It also proved to be of immense political importance. It freed Dudley to marry the queen. But at the same time it spread over both of them the dark question of whether they had somehow conspired to eliminate the one person who stood between them. People were not slow to note that, at the time of her death, Amy had not been visited by her husband in more than a year. And that Dudley, who now became sole owner of his late father-in-law's holdings in land, neither attended his wife's funeral (that was actually not unusual at the time) nor arranged for the kind of memorial customarily created when a member of a prominent family died. Gossip turned to scandal, not only across England but in Europe. People eager to believe that Anne Boleyn had been a slut were easily persuaded that her daughter was a slut as well. Even people close to the queen—even Cecil, her trusted secretary—encouraged the foulest of the rumors in hopes of making the marriage impossible.

THE FALL AND RISE OF ENGLISH THEATER

WHEN ELIZABETH BECAME QUEEN, TWO VERY DIFFERENT kinds of theater were alive and well in England. One was old and religious in impulse and tightly woven into the lives of the people. The other was new and boisterously secular and more than a little disreputable. Both were regarded, from Elizabeth's first days on the throne, as serious problems—as threats to domestic peace if not to true religion, to the morals of the community if not to the efficient functioning of the economy. Over the next forty years the government would systematically suppress the old kind until finally, despite dogged popular resistance, it was extinguished. By the end of the Tudor era the new kind, in spite of a state censorship so strict as to amount almost to persecution, would be emerging as one of the supreme achievements of English cultural history.

Drama, like so much of life in England, had its roots in the early Middle Ages. It made its first, almost childishly simple appearance no later than the tenth century, in the form of little scenes from Scripture acted out by priests and worshippers inside their parish churches. Over the next few centuries these performances grew larger and more elaborate, finally spilling out of the churches and being taken over by the guilds. Three types evolved: mystery plays, in which stories from the Bible were acted out; miracle plays, based on incidents from the lives of saints; and finally morality plays, forerunners of modern drama, in which characters representing good and evil struggled to win the soul of some Everyman. (Mystery plays, by the way, took their name not from the Latin word *mysterium*, meaning "secret," but from *misterium*, meaning "occupation" or "trade." The name reflected the importance of the various occupational guilds—of silversmiths or bakers or carpenters or whatever—as sponsors, underwriters, and producers of dramatic performances, especially in the cities and larger towns.)

Ultimately, and without losing their religious content and purpose, such productions became a major form of popular entertainment and communal celebration. Whole cycles of plays were developed; some cycles included as many as twenty-five or even fifty separate tableaux (enactments of the Genesis account of creation, say, or of Jesus raising Lazarus from the dead). The sets for these miniplays would be mounted on wagons called "pageants," which could be wheeled from place to place in sequence so that in the course of a day spectators could see an entire cycle without having to move. It was not unlike the passage of floats in a parade. The cycles became central to observances of the major events in the liturgical calendar: Christmas of course, but also Twelfth Night (January 6, the feast of the epiphany), Candlemas (February 2), Holy Week with its culmination in Easter, Whitsun (the seventh Sunday after Easter), the feast of Corpus Christi (the Thursday after Trinity Sunday), and Hallowtide at the beginning of November. Schools, too, put on regular theatrical productions—which must have been a hugely welcome break from the tedious recitations that formed the core of classroom instruction—as did the universities and the Inns of Court.

As in any society where even simple forms of theater thrive, some individuals found themselves prepared to sacrifice security and stability in order to spend their lives performing. Tiny companies of professional players began to form and to scratch out a living by traveling from place to place. These groups would put on shows wherever they were allowed to, occasionally finding employment in the universities' Christmas productions or at the courts of the great nobles or even the king. Thus did the professional actor first emerge in post-Roman Britain. With him, inevitably, came nonreligious dramatic works. Few early examples have survived; those available to us tend toward the crude, rude, and unrestrainedly vulgar, but they are also funny enough in their Three Stooges slapstick way and sometimes surprisingly accomplished in character development. One of the oldest survivals, *Gammer Gurton's Needle,* is believed to have been written as late as the 1550s but to be one of the first comedies ever written in English. This dating, if correct, puts the play little more than a generation before the start of Shakespeare's career and marks the beginning of a period of astonishingly rapid artistic development.

At the beginning of Elizabeth's reign, in any case, the mystery, miracle, and morality plays were still a central, much-loved element in En-

glish community life, and professional theater was becoming increasingly popular both in London and in every place where local authorities
would permit touring companies to put on shows in exchange for
money. The new queen's council, its evangelical members especially,
was uncomfortable with theater of any variety and decided almost
before doing anything else that limits had to be imposed. The main problem with the religious plays was their traditional—meaning Catholic—
content. As for the newer, more secular performances, the Puritans
believed that, even if their content was not idolatrous or superstitious,
they wasted time that could better be devoted to work or prayer. Secular
theater suffered also from a growing perception on the part of the ever-
more-respectable middle classes that the kinds of people who engaged
in it were distinctly undesirable. Such opinions were not entirely unfair.
Plays were presented, usually, in neighborhoods where rents were cheap
and houses of prostitution and bear-baiting pits were leading forms of di-
version.

Officialdom's first response was a 1559 proclamation to the effect
that no plays were to be presented anywhere unless licensed either by
the mayor of a city or town or by a titled nobleman. The sternest of the
Puritans undoubtedly would have preferred simply to ban all theater
outright, but this was rendered impossible by the inconvenient fact that
drama had established itself at court. Those responsible for providing
amusements for the queen and her courtiers were learning that hiring a
company of players to perform works already written and rehearsed was
easier—and vastly less expensive—than developing new entertainments
from scratch. Queen and courtiers, for their part, responded enthusiastically to theatrical performances—to the best of them at least.

Theater continued to be regarded as intrinsically disreputable, however. The Privy Council observed it through narrowed eyes, imposing increasingly firm controls. Eventually it limited the authority to license
companies to the titled nobility, in part, no doubt, because nobles were
far fewer in number than mayors and judicial officials and more easily
monitored and subjected to pressure from the Crown. But another reason must have been the fact that England's increasingly well-educated
nobility found pleasure in quality theater, displayed a willingness to support it, and would not have accepted its elimination without complaint.
By the 1560s the Earl of Leicester, the same Rob Dudley who stood first

among Elizabeth's favorites, was sponsoring one of the most successful companies. This weighty endorsement was given even more force by Dudley's status as a prominent evangelical.

As the 1560s proceeded, men more puritanical than Dudley were moving into positions of leadership in cities and towns including London. Such men were repelled by the traditional religious theatricals so loved by their neighbors, and they refused to issue licenses except for scripts cleansed of all vestiges of the old religion. Finally they refused to license the productions altogether, and though resistance was widespread and persistent it was itself unlawful and ultimately fruitless. Cycles tailored to the feast of Corpus Christi were still being performed in Kendal in the north in the late 1580s, and in distant Cornwall even in the 1590s, but by the end of the century they were gone. The tradition they expressed was fading. Henceforth the story of English theater was the story of secular drama exclusively. And it, far more than the old religious plays, was concentrated in London.

The capital was becoming the biggest city in Europe; by the end of the century it would have 200,000 residents, four times as many as in 1500. It was a boiling, brawling cauldron of tradesmen and nobles, clerics and domestic servants, sailors and soldiers, idlers and whores and fortune-seekers from every corner of Europe, most of them hungry for entertainment and many with at least a penny or two to spare. Such a place was a magnet for the traveling companies of actors that, as they put on performances in the courtyards of inns and other rented spaces, found themselves attracting large and lucrative audiences. Necessarily, such performances were almost invariably presented in daytime, and naturally they attracted the sorts of people who were free in the daytime—prostitutes, sailors, and other visitors in search of a good time, workers willing and able to slip away from their jobs. The city fathers, appalled, appealed to the council to purge London of such decadence and refused to issue licenses. The theater people responded by moving to downmarket suburbs beyond the reach of city law. Respectable England's attitude toward the whole phenomenon is apparent in the name of the bill with which Parliament, in 1572, sought to impose order: An Act for Punishment of Vagabonds. Now licenses could be granted only by nobles or two "judicial dignitaries of the realm." In due course the lord chamberlain was made responsible for approving dramatic works—which meant banning any play of which he disapproved—and the stationers' guild for preventing the printing of banned works.

None of this even dented the popularity of the theaters. Audiences continued to grow, and venues grew with them. Impresarios stopped renting space and began to build theaters instead; these were ramshackle affairs at first but soon were more substantial, and by the 1580s the largest could hold three thousand people. Admission was a penny in the large roofless amphitheaters, twopence if you wanted a place to sit, while more exclusive indoor performances might charge as much as sixpence per seat—a sum beyond the means of most people. The revenues thus generated were more than sufficient to encourage the construction of increasingly impressive theaters. The frequency with which many people went to the theater created a voracious market for new material, and the licensing restrictions tended to concentrate the best talent in a small number of companies. For many such reasons London's theatrical world not only expanded but grew more accomplished at an extraordinary pace. Its leading figures became almost respectable. Queen Elizabeth herself became patron of a company in 1583, and in 1594 the lord chamberlain was authorized to select two companies to perform within London itself. By then young Shakespeare had been on the scene for five years, having come up to the city from Warwickshire in the hope of making his way as a writer. The hunger for talent was so strong, and the rewards for exceptional talent so great, that when the grand Globe Theatre was built on the south bank of the Thames in 1598, Shakespeare would be one of its five principal shareholders.

8

A Torrent of Miseries

The intrigues surrounding a possible marriage of Elizabeth to Rob Dudley grew weirder and weirder. Henry Sidney, Dudley's brother-in-law and a courtier close to the queen, soon was approaching the Spanish ambassador about a possible deal in which Philip II would support the marriage and England would once again be reconciled with the Roman church. The context in which this astounding scenario was discussed—with Dudley, Cecil, and the queen herself all involved—was predictably complex. In 1559 the combative Pope Paul IV, that great hater of Hapsburgs and heretics, had died and been succeeded by Pius IV, a placid soul in comparison with his predecessor and more inclined to seek an understanding with schismatics than to condemn them out of hand. It would have seemed distinctly likely that this new pope would be receptive to an arrangement that had the endorsement of the king of Spain and promised to heal the breach with England. Pius was just then making preparations to reconvene the Council of Trent. He intended to invite England, hoping (against hope, one might think) to bring it back into the fold as a partner rather than a rival in reform.

Other parts of the background were the aforementioned deaths of Marie of Guise and young Francis II of France, Mary Stuart's demotion from queen consort to widow and dowager, and the consequent unraveling of the connection between France and Scotland. These developments had, from the Spanish perspective, put Mary's claim to the throne of England in a new and more attractive light. Philip II began exploring the possibility of making Mary the wife of one of his Austrian cousins, or even his own son by his first marriage, the boy Don Carlos. Such a union would have transformed the Queen of Scots, once such a threat to Hapsburg interests, into an immensely useful asset. In dangling her own possible marriage to Dudley in front of Philip, Elizabeth may have merely been attempting to draw his attention away from Mary Stuart. This seems a stretch, however; Elizabeth certainly understood that Philip was capable of pursuing both matters simultaneously, and the notion that Philip could reconcile England and Rome only by abandoning the idea of bringing Mary into the Hapsburg family makes very little sense. The whole affair remains cloaked in mystery, as do the motives of the participants. The negotiations were conducted in such deep secrecy that they remained unknown to the world until the nineteenth century, when the historian J. A. Froude turned up the evidence while examining Spain's diplomatic correspondence.

The idea that Elizabeth was merely playing a diplomatic game is undercut by what is known of Cecil's reaction to the negotiations. He wrote to a confidant that he was, for reasons left unspecified but almost certainly having to do with the proposed marriage, so unhappy with the state of affairs at court as to be considering resignation. At the same time he was continuing to try to disrupt the proceedings by discrediting Elizabeth and Dudley, telling the Spanish ambassador that the two had planned Amy Robsart's death. These would not appear to be the actions of a man who knew his mistress to be pretending. They are more understandable if Cecil genuinely feared that the queen might be willing to abandon the Protestant cause in order to marry the one man she wanted as a husband. If somehow he was acting in collusion with the queen, the two were playing a game so deep and devious as to be incomprehensible.

What appears to have happened, in the end, is that Cecil frightened Elizabeth into calling the whole thing off. He announced that his agents had uncovered a Catholic conspiracy against the Crown, made some dramatic arrests including that of a fugitive priest, and claimed to have evidence of Catholic perfidy so outrageous as to destroy any possibility of a restored relationship. The queen was persuaded, on the basis of evidence that at a distance of four and a half centuries looks distinctly flimsy, that she could expect no loyalty from her Catholic subjects and that large numbers of Protestants were prepared to rise if she turned her back on them. The papal nuncio responsible for delivering an invitation to Trent was prevented from crossing to England. Though the affair ended with scarcely a whimper, it marked a watershed in Elizabeth's life. It would be a good many years before she again regarded an offer of marriage as anything more than an opportunity to manipulate and deceive. Dudley would remain her beau ideal, the most important person in her life, but for both of them the hope of marriage had burned down to dead ash. As it became clear that no great royal unions were in the offing and Mary Stuart made preparations for her return to Scotland, the French queen mother Catherine de' Medici urged the pope to excommunicate Elizabeth. Philip, no longer cast in the incongruous role of enemy of the papacy, persuaded him to do nothing.

Some months later Elizabeth was struck down by smallpox, one of the world's great killers until modern times, and became so ill that she was not expected to live. Council and court were made more painfully aware than ever of how difficult a predicament they would be left in if she died without a spouse, a child, or a designated successor. When she emerged from unconsciousness, still in mortal danger, she asked her councilors to appoint Dudley lord protector of the realm with an income of £20,000 annually, a sum sufficient to support him in the most munificent style. The request was poignantly romantic and utterly without foundation in reality; the council would never have agreed to anything of the kind. Even if it had consented for the second time in little more than a decade to deliver the whole kingdom into the safekeeping of a Dudley—an improbable development to say the least—Robert's elder brother would have been the more logical choice. Ambrose by now had been made Earl of Warwick, the title held by John Dudley until he became Duke of Northumberland, while Robert remained a commoner. The comparison was in any case meaningless; only a delirious Elizabeth could have imagined that her council would surrender control to either of the brothers.

The disease passed but left its mark. Elizabeth's face was badly scarred, and patches of her scalp were left permanently bare. It was a melancholy turn of events for a woman not yet thirty who had always been both attractive and vain. Hardheaded political survivalist though she was, for the rest of her life she would be pathetically susceptible to any sycophant who praised her for a beauty she no longer possessed. It was in a sense doubly cruel that council and Parliament now resumed their appeals for her to marry. But from this point forward the business of finding an acceptable consort and inducing Elizabeth to assent took on a perfunctory character. Fresh attempts were undertaken from time to time, but even those making the effort were never terribly hopeful. The queen herself barely pretended interest unless she could see some diplomatic advantage in doing so. The period after her recovery brought a revival of the candidacy of the Hapsburg archduke Charles, younger brother of the newly elected emperor Maximilian II. Cecil's support for this possibility shows once again that the desire for an heir could override even the strongest antipathy toward Rome. The pressure was for a while so intense that Elizabeth came close to agreeing. In the end she was saved less by her own unwillingness than by the refusal of the emperor to compromise Charles's freedom to practice his religion after taking up residence in England.

Eventually the council's focus shifted from trying to get the queen to marry to the presumably more straightforward task of designating her successor. Here again, however, Elizabeth balked. She did so in spite of the fact that her refusal multiplied the dangers of disorder in the event of her death. And so as the life of her cousin Mary Stuart became one of the most dramatic (and also melodramatic and tragic) in the history of English royalty, it also became heavy with significance for everyone who feared and everyone who desired a restoration of the old religion.

Mary, from the day of her arrival in an Edinburgh that she had not seen since age six, a city now ruled by militant Calvinists with no desire for her return, was herself enmeshed in questions of marriage and succession. Like Elizabeth she was probably a virgin, she, too, would leave behind a chaos of contending factions if she died childless, and almost any husband she chose was certain to bring a baggage train of complications trailing behind him. At first she showed impressive political adroitness, especially for a twenty-year-old dealing with enemies more powerful than herself in what was, essentially, a foreign country. With very nearly no trustworthy advisers to guide her, she accepted the settlement that had delivered Scotland's government and church into Protestant hands. She refused, however, to ratify Cecil's Treaty of Edinburgh, because doing so would have involved relinquishing her claim to the throne of England. Using the little power that remained to her, she established religious toleration as Crown policy—the first time that any such thing had ever been attempted in the history of the British Isles. The dignity and restraint with which she handled herself began to erode the distrust with which many of her subjects had received her in 1561 and to build up a store of goodwill.

Mary had no reluctance to marry, and the English court naturally took an interest in her intentions. In 1564, in a bizarre twist that nevertheless made a good deal of sense from the English perspective and offered practical advantages to Scotland as well, Elizabeth offered Mary as bridegroom none other than Robert Dudley, who was made Earl of Leicester to enhance his suitability. Mary replied that she could agree only if recognized as Elizabeth's heir, but Elizabeth would promise only that Mary and Leicester, once married, would be permitted to live at the English court. That was the end of that. It was also the end of the best part of Mary Stuart's life. She now plunged headlong into a sea of troubles from which she would never emerge.

While the Dudley proposal was still in negotiation, a young cousin of Mary's named Henry Stuart, eldest son of the Earl of Lennox and known as Lord Darnley, had arrived at the Scottish court. Like Mary, he was a grandchild of Henry VIII's sister Margaret, who had married twice more and borne a daughter after the death of King James IV. Also like Mary, therefore, he was a blood member of the royal families of both kingdoms; in the event of Mary's death, in fact, he would have had a strong claim to the Scottish throne. He had grown up in England and become a familiar figure at Elizabeth's court, his father having had to flee Scotland after supporting Henry VIII's failed invasions of the early 1540s. On at least two occasions in his youth, undoubtedly at his father's bidding and for the purpose of winning favor for the family if not specifically for himself, Darnley had traveled to France and met the Queen of Scots there. For reasons that remain obscure, Elizabeth eventually took up the Lennox cause, encouraging Mary to admit her kinsmen back into their homeland and restore their confiscated lands. Mary eventually agreed, her reasons, too, being less than clear, and the consequences were momentous. She was soon smitten with Darnley, who was not yet twenty, and with rather unseemly haste they married. Of the many costly mistakes that Mary would make in the course of an epically difficult life, this was by far the worst, the precipitating blunder from which a torrent of miseries would flow.

Objectively, the marriage offered Mary so many advantages that when news of it reached England Elizabeth was deeply angered. Darnley's bloodlines were so good as to strengthen not only Mary's hold on the crown of Scotland but her claim to that of England as well. Formally he was a Catholic, which was important to Mary, but his beliefs, if he had any, were elastic enough to have allowed him to function comfortably at Elizabeth's court; he was not likely to offend the Protestant lords of Scotland with displays of the faith they despised. The marriage was doomed, however, and its flaw was Darnley himself. He was vain, arrogant, and weak, not merely immature but deeply, dangerously foolish. His wife discovered this soon enough, but by the time she did so she was pregnant. The sequence of calamities that ensued requires attention here because of its bearing on the Tudor succession, but could be dealt with in detail only in a different kind of book. Much of what happened remains open to interpretation; who actually did what, and why, is largely shrouded in mystery.

It began, the worst of it, grotesquely. Mary had a private secretary, a strutting and self-important little Italian named David Riccio who had first come to her court as a musician in search of employment. He alienated the Edinburgh nobles by limiting their access to the queen. (Riccio had many of the same powers as Elizabeth's secretary Cecil, but gave no evidence of comparable intelligence or skill.) The disaffected lords had no difficulty in convincing Darnley (now the Duke of Albany but disgruntled because Mary would not make him her co-ruler) that his wife and the gnomish Riccio were lovers. They drew him into a scheme in the execution of which he and a little gang of retainers burst in on Mary and Riccio while they, in company with a court functionary, were innocently having supper. Riccio was dragged out of the room, stabbed dozens of times, and thrown down a flight of stairs. Mary was six months pregnant, and the conspirators may have hoped to shock her into premature labor so that the child would die and she with it. That didn't happen, and early that summer she gave birth to a healthy boy who was given the name of a long line of his royal forebears: James.

There was more, and worse, to come. Almost a year after the Riccio murder, Darnley himself died in spectacular fashion when the house in which he was sleeping was blown up. It was later determined that Darnley was not killed by the explosion but subsequently strangled. Three months after that Mary eloped with James Hepburn, Earl of Bothwell, an alpha male who had earlier been an important source of support in her struggles with the Scots lords and was probably responsible for killing Darnley; the two were married, surprisingly, in a Protestant ceremony. That is one version of the story and for a time it was the only version anyone heard. Another version, more credible when all the known facts are thrown onto the scales, is that Mary was abducted by Bothwell, acquiescing in the marriage only because he had raped her. Within a few months she was the prisoner of the Protestant lords, who tried to get her to repudiate the Bothwell marriage but were unable to do so, probably because she was pregnant. Told that if she refused to abdicate in favor of her infant son she would be executed, she yielded (though later she would say that she did so only after being secretly advised that an abdication coerced under threat of death could never be upheld as valid). A miscarriage of twins followed, then a nervous breakdown, an escape from prison, defeat in battle, and a flight into England that ended with Mary becoming Elizabeth's prisoner. She was subjected to a ludicrously unfair judicial inquiry in which she was confronted with the now-notorious "casket letters," messages to Bothwell that implicated her in the murder of Darnley but were almost certainly artful forgeries. She was, by this time, all of twenty-five years old.

The year when Mary entered England, 1568, also brought the dynastically important death of Catherine Grey. As the younger sister of Jane Grey and the eldest surviving granddaughter of Henry VIII's sister Mary, the Lady Catherine had a claim to the throne and was the favorite of many Protestants. But she, like her elder sister before her and her younger sister after, learned what a poisonous legacy Tudor blood could be. In law, because King Henry's last will had excluded the Scottish branch of the family from the succession, Catherine's claim appeared to be better than Mary Stuart's. But when, early in Elizabeth's reign, Catherine wanted to marry Edward Seymour, son of the brother of Queen Jane Seymour who had become lord protector after Henry's death, she came up against a statute prohibiting the marriage of anyone of royal blood without the queen's permission. Catherine and her young beau, fearful that approval would be denied, wed in secret and in doing so committed treason. Elizabeth was furious when she learned of this (it was characteristic of her to go into a rage whenever someone close to her married) and had the newlyweds confined in the Tower. Catherine was pregnant by then and gave birth to a son while in prison. Afterward the lieutenant of the Tower allowed the couple to see each other in secret, with the result that Catherine had a second son and any hope of receiving the queen's forgiveness was destroyed. Catherine was still in custody, though no longer in the Tower, when she died. Because her marriage was found to be invalid—that was Elizabeth's doing too— her sons were officially illegitimate and not eligible to inherit the throne. Meanwhile the third Grey sister, the misshapen little Lady Mary, had disgraced herself not only by marrying without permission but by choosing a commoner husband, a widower more than twice her age. That union was broken up before it produced offspring. Thus one of the highest hopes of the Protestants, that the last of the Tudors might be followed by one of the evangelical Grey sisters or a child of one of them, was extinguished.

Attention turned all the more intensely back to Mary Stuart, now almost the only living member of the royal family aside from Elizabeth herself and the mother of a son, albeit a son in the custody of his mother's enemies in Scotland. Even as a prisoner Mary was strongly supported—not as a rival to Elizabeth necessarily, but as her rightful heir—by two factions. One was headed by the leaders of the most powerful ancient families of the north of England, Thomas Percy, the seventh Earl of Northumberland, and Charles Neville, the sixth Earl of Westmorland, and included the large part of the northern population that continued to practice the old religion. The other was based at court, took its strength from those councilors and courtiers who resented the dominance of Secretary Cecil, and looked for leadership to Thomas Howard, the fourth Duke of Norfolk (whose sister, not incidentally, was married to Westmorland). He was the grandson of the duke who had narrowly escaped execution at the time of Henry VIII's death and spent Edward VI's entire reign in the Tower of London.

The next chapters in the Mary Stuart story were as rich in drama as everything that had come before, but their details are less important for present purposes than their results. Percy and Neville secretly allied themselves with the Norfolk faction, took fright when a suspicious Elizabeth summoned them to court, concluded that they had no choice except to fight or flee, and therefore hastily raised the standard of rebellion. They certainly hoped to free Mary and to restore Catholic practice, but whether they aspired to remove Elizabeth from the throne is unclear. In any case their rising was so ill prepared and ineptly managed as to be put down quickly and without great difficulty, the earls finding it advisable to abandon their supporters and escape into Scotland. Before that happened, however, they dispatched to Rome a request that Pope Pius bless their undertaking, send support, and declare Elizabeth excommunicated. By the time this appeal reached Rome the revolt was already over, but Pius had no knowledge of this and was being assured that the people of England were eager to cast off their heretic queen and inhibited only by the fear that rebelling against an anointed ruler would be a grievous sin. Pius issued a bull expelling Elizabeth from the church, absolving her subjects of the obligation of loyalty, and providing grounds in canon law for her fellow rulers to attack and dethrone her. It was perhaps in response to the excommunication that the collapse of the northern rising was followed by some eight hundred executions—extraordinarily savage vengeance for a movement that had petered out before becoming dangerous or even notably large. In fact, the revolt soon proved to have brought immense benefits to the Crown. The centuries-old quasi-independence of the northern nobility came to an end from which there would be no return—the Percys and Neville were only the most prominent of the proud old families ruined—and the administration of the north was put in the hands of officers of Elizabeth's choosing.

The excommunication of England's queen was perhaps understandable after ten years in which to be a Catholic in England was very nearly to be an outlaw, and in which Elizabeth and her council had consistently responded with contempt to overtures from Rome. It was a monumental blunder nevertheless, by far the greatest mistake made by either side during the long conflict between the Tudors and the popes, and England's Catholics paid a high price for it. Immediately their situation was

made desperate: they were left with no alternative except to choose between their church and their queen. Overnight it became plausible for
the authorities to claim that refusal to take the oath of supremacy really
was an act of treason, a declaration of loyalty to foreign enemies committed to making war on England. Intense persecution followed swiftly,
beginning with the execution of the bold character who had posted the
bull of excommunication outside the bishop of London's residence.
New legislation followed also—a Treasons Act increasing penalties for
denial of the supremacy, for example, and an Act Against Papal Bulls.
For the radical Protestants who were just now coming to be known as
Puritans, these new opportunities to attack Catholics could not have
been more welcome. They were exasperated, therefore, when Elizabeth
refused to go as far as they wanted, blocking the implementation of
statutes that would have made it a crime not to receive communion
under the auspices of the Church of England. It was still her hope that
she could gradually, with the sustained application of judicious amounts
of pressure, nudge Catholicism toward extinction while avoiding a repetition of anything as alarming as the revolt of the northern earls. At the
same time, she was refusing to allow the Puritans to reshape her church
to fit their agenda, which was becoming so radical as to include demands for the elimination of bishops. She thereby alienated the Puritans
to such an extent that they began to regard themselves as outside the established church, to spurn that church as beyond hope of reform, and to
direct their energies toward the building of a power base in Parliament.
Thus there emerged three major and irreconcilable religious groupings:
the Catholics, the Puritans, and an approved church the doctrines and
practices of which were determined, essentially, by the queen alone.
Only the second two had access to political power, Catholics having
been barred from the House of Commons as early as 1563 and the practice of their faith now being unlawful and subject to increasingly harsh
sanctions. The Puritans, too, though growing in numbers and clout, felt
excluded and persecuted. Out of these divisions came conflicts and
grievances that would poison the life of the kingdom for centuries.

Looming over it all, a living symbol of unresolvable conflict, was the
forlorn figure of Mary, Queen of Scots. She was Elizabeth's prisoner
though England had no legal grounds for holding her, to the Protestants

she was little better than the Whore of Babylon personified, and yet as Elizabeth grew older she remained—a horrible thought for many—the only plausible heir to the throne. In her person the problem of religion and the problem of the succession merged to become a quandary for which there appeared to be no answer.

THE TURKS

IT IS EASY, IN THINKING ABOUT THE INTERNATIONAL POLITICS of the Tudor century, to overlook the fact that there was another major player besides the Hapsburgs, the kings and queens of France and England, and a papacy that at various times became involved as referee, cheerleader, or freelance utility infielder.

Easy, but a serious mistake. Because throughout the entire period a fourth force was at work, one more aggressive, more dangerous, and more powerful overall than any of the others. It was the Islamic empire of the Ottoman Turks, which at midcentury reached the zenith of its six-hundred-year history, controlled eastern Europe south of the Danube, and directly or indirectly was affecting the destinies of all the Christian powers. The fields of force that it projected, like some vast dark star at the edge of the universe of European nations, are a major reason why Elizabethan England was able to preserve its autonomy in spite of being smaller and weaker than France or Spain and potentially a pariah kingdom in the aftermath of its withdrawal from the old church. By sapping the strength of its principal rival, the Hapsburg empire, Ottoman Turkey contributed importantly to the survival of Protestantism across much of northern Europe.

When Elizabeth became queen, the Ottomans either ruled directly or controlled through puppet regimes not just Turkey but Greece, Serbia, Bulgaria, Romania, and much of Hungary. And that was only the European segment of their dominions, which also encompassed Egypt and Algeria and other strongholds in North Africa, Syria, Palestine, Iraq, the Arabian Peninsula, and some of the most important islands in the Mediterranean. They had been ferociously expansionist since their first emergence among the Turkic-Mongol peoples of Anatolia in the thirteenth century, and generation after generation they had consistently demonstrated their ability to outfight formidable adversaries on land and at sea. In 1453 they captured Constantinople, which had remained the capital of the Eastern Roman Empire and of the Orthodox Church for centuries after Rome itself fell, turning it into the principal metropolis of the Islamic world. And because they were Muslims with entirely non-Western cultural roots, their success in pushing northward and across and even beyond the Balkans was seen, not without reason, as a mortal threat to European civilization itself.

The tenth and greatest of the Ottoman sultans, Suleiman I, was in the thirty-ninth year of his reign when Elizabeth began hers. To his subjects he was Suleiman the Lawgiver, having in the course of his awesomely fruitful career rewritten his empire's entire legal code. Europe called him Suleiman the Magnificent, a title he richly deserved. Like his forebears, he was above all a soldier, having personally led campaigns that crushed a revolt in Damascus, captured Belgrade in Serbia and Buda in Hungary, taken much of the Middle East from the shah of Iran, expelled the Knights Hospitalers from the island of Rhodes, and twice laid siege to the Hapsburg capital of Vienna. But he was also much more than a soldier: an accomplished poet and goldsmith, a lifelong student of philosophy with a particular devotion to Aristotle, the guiding patron of a remarkable efflorescence of Islamic art, literature, and architecture. Impressive and even admirable as he was, however, he should not be sentimentalized. At the heart of his regime—of the entire Ottoman enterprise—lay something worse than barbarism. Suleiman's father, Selim I, himself a great conqueror who nearly tripled the size of the empire in only eight years as sultan, cleared the way for his favorite son to succeed him by killing his own brothers, his brothers' seven sons, and all four of Suleiman's brothers. Suleiman, decades later, would watch through a peephole as his eldest son and heir, a young man much honored for his prowess in war and skill as a governor, was strangled by court eunuchs to make way for a different, younger, and (as time would show) totally worthless son. Fratricide on a grand scale became standard Ottoman practice; each new sultan, upon taking the throne, would have all his brothers and half-brothers murdered and those members of his predecessor's harem who happened to be pregnant bundled up in sacks and thrown into the sea. Conquered peoples were treated little better. Eventually the viciousness of the regime would lead the whole empire to shocking depths of cruelty and degeneracy and finally, in the First World

War, to collapse. But through much of the sixteenth century, under Suleiman, it appeared to be almost invincible. The possibility that it might break through into central Europe, and continue onward from there, not only seemed but was terrifyingly real.

The threat fell first and most heavily on young Charles Hapsburg, who became the seventeen-year-old king of Spain in the same year that Cairo fell to the Turks. By the time he was elected Holy Roman emperor two years later, the Turks had taken Algiers from Spain, the trade routes of Venice and the other seafaring cities of the Italian peninsula were in danger of being cut off by Turkish raiders, and the southern Hapsburg kingdoms of Naples and Sicily were under direct threat. Francis I was king of France by then and Suleiman was about to become sultan, and for the next three decades they and Charles (the three had been born within six years of each other, and all came to power between 1515 and 1520) would be locked in an almost continuous, endlessly complicated struggle. Henry VIII, from his safe haven on the far shore of the English Channel, would join the fray and withdraw from it as the mood struck him and the state of his treasury dictated.

Despite the size of his empire, Charles V usually found himself on the defensive, with Francis repeatedly trying to pry away substantial chunks of Italy and Suleiman both pressing northward out of the Balkans and seeking to clear the Mediterranean of European ships. Charles's successes were almost always limited and his defeats were occasionally serious, but when the number and strength of his adversaries are taken into account (Germany's increasingly numerous Protestant states were soon joining forces to oppose him), he merits recognition as one of the great commanders of the age. When Francis launched an attack on Milan in 1525, Charles not only destroyed his army but took him prisoner. But just a year later, with Charles occupied elsewhere, Suleiman invaded northward, inflicted a ruinous defeat on the Hungarians, and seized territories that the Hapsburgs regarded as theirs by ancient right. Next came Suleiman's 1529 siege of Vienna, which Charles and his brother Ferdinand were barely able to lift after both sides suffered heavy losses, followed by the sultan's attempt to take the island of Malta from the same order of crusader knights from whom, some years earlier, he had taken Rhodes. Emboldened by his success in saving Malta and killing thirty thousand Ottoman troops in the process, Charles decided to carry the

war into enemy territory. He crossed to North Africa and, at Tunis, succeeded in expelling Suleiman's client regime and installing one of his
own.

The contest seesawed back and forth year after year, as Charles and
Suleiman traded blows along the Danube and in the Mediterranean but
neither could gain a decisive advantage. For a time Henry of England
joined with Charles against Francis, later switching sides and finally
turning away from the continent to focus on Anne Boleyn and his conflict with the church. One development that shocked many Europeans,
who saw in it a betrayal of all Christendom, was Francis's entry, in 1536,
into an alliance with Suleiman and the Turks. Once again he was grasp-
ing at Milan, though he like Charles was very nearly at the end of his financial resources. An important side effect was that Henry VIII was left
alone and unthreatened as he completed his break with Rome and fat-
tened on the wealth of the church. Under other circumstances a crusade
against England's schismatic king by the Catholic powers of the continent might have been at least possible. Under the circumstances actually prevailing in the mid-1530s, nothing of the kind could be seriously
considered. Neither Charles nor Francis was in any position to make
trouble for England. Either would have been grateful for Henry's active
friendship.

In 1538 Suleiman's great admiral Khayr ad-Din, called Barbarossa by
Westerners because of his red beard, defeated the Hapsburg navy in a
battle so conclusive that it made the Turks dominant in the Mediterranean for the next thirty-three years. In 1541, as Charles tried and failed
to restore Algiers to Spanish control, Suleiman resumed offensive operations in the north. He had sufficient success to impose a humiliating
peace on the Hapsburgs: Archduke Ferdinand was obliged to renounce
his claim to the throne of Hungary and to become a Turkish vassal,
pledging to pay an annual tribute for the portion of Hungary he was permitted to retain. In 1542 Charles and Francis were once again at war,
and when the French king asked Suleiman for assistance, the sultan
cheerfully agreed. He dispatched a fleet of one hundred galleys, warships powered by oars, to France's south coast, permitting them to pause
along the way to pillage Charles's kingdoms of Naples and Sicily and the
city of Nice, also a Hapsburg possession. On all fronts, Suleiman appeared to be gaining in strength.

Fortunately for Europe, Suleiman like Charles had multiple enemies and more than the conflict between their two empires to deal with. By the late 1540s the shah of Iran had recovered much of the power that had been shattered by Suleiman's father thirty years earlier, and was making himself troublesome. From 1548 to 1550 Suleiman waged war on the shah, and must have been taken aback to find himself making little headway. He settled in for a time at his sumptuous Topkapi Palace, indulging in the pleasures of the court and involving himself in domestic-dynastic intrigues. (It was during this interlude that he had his son Mustafa murdered, so that the son of the Russian slave girl he had made his wife could become heir.) In 1554 he returned with his army to Iran, finally securing a peace in which he received Iraq and eastern Anatolia but relinquished any claim to the Caucasus. By this time his old ally Francis, along with the distant Henry of England, had been dead for seven years. The emperor Charles, spiritually and physically exhausted, was beginning the process by which, over the next two years, he would give the crown of Spain to his son and that of the Holy Roman Empire to his brother and retire to a monastery. Suleiman alone—older than any of the others except Henry—remained vigorous and actively in command. His enemies were not free of him until 1566, when, at age seventy-two, he suddenly died. At the time, he was leading an army northward to Hungary, making ready to reopen the war there. We can only guess at what Europe may have been spared by his passing.

After Suleiman the Ottoman dynasty went into an abrupt decline. His successor, for whose sake the splendid young Mustafa had been eliminated, was a drunkard who reigned in a stupor for eight years before falling in his bath and fracturing his skull. *His* successor specialized in copulation, fathering 103 children in his twenty years as sultan, and every Ottoman ruler after him proved to be utterly incompetent or deeply degenerate or both. The empire, however, was slower to decay; its administrative machinery would wind down only gradually over the next three centuries. To the end of Elizabeth's reign it would remain a formidable presence.

A major turn in Europe's favor came just five years after Suleiman's death. In 1571, off the western coast of Greece, the Ottoman navy met the forces of Christendom in what was, for the latter, a desperate last stand. On the Turkish side were 222 galleys supported by numerous smaller vessels and carrying some thirty-four thousand soldiers. Opposing them was a smaller fleet contributed by members of what called itself the Holy League: Venice, Spain, Naples, Sicily, Sardinia, the Knights of Malta, the Papal States, and such places as Genoa and Savoy.

It was the last major battle ever fought entirely with ships powered by oarsmen, one of the biggest naval battles in history, and according to some historians the most important since Mark Antony lost the Battle of Actium in 31 B.C. and his rival Octavian became master of Rome as the emperor Augustus Caesar. When the Battle of Lepanto was over, all but forty of the Turkish galleys had been captured or destroyed, perhaps twenty-five thousand Turks had been killed or captured, and ten thousand Christian slaves had been freed. The league, by contrast, had lost only twenty galleys and thirteen thousand men. It was not the end of the Ottoman Empire, not even the end of the empire as a great power, but it did bring the empire's mastery of the Mediterranean to a permanent close. The momentum of Turkish expansion was not yet entirely exhausted—the capture of Cyprus and recapture of Tunis still lay ahead—but the Ottomans would never again be quite the threat they had been in Suleiman's time, and they had been deprived of the vast opportunities that a victory at Lepanto would have opened to them.

The commander of the Holy League fleet was the twenty-four-year-old Don John of Austria, Charles V's illegitimate son by a Bavarian girl of common stock. Second in command, himself only twenty-six, was Alessandro Farnese, great-grandson and namesake of Pope Paul III, son of Charles V's illegitimate daughter Margaret, future Duke of Parma. The two, though scarcely more than boys, had changed the course of history. We will encounter both in connection with another of the great conflicts that shaped the Tudor century.

9

Actions, Reactions, Provocations

It would be fatuous to deny that Pope Pius V, in excommunicating Elizabeth, intended to destroy her. Or that he hoped to recruit the leading Catholic powers for a crusade aimed at removing her from her throne.

Nor were such hopes ridiculous. Three decades before, the Pilgrimage of Grace had exposed the unpopularity of Henry VIII's religious innovations and left hanging the question of what a rising might accomplish if given strong enough leadership and sufficient encouragement and support. The rebellions of Edward VI's reign, and the ease with which Mary I had overcome John Dudley's attempted coup, bolstered the credibility of those wanting to make Rome believe that Elizabeth's regime, if given a firm shove, might fall almost of its own weight.

As for the idea of involving France and Spain, here again hope was not entirely without a footing in reality. Though Pius V had become pope with little experience in politics and even less in diplomacy (it is a measure of how rapidly the church was changing that he had grown up in poverty and spent much of his life as a Dominican friar known for austerity), he was not naïve enough to expect kings to sacrifice their thrones on the altar of religion. But in Philip of Spain he had an ally who genuinely believed that if he could save England from the Protestants he would save her people from eternal damnation. And Pius could hope to find support at France's Valois court if he could point to practical advantages of removing the English queen.

Thus it is entirely understandable that Elizabeth and her council went to great lengths to prevent a Catholic combination from forming. If they can be faulted, it is for going too far with their meddling in continental affairs, thereby helping to bring into existence something very like what they most feared. The worst of their mistakes was to overreact, bringing down upon England hardships that might and even should have been avoided.

For in fact their position was less dangerous than they understood. Under any circumstances it would have been difficult in the extreme for France and Spain, locked in a struggle for European domination that was already half a century old, to join forces for any shared purpose involving sacrifice and risk. They had already shown themselves to be incapable of organizing a common defense even against the Ottoman Empire, which unlike England posed a threat to the very survival of their civilization. And that was only half the story. The Reformation had come to France by this time, giving rise to conflicts that were draining away the kingdom's power. Yet another new phenomenon, nationalism, had come at the same time to the Spanish possessions in the Netherlands, sparking a rebellion that Philip would need all the resources of his sprawling empire and all the gold being stripped from the New World to keep from overwhelming him. France and Spain alike—though France more than Spain—rarely ignored an opportunity to exploit and worsen the other's problems and to ally themselves with England whenever it seemed advantageous to do so. Neither was easily drawn into fantasies of returning England to the universal church by force of arms. Philip, though more the idealist than Marie de' Medici, understood from personal experience that, in the almost forty years since Henry VIII's break with Rome, the number of Englishmen likely to see any sense in fighting to repair that break had shrunk severely.

The brilliant success of Elizabeth's first international adventure, the 1560 foray into Scotland, served to encourage further enterprises more distant from home. An opportunity came just two years later with the eruption of France's first religious war, which pitted Calvinist Huguenots against the regime headed by the queen dowager Catherine de' Medici in the name of her sickly and ineffectual second son, the adolescent Charles IX. It was easy to argue that England could both help itself and do God's work by becoming involved on the Protestant side, and the Dudley brothers, ambitious and eager for action, argued exactly that. Intervention could frustrate Philip of Spain, who was supporting the royal Catholic party in the hope of building a lasting alliance. At the same time it could undermine the Valois by enhancing the strength of their internal enemies. Conceivably it could lead to the recovery of Calais, which would be a tremendous propaganda coup for Elizabeth, a demonstration of the superiority of her rule to that of her late sister.

William Cecil, who by pushing the Scottish incursion to its conclusion had laid at the feet of his queen an achievement of genuine strategic importance, was not enthusiastic about making war on France. As a committed Protestant he naturally favored the Huguenots, but he was not as confident as the Dudleys that providing assistance required going to war with a kingdom whose population was several times that of England. The queen, however, approved the sending of an expeditionary force. She disappointed Robert Dudley, who wanted command, by selecting his brother the Earl of Warwick instead. He was to land his troops at, and take possession of, the port of Le Havre—the English called it Newhaven—on the Normandy coast. The plan, from that point, was to win the gratitude of the Huguenots to such an extent that they would exchange Calais for Le Havre. Exactly how this was to be accomplished appears to have been left rather vague.

All did not go according to plan. Ambrose Dudley showed himself to be an effective enough leader, maintaining order and discipline in his little army under difficult conditions and establishing good relations with the inhabitants of Le Havre. But his instructions from the queen made it impossible to achieve anything. Throughout the first two months following his arrival in France, Dudley remained under orders to take no action. Then, when the opposing French sides surprised him by making peace, the earl was ordered to hold on to Le Havre until a trade for Calais could be arranged. This led—a crowning absurdity—to his erstwhile allies joining forces with the Catholics to drive him out. After several months of standing their ground in spite of the inadequacy of Le Havre's defensive works, the English were so ravaged by plague that Dudley was left with no choice but to surrender. A final, tragic chapter was added when the remnants of his expeditionary force returned to England and brought the plague with them. In the subsequent Peace of Troyes, England abandoned forever its claim to Calais. Robert Dudley, as responsible as anyone for putting the whole debacle in motion, was rewarded with appointment to the Privy Council. Perhaps because Elizabeth's refusal to part with him had spared him exposure to the hardships of the campaign, his appetite for war was undiminished. Cecil, whose responsibilities made him acutely aware of the strain the affair had put on the treasury, would henceforth be incapable of mustering much enthusiasm for sending armies across the Channel for any purpose.

Cecil was not averse, however, to tweaking the tail of the despised king of Spain whenever he found opportunities to do so without excessive risk. This tendency became increasingly pronounced, in fact, as the first decade of Elizabeth's reign approached its end and Cecil persuaded himself that France and Spain were preparing a great joint invasion. About this he was consistently, demonstrably wrong—a rare and even weird miscalculation by one of the most astute, careful, and successful politicians of the age. Above all it was a misreading of the king of Spain. Perhaps Cecil could not understand Philip, could think only the worst of him, simply because his contempt was so deep. Probably he had no idea that Philip had concluded, during his years as England's uncrowned king, that it was an alien and treacherous place and best left alone. At this stage Philip was, despite his religious convictions, almost desperately eager for England's friendship, and if he could not have that he wanted her neutrality. He had more than enough other matters demanding his attention, more than enough other uses for resources that never seemed sufficient to his needs, and little reason to be confident that he stood to gain anything by deposing Elizabeth and replacing her with Mary, Queen of Scots. Cecil might have benefited from remembering how supportive of Elizabeth Philip had been both before she became queen and during the uncertain early days of her reign. He might have asked himself if conditions had changed enough to turn Philip into an actively aggressive foe. Instead he allowed his concerns to grow into something akin to paranoia, and to drive him—and with him England— into dangerously provocative actions that could serve no significantly good purpose and for which there was absolutely no need.

A particularly dangerous temptation came within Cecil's grasp late in 1568, when a fleet of Spanish ships traversing the Channel en route to the Netherlands found itself threatened by pirates and took refuge in English ports. The fleet's commander had good reason for wanting to avoid capture: he was carrying a fortune in gold and silver that Philip had borrowed from his Italian bankers and was sending to the Low Countries to pay the troops he had stationed there. Cecil, when he became aware of what had fallen into his clutches, did not hesitate. He ordered the money seized and locked away. The Spaniards, needless to say, were outraged. Philip's governor in the Netherlands, the tough old Duke of Alba, responded by seizing English trade goods. England retaliated in its turn, and the dispute escalated until there was a real danger of war. Alba, however, had a turbulent region on his hands and so dispatched envoys with instructions to make themselves agreeable to the English. Cecil for his part wanted nothing less than outright war, and gradually the situation was defused.

The Privy Council then fell into an angry dispute over what Cecil had done. A substantial number of its members, Robert Dudley prominent among them, accused him of having recklessly put England in danger. There followed a contest over whether he should retain his position as secretary and with it his control over what information was allowed to reach the queen, what business was brought before the council, and how the council's decisions were translated into action. This became the decisive crisis of Cecil's long career. It ended with Elizabeth intervening so decisively on his behalf that it was no longer possible to doubt that he enjoyed her full confidence. He became and would remain unassailably secure. Not coincidentally, by protecting him the queen implicitly endorsed his policy of harassing the Spaniards by almost every possible means while pretending innocence. She and her government were turning a benignly blind eye to the raids that freebooters like John Hawkins and his cousin Francis Drake, privateers destined to rank high among the immortals of the Elizabethan age, were making on Spanish ports and shipping. It seemed an ideal arrangement: Cecil and even Elizabeth herself not only provided the pirates with a secure home base but helped to finance their voyages in return for a share of the profits. When Spain protested they claimed, unconvincingly, to know nothing and to be unable to do anything. Philip's restraint through years of this unde-

clared naval war is the strongest possible indication of just how badly he
wanted to avoid conflict.

Soon it was again France's turn at center stage. The end of the 1560s
brought a resumption of the increasingly bitter and bloody conflict between the Huguenots and the Catholic government in Paris. (It might
be appropriate to speak of the *ostensibly* Catholic government, the
young king Charles showing at this point more inclination to accept the
counsel of the Protestant leader Admiral de Coligny than that of his
mother, Catherine; the alignments were rarely not confusing.) These
wars were dangerous because of the pull they inevitably exerted on
other countries: Spain was always drawn to what Philip judged to be the
Catholic side, England to the Calvinists. The latest round of hostilities
ended in 1570 with the Peace of St. Germain, but on terms that offered
little hope of lasting amity. Catherine de' Medici agreed, over the objections of Philip, to the marriage of her daughter Margaret to the bride's
royal cousin Henry of Bourbon, more widely known as Henry of
Navarre. The Guises, still the driving force behind Catholic militancy in
France, were not alone in complaining that such a marriage would be an
outrage: Navarre was a Protestant and therefore judged to be no fit
spouse for a princess of the blood. The Huguenots, by contrast, rejoiced; Navarre would be next in line to the throne if (as must have
seemed possible by this time) none of Catherine's diminishing supply of
sons produced a male heir, and a Valois bride could only strengthen his
claim. Elizabeth and Cecil were untroubled by the prospect of peace.
They were content to be relieved of the obligation to support the
Huguenots financially, and ready to try to wedge themselves between
Spain and France by building a friendly relationship with the Valois.
Their first steps in this direction gave rise to a possible new way of solving England's festering succession problem. King Charles's heir presumptive—his heir, that is, if he died without a son—was his brother
Henry of Anjou, not yet twenty years old. Elizabeth being in her late
thirties now, negotiations of a possible marriage got under way with
some sense of urgency on the English side: those still hopeful that the
queen might have a child knew that, for such a thing to happen, she
would have to act soon.

Elizabeth probably had as little interest in marrying now as at any
point in the preceding decade; she allowed the talks to proceed simply to

distract the French from rapprochement with Spain. Anjou definitely had no interest, speaking contemptuously of his prospective bride as a "public whore" and (after being told that varicose veins were causing her to limp) as "an old creature with a sore leg." If somehow the two had married, the consequences could only have been disappointing for both sides. Anjou was more militantly, aggressively Catholic than Elizabeth was Protestant. His irregular personal behavior, including a passion for extravagantly lavish, sometimes shockingly feminine attire and a refusal to engage in hunting or the other customary pastimes of male royalty, had won for him the epithet "Prince of Sodom." His very appearance would have stunned Elizabeth's court and mortally offended every Puritan in England. As for his breeding potential, he would live a good many years more but never have a child in or out of wedlock.

The following year, 1572, brought convulsions that would briefly make an Anglo-French marriage alliance seem more plausible but then drive the two countries apart. In March the conflict between the people of the northern Netherlands and their Spanish masters erupted into open revolt. In short order four provinces made themselves functionally independent under the leadership of William of Orange (William of Nassau if you prefer, or William the Silent), a onetime Catholic and protégé of the Hapsburgs who had gone into exile and become a Calvinist in reaction to Spanish demands for the surrender of what the Dutch regarded as their inalienable liberties. Elizabeth, for obvious reasons, always regarded loyalty to the sovereign as a sacred duty of all subjects everywhere, and so now as in other, similar situations she found it difficult to support or even condone rebellion. At first England's ports were closed to the seafaring Dutch renegades. But the temptation to create trouble for Philip once again proved irresistible, all the more so when the rebels demonstrated that they were not going to be easily suppressed. Soon the English authorities were coyly noticing nothing as Protestant volunteers and money began streaming out of the country in aid of the revolt. The French, too, could find nothing objectionable in a war that soaked up so much Spanish manpower and treasure, and they saw new reason to make common cause with England. In April the two countries entered into the Treaty of Blois, by which they pledged to assist each other if either were attacked. The Duke of Anjou having conclusively removed himself from contention for Elizabeth's hand, a new candidate emerged in the person of his younger brother Francis (at birth he had been given the name Hercules), the Duke of Alençon. He was sixteen years old; Elizabeth was thirty-nine.

August was when it all blew up. The explosion came in Paris on the feast of St. Bartholomew, and it was horrific. From all around France thousands of Huguenots, many of them people of considerable wealth and social standing accompanied by their private security forces, had gathered in the capital to celebrate the wedding of their champion and hope for the future, Henry of Navarre, to the sister of a childless king. The city was electric with tension between the visitors, who continued to parade through the streets long after the wedding was over, and the local population. Four days after the ceremony there was an attempt on the life of the Protestant leader Admiral de Coligny, who, to the indignation of powerful Catholics including the Guises, had been readmitted to the national governing council as part of the reconciliation between the contending factions. Coligny escaped with relatively minor gunshot wounds, but on the third day of his recuperation one of the Duke of Guise's ruffians burst into his room, pulled him from his bed, stabbed him to death, and threw the body out the window. The killing was like a spark put to gunpowder. There followed days and then weeks of wholesale butchery; Protestants were hunted down first in Paris and then in other cities as well. The generally accepted best guess puts the number of dead in the neighborhood of ten thousand, and the total may very well have been higher. Who exactly was responsible, and why the slaughter was carried to such extremes, remains unclear. That the Guises were responsible for the killing of Coligny cannot be doubted. The involvement of Catherine de' Medici, and through her of her son King Charles, is likewise beyond dispute; she appears to have been frightened into thinking that the Huguenot leadership had to be eliminated to abort an investigation that would have revealed her approval of the original assault on Coligny. The Duke of Alba may have encouraged the attack on Coligny because the admiral had been urging French support of the Dutch rebels and appeared to be winning the young king's agreement, but we have no conclusive evidence that any of these people intended a massacre. More likely the original plan was to eliminate Coligny only, and the scheme was broadened to include a number of his associates only after the failure of the first attempt on his life stirred up fears of reprisals, a damaging investigation, or even a coup d'état. But the people of Paris were Catholic and poor, they had been experiencing hardship that year as a failed harvest inflated the price of food, and their resentment had been inflamed by the spectacle of so many prosperous Protestant outsiders, some of them guarded by armed men, ostentatiously showing themselves off in the streets. Catholic preachers were warning of a Protestant takeover, no doubt in inflammatory ways, and apparently some of their listeners took the news of the first killings as license to go on a rampage. Within a few days the disorder had spread to Rouen, Lyon, Orleans, and Bordeaux, and in all these places royal orders for it to stop were ignored.

The religious divisions of France were even more hateful than those in England and obviously much more dangerous. Open war had erupted between the contending parties three times in the previous decade, with much criminality on both sides. That the 1572 calamity began on the feast of St. Bartholomew was probably not a coincidence. On the same day three years earlier, in the south of France, Henry of Navarre's mother, a woman whose contempt for the old religion made the evangelicals of England seem models of toleration by comparison, had ordered the execution of a company of Catholic nobles who had surrendered after receiving assurances that their lives would be spared. The young Duke of Guise, if in fact he ordered Coligny's murder, was undoubtedly spurred less by theology than by a hunger for revenge: the admiral had earlier been responsible for the killing of Guise's father. In France the Reformation was becoming a sordid chronicle of atrocities and reprisals, treachery was by no means exclusive to either side, and the complications were almost as endless as the provocations. What matters here is that the massacre of 1572 horrified the Protestants of England, seemed to provide rich justification for their insistence that Catholicism had to be extinguished, and made it impossible for Elizabeth even to feign interest in marriage to any son of Catherine de' Medici.

In that same year the increasingly discontented, increasingly unmanageable Puritans began bullying Elizabeth to destroy Thomas Howard, fourth Duke of Norfolk. Son of the Earl of Surrey whose execution was one of the last acts ordered by Henry VIII, grandson of the duke whose life was saved only by Henry's death, great-grandson of the earl who restored the family's fortunes by crushing the Scots at Flodden, and great-great-grandson of the duke who died fighting for Richard III at Bosworth, this latest Norfolk was a somewhat feckless individual who lacked the strength to resist being drawn into dark schemes that he could neither control nor, probably, understand. Secretary Cecil had put him on the council in 1564 as a conservative and presumably manageable counterweight to Robert Dudley, who also became a member that year and was obviously not going to be managed by Cecil or anyone else. Things did not work out as Cecil planned, however. Instead of helping to neutralize Dudley, Norfolk joined him in trying to get Cecil dismissed after his seizure of the Spanish king's gold. He also opposed the secretary's policies with respect to Mary Stuart, aid to the French Huguenots, and the harassment of Philip II. He had given Cecil no reason to support him—or even, in a pinch, to do anything to save his life.

What made Norfolk a prime target of the Puritans was his involvement with Mary, Queen of Scots, and a faintly asinine (unless he was instead profoundly devious) Florentine banker named Roberto di Ridolfi. After Mary became a prisoner of the English Crown, a group of courtiers (including, somewhat oddly, Robert Dudley) hatched the idea of neutralizing her as a threat to Elizabeth and at the same time solving the succession problem by marrying her into the English, and Protestant, nobility. Norfolk, a youngish widower who as the only duke in the kingdom was its premier noble, was an obvious possibility. And he was immediately, if foolishly, interested. Most of the Puritans, uncomfortable with anything that might even tend to legitimate Mary as heir, were so hostile to the proposal as to cast Norfolk into the role of mortal enemy. William Cecil, as always, was opposed to anything that might lead to Mary Stuart becoming queen of England.

The marriage scheme became, in ways far too arcane to be unraveled here, intertwined with the revolt of the northern earls. Norfolk, as a result, fell into deep disfavor at court. It is at this point that Ridolfi enters the story. A busybody who had first come to England as a moneylender, much too restless a spirit to be satisfied with dabbling in the currency markets, he began intriguing in so many directions that in due course he became a paid informant of the French and Spanish governments and the pope's "secret nuncio." Like Norfolk he got into trouble in connection with the northern rising, and for a time he was in custody and under interrogation by Cecil and the head of Elizabeth's intelligence service, Francis Walsingham. After his release Ridolfi appears to have made it his mission to win papal approval for the marriage of Mary Stuart and Norfolk and, probably, to arrange a good deal more than that. He began weaving a web of conspiracy that extended from the English to the Spanish court, from Mary's place of confinement to Rome and the Netherlands. In 1571 he crossed to the continent, traveling from place to place presumably to make arrangements for a Spanish invasion to occur simultaneously with a rising of England's Catholics, the marriage of a liberated Scots queen to Norfolk, and Elizabeth's removal. In actuality it was all talk—no one was doing anything serious in preparation for either an invasion or a rebellion—and almost all of it came from Ridolfi himself. He was so free in telling everyone who would listen about his plans that there has hung over him, ever since, the suspicion that when Cecil and Walsingham had him in custody, they may have bribed or blackmailed him into becoming their agent. Certainly no agent provocateur could have done more to lure Norfolk and others into incriminating themselves, or to make certain that nothing about his scheme was truly secret. Cecil was fully aware of what Ridolfi was up to: Grand Duke Cosimo de' Medici of Florence even sent him a warning immediately after being visited, and confided in, by Ridolfi. Norfolk was arrested and put on trial for treason. Slanted in favor of the prosecution as all treason trials were in those days—the accused were allowed neither legal counsel nor any opportunity to prepare a defense—in this instance guilt was undeniable, and the duke was quickly sentenced to death. For four months, however, the queen refused to approve his execution. Parliament and council, meanwhile, badgered her relentlessly to allow Mary Stuart to be condemned as well. To this she absolutely would not agree. Her unwillingness to see even a deposed queen put to death was even more powerful than her reluctance to kill dukes. Though Norfolk had to be sacrificed at last, Mary was too valuable a prisoner to be dispensed with. So long as she remained alive, England's Protestant subjects would have strong reasons for wanting Elizabeth to remain alive as well. And of course Elizabeth may have felt compassion for her fallen cousin, who was passing her life as a prisoner in spite of having been charged with no crime.

TORTURE

IT IS A MISTAKE TO ASSUME, UPON BECOMING AWARE OF
how extensively Henry VIII and Elizabeth I used torture to terrorize their
subjects and extract information about real or imagined enemies, that
they were simply continuing a standard practice of the English Middle
Ages.

They were doing nothing of the kind. Though inflicting physical pain
on captives to achieve some political purpose goes back further than
recorded history, and though it was certainly not unknown in England
before the Tudors, it was never legitimized by law there or allowed to become accepted practice. English rulers never used torture as an instrument of state in anything approaching a systematic way until Henry VIII
and Thomas Cromwell began doing so in the mid-1530s. Half a century
later, when Elizabeth surpassed her father in the intensity and frequency
of the tortures inflicted on people perceived to be a threat to her survival
and even began to torture people because of their religious beliefs, the
population was so repelled that after her death such practices soon fell
into disuse and in due course were banned—forever, as it turned out—
by Parliament.

Being an inherently loathsome thing—church leaders condemned its
use from the earliest centuries of the Christian era—torture inevitably required Elizabeth and her henchmen to employ singularly odious men.
Not much is known about her first principal torturer, a member of Parliament called "Rackmaster Norton," but whatever atrocities he may have
been capable of must have been almost trivial compared to those of the
man who replaced him in 1572, Richard Topcliffe. A Yorkshire landowner who appears to have won Elizabeth's favor early in her reign or
possibly even earlier, Topcliffe was not only a dutiful torturer but an
eager one—a sadist to the point of psychosis. Having begun his public
career as a kind of intelligence agent for Francis Walsingham, who en-

tered royal service as an associate of the queen's secretary William Cecil and rose to secretary himself when Cecil became lord treasurer, Topcliffe distinguished himself first as a hunter of fugitive Catholics and then as an interrogator of the people he captured. He was so passionate in his hatred of Catholics and all things Catholic that there appear to have been no limits to what he was willing to do; in devising new ways of inflicting pain he was always confident of doing God's work. The relish with which he approached his duties—he participated personally in the disemboweling and quartering of condemned men in spite of the fact that there was no need for him to do so—made him so useful to Cecil and Walsingham (not to mention the queen) that he was permitted to install a torture chamber in his Westminster home. Though by no means the Crown's only torturer (the Tower of London's warders or "Beefeaters" customarily operated such machinery as the rack, the scavenger's daughter, and the iron maiden, while gentlemen merely did the questioning), he easily established himself as the leading practitioner of his dubious trade. He wrote with a kind of pornographic glee of the mastery required to push victims up to but not quite across the threshold of death, comparing the prolongation of unbearable agony to a skilled lover's ability to sustain sexual ecstasy.

A number of the best-known priests to fall into the Crown's hands in the 1580s and early 1590s, the Jesuit poet Robert Southwell among them, spent long periods in Topcliffe's custody (some were apprehended by Topcliffe himself) before finally being put to death. If challenged about his methods and the validity of confessions made under torture, he always replied—not truthfully, it is clear—that his objective was always to obtain information, not mere confessions. No one was ever tortured, he absurdly claimed, whose guilt had not already been established beyond doubt.

Two stories, one nightmarishly horrible and the other merely disgusting in a sardonically amusing way, reveal as much as any normal person could ever want to know about Topcliffe's character. The first happened in 1592, when he had been pursuing Southwell without success for six frustrating years. His search led him to the home of a family named Bellamy, several of whose members were already in prison (two would die there, and a third would be executed) on suspicion of harboring priests. Somehow he learned that one of the daughters of the household, Anne

Bellamy, supposedly had information about Southwell's plans. When the girl would tell him nothing, Topcliffe made her his prisoner, but instead of using the usual instruments of torture he adopted a method that must have been vastly more painful and infinitely humiliating. He raped her repeatedly until at last, broken, she gave up her secret (which was that Southwell had promised to return to the Bellamys' house on June 20, in order to say mass). Southwell was captured as a result. He was tortured on thirteen separate occasions, first at Topcliffe's home and then in the Tower. After refusing to answer questions even about the color of his horse—he feared that anything he said might compromise the people who had sheltered him—the priest was taken to Tyburn to be hanged, drawn, and quartered. When Anne Bellamy found that she was pregnant, Topcliffe was able to avoid disclosure of what he had done by forcing her to marry his assistant. One can only speculate as to what sort of bridegroom a torturer's assistant must have been. Nothing is known of what finally happened to the girl, one of history's forgotten victims.

The second Topcliffe story involves another of his assistants, one Thomas Fitzherbert, whose family were landowning Catholics. Topcliffe and Fitzherbert concocted a scheme for making a tidy fortune quickly. Fitzherbert would accuse his father, his uncle, and a man named Bassett of treason, thereby providing an excuse for their arrest. Topcliffe would then torture the three to death, Fitzherbert would inherit their property, and the two of them would split the proceeds. All went according to plan, apparently, until Fitzherbert refused to pay up. Amazingly, Topcliffe then had the temerity to go to court, explaining the nature of the bargain and suing Fitzherbert for £5,000. In defending himself, Fitzherbert complained that Topcliffe had not done his part: that Bassett was still alive, and the father and uncle had died not of torture but of a fever contracted in prison. Even more amazingly, thanks no doubt to his excellent connections at court, Topcliffe won the case instead of being arrested for conspiracy to commit murder or worse. Fitzherbert was obliged to surrender his inheritance.

One would like to think that the queen knew nothing of such matters and little of what was being done in her name. Where Topcliffe is concerned, unfortunately, it is not possible to believe anything of the kind; the records make clear that the torturer had ready access to Elizabeth over a great many years, that at least some of his foul work was done with her knowledge and possibly at her direction, and that he was well rewarded for his labors. He wrote of being encouraged by Elizabeth, quoting her as complaining about "sundry lewde popishe beasts." He always claimed that he acted not on Walsingham's or Cecil's authority but on that of the queen herself, and that he was accountable to her only. This is not implausible, though it is not likely that Topcliffe ever had to bypass either Cecil or Walsingham in the performance of his duties; those two shared a fear and hatred of Catholics that, if not pathological like Topcliffe's, certainly gave them no reason to interfere with his work. Perhaps it was thanks to Elizabeth that Topcliffe was given a seat in the House of Commons, that Crown and local officials always treated him with more deference than the offices he held warranted, and that he was set free after Burghley had him arrested for appearing to threaten members of the Privy Council. He was always treated generously. When the queen decided for some reason that the bumbling patricide Fitzherbert should have his inheritance after all, Topcliffe was given a generous grant of Crown lands to compensate him for his loss.

It is hardly surprising that historians wishing to emphasize the glories of Elizabethan England have rarely given much attention to the career of Richard Topcliffe. He is nearly as forgotten as Anne Bellamy, though in his own lifetime he became all too well known. At the time of his death—like that other reptilian arch-villain Richard Rich, he died in his bed, an old and wealthy man—he was everywhere reviled. His own nephew had by then changed his name to escape the ignominy of being a Topcliffe.

10

A Horrific Tangle—
And War at Last

By the early 1570s the Puritans had grown significantly in numbers
and in economic and political clout. They were not only unsatisfied,
however, but increasingly discontented. At the same time that they were
trying and failing to pressure the government into killing Mary Stuart,
some of the more adventurous among them surreptitiously printed and
distributed a First and then a Second Admonition to Parliament. These
were bold, even treasonous complaints about how far the church had,
under the Elizabethan settlement, departed from the gospel and from
true religion. They reflected John Calvin's absolute rejection of everything that the English reformers had retained from the time before
Luther's revolt, and they expressed the conviction that even the office of
bishop was an abomination little less repulsive than the papacy itself.
The authors of the Admonitions declared that in the pure first years of
the Christian era the communities of the faithful had been led by dea-
cons and elders, not by bishops, and that fidelity to Scripture and to
Christ himself required a return to that aboriginal system. This was, in
England, the genesis of Presbyterianism. Because it challenged the legitimacy of the church that Elizabeth had established upon becoming
queen, it was taken as a challenge to Elizabeth herself. Her reaction
should have surprised no one. Those responsible for publication of the
Admonitions became hunted men, finally having to flee to the continent. They continued, from exile, to produce pamphlets condemning

the Rome-ish corruptions of the Elizabethan church. That church became a dangerous environment for clergy of Calvinist-Presbyterian inclination, but their beliefs continued to spread.

Meanwhile the government's program of killing Roman Catholicism
through a slow process of discouragement, through harassment and
disdain rather than murderous persecution, was not working out as
hoped. The lifeblood of Catholic practice was the sacraments, and that
loftiest of sacraments, the Eucharist, was not possible in the absence of
a priest empowered to consecrate the bread and wine. Elizabeth and
Cecil were not being foolish in expecting that, deprived of its priests, the
Catholic community would atrophy, especially if at the same time it
were punished in large ways and small and repeatedly accused of being
disloyal to England and the queen. But eliminating the priesthood
turned out to be considerably more difficult than it must at first have
seemed. Among the Catholics purged from the English universities after
Elizabeth ascended the throne was Oxford's proctor William Allen, already well known as a scholar and administrator though not yet quite
thirty years old. Like many of his academic coreligionists Allen drifted
back and forth between England and the continent in the early 1560s,
eventually deciding to become a priest and fixing his attention on the
large numbers of onetime Oxford and Cambridge teachers and students
who were now as adrift as he was. Many of these men had been drawn
to the Catholic Low Countries, particularly to the universities at Lou-
vain and Douai. It was at the latter that, in 1568, Allen found the financial support to start Douai College, a seminary where the faculty and all
the candidates for the priesthood were English.

It is not clear that Allen began with the idea of developing a cadre of
missionary priests to be sent back into England. His goal, rather, seems
to have been to keep the intellectual life of the English Catholic community intact in preparation for a time when it would once again be
welcome at home, and to engage the Protestant establishment in disputation while preparing a Catholic translation of the Bible. His college, in
any case, attracted so many exiles that soon it was filled beyond capacity,
and other seminaries were established elsewhere, most notably in
Rome. As the students completed their studies and were ordained, some
naturally yearned to return home and minister to the priest-starved
Catholics of England. Such requests were granted, and the first of the

young "seminary priests" slipped quietly across the Channel in 1574. As soon as the authorities became aware of their presence, the hunt was on. Inevitably the likes of Cecil and Dudley and Walsingham saw the products of Allen's school as spies and instruments of subversion and wanted the queen to see them in the same way. Certainly the priests were a threat to the policy of trying to bleed English Catholicism dry with a thousand tiny cuts; almost from the moment of their arrival they infused fresh vitality into a community that was supposed to be dying. The first to be caught, Cuthbert Mayne, was a Devon farmer's son who had taken two degrees at Oxford and become a Church of England chaplain before converting to Rome. He had then departed for Douai, where, in his early thirties, he enrolled in Allen's seminary. Within months of his ordination he was back in the west of England and, under the patronage of a wealthy Catholic landowner, taking on the public role of steward in order to travel the countryside and deliver the sacraments. Captured inside his patron's house by a posse of more than a hundred men, he was charged with six counts of treason, convicted, and offered a pardon in return for acknowledging the queen's supremacy. Upon refusing, he was made an object lesson in how religion was once again a matter of life and death in England. He was hanged, cut down alive, and thrown to the ground so violently that one of his eyes was put out. He was then disemboweled, castrated, and quartered. By hanging him as a traitor rather than burning him as a heretic, the government was able to deny that it was returning to the Marian persecutions. In Mayne's case as with the hundreds of priests who would follow him to the scaffold, the queen and her council maintained the fiction that they were killing Englishmen not for their beliefs but for seeking to deliver their homeland into the hands of foreign enemies.

As the suppression of Catholics entered a new, more desperate phase, so, too, and almost simultaneously, did the conflict with the Puritans. By the mid-1570s the queen had run out of patience with the practice known as "prophesying," which was not a matter of making predictions but simply of preaching with a pronouncedly evangelical slant rather than staying within the boundaries prescribed by the Book of Common Prayer. Somewhat oddly for a Protestant of her time, Elizabeth throughout her reign displayed a strong distaste for preaching and a determination to retain many of the trappings—clerical vestments, for example, and crucifixes—that growing numbers of her subjects were coming to regard as insufferable carryovers from the age of superstition. Such issues generated more and more heat as the 1570s advanced, until finally Edmund Grindal, the archbishop of Canterbury, was suspended for refusing to suppress prophesyings as the queen ordered. Canterbury remained an unoccupied see for years, and at times it must have appeared that Elizabeth was the head of a church of which she herself was almost the sole completely faithful member. It was her good fortune to have two sets of adversaries, the Puritans on one side and the Catholics on the other, who feared and despised each other far too much ever to combine against her. (Grindal, for example, had pleaded with the queen to stiffen the penalties for attending mass.) It also continued to be her good fortune to have the Queen of Scots as her most likely successor. So long as Mary Stuart drew breath, not even the most radical Protestant could possibly wish Elizabeth harm. The church that had taken shape under her direction was a peculiar and even improbable concoction of rather uncertain identity, no more Lutheran than Calvinist or Catholic. For the time being it was able to hang in a state of suspension easily mistaken for stability between the other contending parties.

In order to sell the story that the priests coming into England were the agents of a foreign enemy, England needed to *have* such an enemy. Though the pope would always be the ideal all-purpose bogeyman, no one could take him seriously as a military threat. The same was true of the Holy Roman Empire now that it was detached from Spain, run by a separate branch of the Hapsburgs, and fully occupied by intractable internal problems and external enemies as potent as the Turks. That left France and Spain, and so many factors made Spain the more compelling choice that not even the memory of the St. Bartholomew's Day massacre could neutralize them for long. After the massacre, the Valois regime nominally headed by Charles IX made an effort to capture the Huguenot stronghold of La Rochelle and, upon failing, sensibly gave up on anti-Protestantism as the cornerstone of its domestic policy. Like England, it turned its attention to the most significant thing then happening in northern Europe: the ongoing revolt of the Dutch against Spanish rule, and Spain's difficulty in bringing that revolt to an end. England and France alike were eager to contribute what they could to exacerbating Spain's troubles. And England had a good story to tell in explaining its involvement: it could claim to be protecting the Dutch from the Roman Church (the *Spanish* Roman Church, specifically) and its Inquisition. England and France were also drawn together by the simple realization that it could be disastrous for either of them if the other became an ally of Spain's. The 1574 death of King Charles at twenty-four did nothing to change the dynamics of the situation. He was succeeded by his nearest brother, the flamboyant Duke of Anjou, who as Henry II became the third of Catherine de' Medici's sons to inherit the throne. There remained one more brother, the young Duke of Alençon, who now assumed the Anjou title but is usually referred to as Alençon to keep him distinct from his brother. There was resumed talk, not particularly serious on either side, of marrying the young duke, disfigured by smallpox and bent by a spinal deformation but nearly twenty years old now, to the forty-one-year-old Elizabeth. Each side played the game in the faint hope that the other might attach more importance to it than it deserved.

Philip, meanwhile, was sinking deeper into the quagmire created by his rebellious Dutch subjects, and England and France were being drawn in with him. Philip had received from his father Charles V, thanks to the fifteenth-century marriage of Charles's Hapsburg grandfather to the only daughter of the last Duke of Burgundy, a region of seventeen provinces, much of it reclaimed tidal plain, known for obvious topographical reasons as the Low Countries or—what means the same thing—the Netherlands. The rebellion had started in response to Philip's efforts to impose a Spanish-style autocracy on the northernmost provinces, an almost fantastically prosperous center of trade and manufacturing where the Reformation had taken a strong hold and provided particular reason for resentment of Spanish interference. It had then spread southward as a newly appointed governor, the Duke of Alba, clamped down not only with harsh new taxes but with a reign of terror in which thousands of people, Protestants and Catholics alike, were brutally put to death. Militarily Alba was successful, bringing all but two of the provinces under control in years of hard fighting, but the savagery of his methods made reconciliation impossible. His successor Requesens tried to negotiate with the leader of the rebels, William of Orange, but resumed military operations after his overtures were spurned. In spite of crippling financial problems—Philip's government was essentially bankrupt—Requesens, too, began to have some success, but he died in 1576 with the job of reconquest still incomplete. Much of what he had achieved was thereupon undone when his troops, finding themselves unpaid, went on a rampage of looting and vandalism. Their targets, necessarily, were the only provinces accessible to them: the ones still loyal to, or at least under the control of, Spain. Thus even the most Catholic sectors of the Netherlands were given good reason to hate the outsiders.

At this juncture, with his position in the Low Countries seemingly almost lost, Philip was rescued by the fact that his father, the emperor, had, in the course of his long career, produced illegitimate branches of the Hapsburg family tree on which grew a pair of genuinely brilliant figures. First among them was Philip's younger (and illegitimate) half-brother Juan, known to history as Don John of Austria, a charismatic, even heroic character who in his youth had run off to pursue a military career in spite of being steered toward the church by both Charles and Philip. When he became governor-general of the Netherlands in 1576, Don John was almost thirty and not only a seasoned veteran of the Turkish conflict but the victor of the great Battle of Lepanto. He didn't want the Dutch assignment but accepted it with the thought that it might give rise to an opportunity to fulfill an old romantic fantasy: that of invading England and liberating Mary, Queen of Scots. The situation he found himself in was very nearly unmanageable, but after two years he was making such good progress that William of Orange, in desperate straits and without hope of getting assistance from England, invited the Duke of Alençon, still under consideration as a possible spouse for Elizabeth, to become leader of the rebellion and, by implication, ruler of the Netherlands. Alençon was utterly unqualified to take command of anything, but he was eager to make a place for himself in the world and attracted by the possibility of carving a kingdom out of the Netherlands. The Dutch of course had no real wish to accept such an unprepossessing specimen as their chief but as brother and heir to the king of France he carried with him the implicit promise of substantial help. He eagerly accepted Orange's invitation, discovered that there was no serious chance of getting meaningful assistance from his brother the king, and leaped to the conclusion that nothing could satisfy his needs more quickly and completely than a successful courtship of the English queen. Discussion soon resumed through diplomatic channels, and when word came from England that Elizabeth would never consent to marry a man she had not seen, Alençon made preparations to cross the Channel.

Don John, though continuing to progress inch by painful inch closer toward the defeat of the rebellion, was physically and mentally exhausted by the struggle and chronically short of essential resources. When in October he contracted typhus and died, his loss must have seemed another lethal setback for the Spanish cause. But before expiring he had nominated as his successor yet another product of Charles V's extramarital adventures. This was Alessandro Farnese, a son of Charles's bastard daughter, great-grandson of his namesake Pope Paul III. Farnese was almost exactly Don John's age, had been raised and educated with him as well as with King Philip's son Don Carlos, and had been second in command both at Lepanto and in the Netherlands. Usually remembered as the Duke of Parma, a title he would not inherit from his father until ten years after becoming governor-general in the Netherlands, he was no less gifted a soldier than Don John and a canny diplomat as well. Building on what Don John had accomplished, he began to coax the southern and central provinces (which would remain Catholic and evolve long afterward into Belgium, Luxembourg, and France's Nord-Pas-de-Calais) back into the Spanish camp. The seven northern provinces—the future Holland—proved however to be too strong and too determined for Farnese to overpower them. And so the war went bitterly on, poisoning northern Europe.

Influential members of Elizabeth's council, Robert Dudley among them, were not satisfied with merely assisting the Dutch rebels financially and leaving the military glory to Orange and his countrymen. Elizabeth, however, was still as wary of continental wars as she had been since the Le Havre debacle of a decade and a half before. She was sensitive to the costs of such wars and the unpredictability of the results. She had learned how difficult it was to manage seekers after glory, men convinced that where war was concerned it was absurd to take orders from any woman, even a queen. She sent money to Orange, but only in amounts calculated to keep him from putting himself completely under French domination. A strong French presence in the Low Countries, with their proximity to England across the narrowest part of the Channel, was less unattractive than Spanish dominance there, but not by a wide margin.

From this point forward the Dutch revolt, the religious divisions of France and England, and nagging uncertainty about the English succession all became impenetrably intertwined. The elfin little Duke of Alençon arrived in England, and to the amazement of her court, Elizabeth gave every appearance of being smitten with him. She was easily old enough to be his mother, and there was something pathetic in her infatuation with this youth whom she playfully called her "frog." As it dawned on people that marriage was not out of the question, council and court separated into factions. Elizabeth meanwhile made clear that this time she regarded her choice of a husband as no one's business but her own. When a loyal subject named John Stubbs published a statement of opposition to the much-talked-of marriage, both he and his printer had their right hands chopped off.

Robert Dudley was opposed, too, and probably for a multitude of reasons. He wanted to make war in the Netherlands, but he was sure that he and not the absurd Alençon should be the commander. To this wish were added his evangelical leanings, and a consequent dislike of the idea of a Catholic consort for the queen. But Dudley had kept his antipathy for Catholics within bounds when other possible husbands were under discussion, and this time more personal factors undoubtedly were in play. In 1578, after years of widowhood during which he had lived at the queen's beck and call and lamented the fact that because neither he nor his brother Ambrose had children the Dudley line seemed doomed to end with them, he had impregnated the beautiful Lettice Knollys, daughter of the veteran privy councilor Sir Francis Knollys and widow of the Earl of Essex. The two were secretly married—secretly because Dudley knew what the queen's reaction would be—and when Elizabeth learned she was angry and hurt. She arranged to complicate Dudley's life financially by withdrawing certain remunerative favors, but he was allowed to remain at court and soon was restored to his old place as favorite. His bride, already the mother of several children by her first husband, gave birth to a son who was christened Robert. But she was forbidden to appear at court. (The boy, Lord Denbigh, would be the last child born legitimately into the Dudley family and would die at age three.) All this could well have injected an element of spite into Dudley's reaction to the queen's marriage plans.

By the early 1580s Elizabeth's uncertainties, hesitations, and ambiguous policies had enmeshed her in a tangle of political, military, and religious conflict. In 1585 it all finally blossomed into a war that would consume the last eighteen years of what increasingly looked like an overlong reign. Much of the trouble grew out of the determination of the government's most influential and militant Protestants—Cecil certainly, but even more his protégé Francis Walsingham—to make the queen believe that the survival of Catholicism in England posed a threat not only to domestic peace but to her very life. As early as 1581 Walsingham was asking Lord Hunsdon, Elizabeth's cousin and one of the men to whom she had entrusted the management of the north after the revolt of the earls, to amend his reports so as to give a darker—and to the queen more alarming—appraisal of the loyalty of the region's still-numerous Catholics. In that same year Parliament, with Cecil ennobled as Baron Burghley and dominating the House of Lords while continuing to control the Commons through his agents, passed bills making it high treason for a priest to say mass and condemning anyone attending mass to life imprisonment and confiscation of property.

This was more than Elizabeth was prepared to approve, and the penalty for "recusancy" was reduced to a fine of £20 per month—a sum so impossible for most subjects as to be no different from confiscation. The queen's efforts to find a middle ground, to avoid being so soft on the old religion as to outrage the evangelicals or persecuting the Catholics so savagely as to leave them with nothing to lose, resulted in a policy that sometimes seemed incoherent. An innovation called "compounding," which permitted Catholics to elude the statutory penalties by purchasing what amounted to a license to practice their faith, was soon followed by a royal proclamation declaring all the priests entering England to be traitors regardless of what they did or refrained from doing. Life became increasingly difficult for Catholics, but the Puritans complained that it was not being made nearly difficult enough. As the queen refused to approve the most draconian of Parliament's anti-Catholic measures, the conflict between her church and her growing numbers of Puritan subjects became chronic and deeply bitter. When the archbishop of Canterbury whom she had suspended years earlier died in

1583, Elizabeth was able at last to appoint a primate, John Whitgift, whose views accorded with her own. He soon began a program aimed at purging the clergy of Puritans and suppressing Puritan practices. The Elizabethan church, therefore, was soon waging religious war in one direction while Elizabeth's government did so in another.

And the fighting in the Netherlands dragged wearily on. Philip II's financial problems had eased in 1580 when the king of Portugal died without an heir and he, as the son and onetime husband of Portuguese princesses, successfully laid claim to that crown. This gave him control of the Portuguese fleet and the vast overseas empire that went with it. The following year, when the so-called United Provinces under William of Orange formally repudiated Spanish rule, Philip had the wherewithal to respond by putting more resources into the capable hands of his governor-general and nephew Farnese. The result was a sequence of successes for the Spanish army and calamities for the rebellion, all of it deepening the difficulties of the English. The little Duke of Alençon, whose dalliance with England's queen had advanced to the point where a betrothal was announced by both parties only to founder on the old religious obstacles (how could even the queen's husband be allowed to hear mass at the Elizabethan court?), went off to try his hand as leader of the rebellion. He showed himself to be even more inept than his worst critics had expected, and died of a lung ailment not long after returning to France a thoroughly discredited figure.

In that same year, 1584, William of Orange was assassinated by an apprentice cabinetmaker eager to strike a blow for the Catholic faith, the Guises allied their Catholic League with Spain, Farnese took the city of Antwerp from the rebels, and English policy lay in ruins. Philip meanwhile was repeatedly being goaded by the raids of Francis Drake and other English pirates—if *pirates* is the right word for thieves who found financing at the English court and were welcomed as heroes when they returned from their raids—on ports and treasure fleets from the coast of Spain to the New World. Now he appeared to be near victory in the Low Countries, and if he achieved his aims there the English had given him an abundance of reasons to turn his army and navy on them. When Drake, on a 1585 West Indies voyage financed by Elizabeth and Robert Dudley and others, burned and looted Cartagena and Santo Domingo and other Spanish ports and brought his ships home loaded with booty, it was the last straw for Philip. He ordered work to begin on the assembly of a great fleet and the planning of an invasion of England.

For Elizabeth and her council it was a nightmare scenario, though undeniably they had brought it on themselves. They had provoked the Spanish king's open enmity at last, and had done so in such a penny-pinching way as to leave their rebel clients virtually at his mercy. The prospect that Philip might soon subdue the Low Countries was, under these circumstances, vastly more frightening than it had been when the revolt began. And so at last there seemed no alternative except to do exactly what Elizabeth had never wanted to do: send troops. Robert Dudley was delighted, especially when he was ordered to take command. He was well into his fifties by now, however, and his experience of war was decades in the past and not really extensive. But his enthusiasm was such that he took on a ruinous load of personal debt to cover his expenses—Elizabeth was not going to pay a penny more than she was forced to—and once in the field he found that he was neither receiving satisfactory support from home nor able to outwit or outfight his seasoned Spanish adversaries. The arrival of English troops was sufficient to avert the collapse of the rebellion but not sufficient to produce victory; the result was the further prolongation, at greatly increased cost, of a conflict that offered vanishingly little hope of a truly satisfactory outcome. England's intervention had persuaded Philip, meanwhile, that he could never recover his lost provinces—might never again know peace within his own domains—unless England was humbled. The invasion that he had in preparation began to seem not just feasible but imperative.

Overt war with Spain provided a new basis for portraying England's Catholics as agents of a foreign enemy and therefore as traitors. Suppression, along with the hunting down and execution of missionary priests, intensified. Inevitably, persecution further eroded the number of practicing Catholics, but at the same time, it gave rise to a cadre of young fanatics desperate enough to plot against the queen's life. This development—like Philip's anger a direct outgrowth of the government's actions—was the best possible news for Francis Walsingham with his network of spies, torturers, and agents provocateurs. It gave him new evidence to draw on in making Elizabeth believe that it was necessary to do more to exterminate the old religion. None of the most notorious and supposedly dangerous plots against Elizabeth had the slimmest chance of success, and Walsingham himself probably actively encouraged at least one of them in order to entrap gullible young true believers. He may even have concocted the last of the conspiracies (the so-called Babington Plot, which led to Mary Stuart's confessing to planning an escape and being accused, but not really proved guilty, of assenting to Elizabeth's assassination) in order to get a deeply reluctant Elizabeth to approve Mary's execution. Historians have often argued that the need to eliminate the Queen of Scots is demonstrated by the fact that after she was beheaded in February 1587 there were no more plots against the queen's life. But it is possible that, once Mary was dead, Cecil and Walsingham no longer saw any need to put such plots in motion, nurse along the ones that they discovered, or exploit their propaganda value when the time was ripe for exposure.

What is often depicted as the apotheosis of the Elizabethan Age, the turning point at which the wisdom of everything the queen had done was made manifest and the way was cleared for England's emergence as the greatest of world powers, came in the third week of July 1588. It was then that Philip's mighty Armada came plowing up the Channel into England's home waters, found Drake and Elizabeth's other sea dogs waiting, and was put to flight. It was indeed an escape for England, even a victory, though it was accomplished as much by weather and Spanish mistakes as by weapons. But it changed very little and settled nothing. It was less a culmination than a bright interlude, and it led only to the fifteen years of trouble and decline that would be the long final third of Elizabeth's reign.

THE PUNISHMENT OF THE INNOCENT

TUDOR ENGLAND WAS A WORLD IN WHICH THE RICH GOT richer while the poor got not only poorer but much, much more numerous. Twenty years into Elizabeth's reign she had so many seriously poor subjects, and the situation of many of them was so desperate, that figuring out what to do with them had become one of the challenges of the age.

There were many reasons why the condition of ordinary English families deteriorated precipitously during the Tudor century: the destruction of an ecclesiastical social welfare system that for centuries had reached out from the monasteries and parish churches into every corner of the kingdom; the ongoing enclosure of arable land and the expulsion of the people who had long farmed it to make way for sheep; an unprecedented concentration of wealth in the hands of a gentry class that was only a tiny part of the population; and a toxic mix of economic forces that caused real wages to fall decade after decade even as prices relentlessly rose.

Added to all this was the emergence of a new set of social values—call it the Protestant ethic—that encouraged the prosperous to equate wealth with virtue and to regard the destitute as responsible for (even predestined to) their predicament. An older worldview in which society was expected to provide a place for everyone, in which the poor were believed to have a special relationship with God and caring for them was supposed to be one of the primary moral obligations of every person, was inexorably passing away.

Poverty did not begin with the Tudors, obviously. Parliamentary statutes dealing with the homeless and unemployed had first appeared as early as the reign of King Richard II, late in the fourteenth century. Such persons were described as "vagabonds" even then, and if they were "sturdy vagabonds"—drifters capable of working—they were to be put into the stocks wherever they were found and then ordered to go back to where they had come from. Only the "impotent" were permitted to beg—only, that is, the very young and very old and those otherwise genuinely unable to earn a living—and they needed a license and were forbidden to beg very far from home. In these first poor laws as for centuries thereafter, one of the government's chief objectives was to prevent idlers from roaming wherever they wished.

Implicit in all this was the assumption that even the poorest could find at least minimal subsistence in their home districts, and that appears to have been generally true. That there were no new laws dealing with the poor for almost a century after Richard II, and that when Henry VII revised the old law in 1495 he did so to ease the prescribed penalties, seems a clear indication that poverty remained a negligible problem, for the government at least, for a very long time. The introduction of new measures in 1531 had less to do with Henry VIII's quarrel with Rome than with the economic problems of the late 1520s, which had driven streams of people out of their homes and onto the roads in search of food and work. Soon thereafter, however, the expropriation of the resources of the church destroyed the one traditional refuge of the English poor, and poverty became a significant policy issue. What is striking about the new laws that followed is the contempt for the poor that they reflect. This was something new to English life. An inclination to treat poverty as an offense deserving punishment came to dominate the Privy Council's actions.

From the early 1530s on, anyone judged to be a vagabond was to be not merely put in stocks but given a public whipping before being driven away. It was a curiously cold-blooded way to deal with people who no longer had homes, could not find work, and could find no way to escape starvation. But it set the pattern for what lay ahead: a national system of laws and proclamations designed not to help the poor but to keep them confined: to limit their mobility, increase their difficulties in entering a skilled trade, force them to take any available work on whatever terms were offered, and punish and humiliate those able to find nothing. Everything was slanted to the advantage of the property-owning classes—Parliament not only put limits on wages but made it a crime to either demand or pay more—and only the immediate threat of civil unrest could on rare occasions force council or Parliament to intervene even briefly on behalf of workers or the unemployed.

A theme that runs through all the poor laws from the 1530s on is fear of the itinerant homeless. This was not irrational; people living on farms or in tiny villages had reason to be concerned when ragged strangers suddenly appeared, whether singly or in groups. It is no coincidence, therefore, that one of the most savagely repressive measures of the whole Tudor era was passed in 1547, a time when thousands of men had recently returned from the last of King Henry's continental wars. These were hardened cases, many of them, and penniless, and often resentful of the callous treatment that was the lot of soldiers in those days. Many of them had little option but to take to the highways, begging as they went, looking for work or, failing that, for something to steal. The scare that they put into the gentlefolk of southeastern England was a factor in Parliament's passage of a law unlike any other in the recorded history of England—one that prescribed branding for vagrancy and enslavement for those who failed to mend their ways. When this law was repealed after two years—it was simply too repulsive to be enforced or defended—whipping and expulsion once again became the standard punishment for poor people who showed up where they were not wanted.

As the years went by and unrelenting punishment failed to solve the poverty problem, local authorities and central government alike were slowly, grudgingly forced to the realization that some people were poor not because they were lazy but as the result of conditions beyond their control. It became impossible to believe that force alone was going to maintain public order. Thomas Cromwell seems to have understood this as early as the 1530s: he drafted a bill that would have required parishes to collect alms for the support of the impotent and assigned the able unemployed to public works projects supervised by "councils to avoid vagabonds." He was ahead of his time, however, and the bill never became law. Finally, in 1552, begging was banned completely, parishes were admonished to take up collections for the impotent, and so for the first time the helpless no longer had to fend for themselves. Five years later, during the reign of Queen Mary, a system was established to provide the unemployed and their families with materials—hemp, flax, wool— that they could fashion into items for sale and so support themselves.

With numerous short-term ups and downs, general conditions continued to deteriorate during Elizabeth's reign. The Statute of Artificers of 1563, while making contributions to parish poor boxes compulsory and thereby establishing the rudiments of a national tax system, went to new lengths to keep the poor in their place, in some ways quite literally. Upward mobility, already reduced by the disappearance of many schools, was further curtailed by a tightening of the property qualifications for apprenticeship. Responsibility for putting limits on wages was transferred from Parliament to the justices of the peace, but it remained unlawful to exceed those limits or even to ask for more than the law allowed. Nine years later Parliament put sharp new teeth into the punishment of vagabonds. The penalty for a first offense was now not whipping alone but also the boring of a hole into one ear—an ineradicable sign that one was not a respectable person. Second offenses were treated as felonies, and anyone found guilty of a third could be put to death. These provisions remained in effect for more than twenty years, but in 1576, with a conspicuous lack of enthusiasm, Parliament established a new category called the "deserving poor"—people who were not only able but willing to work, but could find no employment. The Marian practice of providing such people with raw materials to be fashioned into merchandise was revived, but in reviving it Parliament scornfully stated that its motive was not to help anyone but to assure that "rogues may not have any just excuse in saying that they cannot get any service or work." In the eyes of the governing elite, the poor remained a nuisance that unfortunately could not be ignored.

By the late 1590s the state of the economy had become so alarming that chaos seemed to threaten. Failed harvests, raging inflation, unemployment caused by war in the Netherlands, and a continuing decline in the standard of living combined to spark food riots in London and its environs in 1595, and in East Anglia, Kent, and southwestern England in the two following years. The capital and the roads leading into and out of it had become notoriously unsafe, with much of the trouble caused by soldiers returning from the continent. The authorities, in a panic, began cracking down ruthlessly on almost any sign of discontent. When an attempt at an uprising fizzled in Oxfordshire—only four men responded to the call, and upon finding themselves alone they returned to their homes—the Privy Council nevertheless demanded arrests. That led to some suspects being tortured (possibly to death in two cases), and to others being executed. The use of the death penalty rose sharply in many jurisdictions, provost marshals were commissioned to conduct sweeps aimed at clearing the roads of "base persons," and a statute of 1597 ordered that "dangerous rogues" were either to be banished from the kingdom or put to work as oarsmen on the queen's galleys.

As the century came to an end economic conditions improved somewhat, and social tensions lessened. But for an overwhelming majority of the men and women of England, the great Elizabethan Age was limping to a distinctly miserable conclusion.

11

The Last Favorite

I f the failure of Philip's great Armada was the zenith of Elizabeth's reign that it has so often been depicted as being, if it really did carry her to the heights of glory and provide proof of God's favor, she was not slow to return to the lower altitudes at which she had been accustomed to operate throughout the previous thirty years.

Her navy had barely broken off its pursuit of the fleeing Spaniards, in fact, when Elizabeth exposed her bred-in-the-bone selfishness, her cold indifference to the well-being of the subjects whose supposed love for her she and the royal propagandists endlessly celebrated as one of the wonders of the age. The commander of the Spanish fleet, upon abandoning hope of being able to land his troops on English soil, had decided not to run the gauntlet of the Channel in returning to his home ports but to take the much longer, presumably safer route all the way around England, Scotland, and Ireland. He therefore set a course for the north. The English kept pace with him as far as the waters off Scotland but then, being virtually out of ammunition and no better equipped than any of the ships of the time for long periods at sea, turned back south. It was well that they did. Plague was breaking out among the crews, and soon the ships were hauling into whatever havens they could find and unloading hundreds of desperately sick men. These were the heroes of the hour, the sailors who had saved their homeland from invasion, but now they were carrying deadly contagion. It is hardly surprising that they were not welcomed when they came ashore. What *is* surprising, not to say appalling, is the queen's failure to do anything to help them. Her admiral, Lord Howard of Effingham, wrote urgently of how "sickness and mortality begins to grow wonderfully amongst us, and it is a most pitiful sight to see, here at Margate, how the men, having no place to receive them into here, died in the streets . . . It would grieve any man's heart to see them that have served so valiantly, to die so miserably."

Howard was a court insider, not only a grandson of the Duke of Norfolk who had defeated the Scots at Flodden but the husband of one of Elizabeth's Carey cousins, and messages from him were not likely to be casually disregarded. He wrote the day before Elizabeth paid a visit to an encampment of her soldiers at Tilbury on the lower Thames, where nearly twenty thousand troops had been positioned to engage any Spanish force that might enter the river's mouth and attempt a landing. Here she supposedly delivered one of the greatest of her orations.

Characteristically, she focused her words on herself ("resolved in the midst and heat of the battle to live and die among you all") and her superiority to ordinary mortals ("I have the heart and stomach of a king, and of a king of England too"). This took place, if it *did* take place, fully one week after Howard broke off his pursuit of the Spanish and therefore even longer after the Armada had switched over from attack to escape. Possibly her main reason for going to Tilbury was that Rob Dudley was in command there—hating as she did to be apart from him at any time, she must have felt a particular need for his company in the middle of such a crisis; she and Dudley must both have known that the danger was now past, the enemy scattered. But it was an occasion for the kind of theater that Elizabeth loved, a gesture that cost nothing except a costume or two. (In pictures of her Tilbury performance, she is often shown wearing a metal breastplate and brandishing a sort of toy sword.) Trying to do something for the men who had saved her and were now dying in barns and sheds and gutters, by contrast, would have been both expensive and lacking in opportunities for drama. The admiral's appeal fell on deaf ears at least in part, apparently, because of the fact—an attractive one to Elizabeth and her hard-pressed treasurer Lord Burghley—that dead seamen were unlikely to demand back wages.

That was the worst of the government's conduct in the immediate aftermath of the Armada, but just barely. During the period when invasion seemed imminent, England's Catholics had rallied to the queen and volunteered to join in the defense. This behavior fit badly, of course, with what the Cecils and Walsinghams wanted Elizabeth and the nation to understand about the dangers of papist sedition. And so, rather than being mustered, Catholics were forcibly and humiliatingly disarmed. Between July and November twenty-one imprisoned priests, eleven Catholic laymen, and one woman were put to death. The Protestants needed little persuasion that these people were traitors and had to be eliminated.

Just a few weeks after Tilbury, Rob Dudley died unexpectedly while traveling from London to join his wife, his brother Ambrose, and Ambrose's wife (herself one of the ladies of the queen's privy chamber). He had been on his way to a period of rest in the country. The immediate cause of death appears to have been malaria, but Dudley's health had been undermined by the military campaign in the Netherlands, the difficulties of dealing with distrustful and sometimes resentful Dutch rebels, and the strain of being criticized by Elizabeth for almost his every move. His small son had died in 1584, he had mortgaged his estates and borrowed heavily from the Crown to help cover his expenses in the Low Countries, and in October 1586 his nephew Sir Philip Sidney, the apotheosis of the Elizabethan warrior-poet-gentleman, had died an agonizing death almost a month after being shot in the thigh in a skirmish at Zutphen. Quite apart from being the most important man in Elizabeth's life through the first three decades of her reign, the one man from whom she could scarcely bear to be separated, Dudley had sacrificed much, at least partly for her sake. He had never been disloyal, unless daring to marry after many years of enforced widowhood can be considered disloyalty. Elizabeth of course was genuinely hurt by his death, but on the practical level her response was once again frigid. She did nothing to relieve Dudley's widow, the despised Lettice, who was left to struggle alone with the ruinous financial consequences of her husband's service.

Dudley's death had broad consequences. It removed from the Privy Council one of the last influential members with a real attachment to the Puritan cause. Thereby it removed also one of the few remaining obstacles to the conservative program of the only prelate that Elizabeth ever appointed to her council, John Whitgift, archbishop of Canterbury.

Though theologically Whitgift was a Calvinist, in matters of church structure and practice he abhorred many of the positions taken by the radicals (their demands for the elimination of bishops, for example). He had the queen's full support in setting out to cleanse the church of radicals, and in undertaking a persecution of the Presbyterians that at times rivaled the ferocity of the hunt for priests: several men were executed for the publication of Protestant tracts. Whitgift himself was ridiculed in a series of widely distributed pamphlets by an anonymous radical who called himself "Martin Marprelate," and the Calvinists separated acrimoniously into rival camps with opposing notions of "sublapsarian" versus "supralapsarian" predestination. With the power of the Crown at his back Whitgift finally destroyed Presbyterianism as a significant element in the established church and drove it underground, where it continued to smolder menacingly and to grow in size.

By dying suddenly and earlier than might have been expected—he was about fifty-five—Dudley left behind a momentously unfinished piece of business: the preparation for public life of the youth whose patron and mentor he had become, Robert Devereux, the second Earl of Essex. It is a curiosity of history that, just as the Dudleys were dying out, the last member of the family to occupy a position of prime importance left a stepson who also, and with surprising speed, vaulted to prominence and power. Even more curious is the possibility, remote perhaps but nonetheless real, that young Essex was actually Dudley's son. His mother, Lettice Knollys, had married Dudley after the death of her husband Walter Devereux, the first Earl of Essex, but she appears to have been involved with Dudley many years before marrying him—even before her eldest son's birth. Intriguingly, Devereux and Dudley became enemies at about the time the boy was born, the rift between them is not explained by anything going on in politics at the time, and in spite of their bad relations Dudley became the child's godfather as well as his namesake. Walter Devereux died in 1576, deep in debt as the result of a failed scheme to establish a "plantation" of English settlers in Ireland. The pregnant Lettice married Dudley two years later, when the boy Robert was entering his teens, and from that point forward, regardless of whether they were connected by blood, the stepfather was advancing the stepson's career not only vigorously but far more speedily than was good for him.

Essex was a young man of high intelligence and authentic intellectual attainment; unusually for a nobleman of the time, he qualified for the M.A. at Oxford before ending his formal education. He was clever and quick and had exquisite manners, and because his mother was a grand-daughter of Mary Boleyn he was related to the queen. He made a brilliant impression when Dudley first brought him to court and was quickly established among Elizabeth's younger favorites. In 1586, when Dudley departed for the Netherlands and command of the English expeditionary force, he took his stepson, barely twenty-one years old, with him as colonel-general in command of the cavalry (and therefore senior even to Lord Burghley's experienced soldier son, the forty-four-year-old Sir Thomas Cecil). A year later Dudley handed over to Essex the court position of master of horse, and among the younger men at court only the dashing Walter Ralegh could rival Essex in the competition for Elizabeth's attention and approval. Like his stepfather, and indeed like Ralegh, Essex wanted more than opportunities to dally with the queen. From the beginning he had a lofty sense of his place in the world and his destiny, and his rapid rise contributed to his expectation that great things lay ahead. He craved military glory and more: while still little more than a boy, he appears to have regarded himself as destined for a place second only to that of the queen herself. He was also desperately hungry for money, not because he was greedy—greed had no part in his makeup— but because both his father and his stepfather had left monstrous debts. At the Elizabethan court one could have little real power without a cadre of followers, and followers were not possible without the ability to reward. It is perhaps essential to Essex's tragedy that he was only twenty-three when his stepfather died. Dudley had lived just long enough to show him the view from the heights and to encourage his belief that he belonged at the pinnacle. But Dudley had not lived long enough to teach him anything of political wisdom—the need for shrewdness and cunning, patience and restraint. Most obviously Dudley had not taught the youngster what he himself knew best: how the mind of the queen worked, what flattery could accomplish with her, above all what she would and would not tolerate. Nearly alone in the world of high politics almost before he was fully grown, Essex had almost all the qualities necessary for the achievement of even his most extravagant ambitions. Some virtues he possessed in excess: he was courageous to the point of recklessness, and he had an exceedingly strict sense of honor. But of the craftiness that makes for longevity in the realm of power politics he had none. If he understood Elizabeth at all, he was too proud to exploit his knowledge.

The story of the last third of Elizabeth's reign is, to a remarkable extent, Essex's story. The war with Spain continued, the two sides alternately delivering blows that settled nothing; France was intermittently drawn in while continuing to be crippled by its religious divisions; and finally Ireland became, from the English perspective, the most important theater of operations. And at every stage, in military or governmental affairs and often in both, Essex was among the leading figures and at the center of the action. He eagerly pursued every opportunity that the queen's affection opened to him, but in the end he so overreached himself, so misjudged the queen and mismanaged his relationship with her, as to bring about his own destruction.

Early in 1589, just months after the failure of the Armada, plans took shape for a great counterstroke aimed at rendering the Spanish incapable of further offensives. A fleet was to be assembled and sent off to the Spanish ports on the Bay of Biscay, where it was to search out and destroy the forty-odd warships that were known to be undergoing repair after the disaster of the previous year. (All the other vessels that had made up the Armada had been lost in storms off Scotland and Ireland.) Upon completing that part of its mission, the fleet was to proceed out into the Atlantic and take possession of one of the islands of the Azores, establishing a permanent base from which England would be able to prey on the transport ships that regularly returned to Spain laden with the treasures of the New World. As ambitious as it was strategically, in broad terms the plan was not unrealistic; Philip's navy being in a state of ruin in 1589, its remnants were incapable of defending themselves or their ports. Just as encouragingly, the English counter-Armada was to be commanded by the redoubtable Sir Francis Drake, already a legend in his own time, and the thousands of soldiers crowded aboard Drake's ships would be led by probably the best English general of the time, Sir John Norris. These advantages were largely neutralized, however, by the financial realities that involvement in continental wars was once again imposing upon the government. Elizabeth had neither enough ships nor enough money to make the venture a success. The old pirate Drake was able to provide ships and money of his own, however, and he had the backing of speculators accustomed to reaping huge dividends by financing the privateers. Preparations moved forward, therefore, but not all the people involved had the same objectives. Queen and council, in contributing tens of thousands of pounds, were motivated primarily by the hope of breaking Spanish power beyond possibility of recovery. Drake and his syndicate were looking for profit first.

Elizabeth, now as reluctant to allow Essex to be absent from court as she had always been to part with Robert Dudley, forbade him to take part. But he had a young man's hunger for adventure, reinforced by a determination to prove himself and to share in the spoils that Drake seemed certain to bring home. He therefore invested in the expedition—invested by borrowing—and sometime after Drake and Norris had set out he sailed off to join them. The queen, when she learned of his departure, was furious. She sent orders for his immediate return, but was too late. The expedition turned out to be a disaster. The main assault force, instead of proceeding to the ports of Santander and San Sebastián where it would have found the core of the Spanish navy disabled and ripe for the picking, sailed instead to La Coruña. There, after destroying a single galleon, its sailors and soldiers were unleashed for weeks of drunken carnage that yielded almost nothing in the way of booty. When the fleet finally set out again, its destination was not the Azores but the Portuguese capital of Lisbon, which Drake and Norris had sworn to stay away from before being allowed to leave England. Drake had with him a pretender to the throne of Portugal who assured him that the city would rise up as soon as he appeared. Essex joined them en route—the ease with which he found them suggests that all of them had planned in advance to rendezvous in defiance of the queen's instructions—and was able to make himself conspicuous in an attack on Lisbon that was, by almost every measure, a fiasco. The long stop in La Coruña had provided the Portuguese with ample warning, there was no rising in support of Drake's claimant to the throne, and the English had brought none of the equipment needed for a siege. A halfhearted pass at the Azores proved equally fruitless, and by the time the thoroughly demoralized fleet limped back to England late in June some eleven thousand of the nineteen thousand men with whom it had set out three months earlier were dead, mostly from disease. The expedition had cost an estimated £100,000, half of which had come out of the royal treasury, and exactly nothing had been achieved.

Everyone associated with the venture was in disgrace, in some cases permanently. (Drake, for one, was never trusted by the queen again.) Essex's situation was especially dangerous because he had participated in direct disobedience of Elizabeth's orders. Nevertheless, he was rehabilitated with surprising speed. As total a failure as the attack on Lisbon had been, it had provided him with numerous opportunities to put his courage and gallantry on display. Upon arrival he had personally led an amphibious assault, wading through chest-high water onto a shore defended by armed enemies. He had challenged the Spanish governor to a duel (the invitation was declined), defiantly hurled a lance against the city's locked gates when the siege was obviously failing, and at one point thrown his own belongings out of his carriage to make room for wounded troops. He more than any other member of the expedition had covered himself with something like glory, his praises were literally sung back in England, and Elizabeth's anger must have been mixed with pride that her favorite had acquitted himself so well. And at court he had influential friends who were willing to speak up for him. Old Lord Burghley, who had taken a hand in Essex's upbringing and education after the death of his father, remained one of his defenders even though the earl was becoming a rival of his own son, Robert Cecil. Among Essex's other champions were his grandfather Sir Francis Knollys, still active on the Privy Council though nearly eighty years of age; his and the queen's cousin Lord Hunsdon; and Ambrose Dudley's wife, the Countess of Warwick, one of the longest-serving ladies of the privy chamber. Such support made it easier for Elizabeth to yield to her own powerful affection for the young hero. She not only allowed him to resume his place at court but conferred upon him the monopoly on sweetwine imports that had previously belonged to his stepfather. This eased Essex's financial problems; renewed in 1593 and again in 1597, it would become essential to his ability to maintain himself as the leader of a significant political faction.

Among the more appealing aspects of Essex's character, and ultimately one of the key factors in his tragedy, was his unwillingness to be a courtier only, or to rely entirely on the queen's favor for advancement and the accumulation of wealth. He could have done well for himself and restored the fortunes of his family by remaining close to the throne and wheedling offices and other streams of income from the needy, aging woman who sat on it. But he was determined to be more and do more than that, and even after his escape from being buried in the ruins of the Lisbon expedition he continued to involve himself in matters that a more prudent man—a Cecil, say—might have left alone. Just days after his return from Portugal, the French wars of religion were ignited yet again by the assassination of King Henry III, who, in spite of being decidedly Catholic in his beliefs, was stabbed to death by a Dominican friar for having arranged the murder of three leading members of the Guise clan, including the duke himself. The last of Catherine de' Medici's sons being thus dead, the crown passed to their cousin, the Protestant Henry of Navarre, who duly became King Henry IV but met such fierce popular opposition that he was unable to enter Paris. One after another the major pieces on the northern European chessboard went into motion, some of them sensing opportunity, others danger. For Spain especially, a divided France whose Protestant ruler was too weak to impose order seemed extravagantly rich in possibilities, and it soon became known that Philip was preparing to intervene. The English had reason to be alarmed. A new expeditionary force was hastily assembled and, under the command of Essex's friend Lord Willoughby, sent across the Channel with a threefold mission: to assist Henry IV and his Huguenots, to discourage aggressive action on Philip's part, and to explore any avenues that might lead to the recovery of Calais. It all happened too quickly, and too soon after Lisbon, for Essex's participation to be possible. He considered Henry of Navarre a friend and ally, having since 1587 been sending him boyishly excited promises of support in the great struggle with the Roman Antichrist, and he followed events in France with passionate interest. At the same time, in cooperation with his sister Lady Penelope Rich (wife of the majestically wealthy grandson of the Richard Rich who had played such a villainous role in the reign of Henry VIII), Essex was secretly communicating with James VI of Scotland about the importance of an international Protestant alliance. He appears to have been calculating, more than a decade prematurely, that the aging Elizabeth and her closest, most trusted ministers were not likely to live a great deal longer. In encouraging the son of Mary, Queen of Scots to prepare for inheritance of the English throne, he appears to have been motivated at least as much by genuine religious zeal as by any wish to promote himself.

The Willoughby expedition ended soon and badly, more because of insufficient support and the diseases that invariably afflicted armies attempting to operate in wintertime than because of any failure on the part of its commander. Nothing had been accomplished that might prevent the Spanish from moving in; by early 1590 everyone could see that such a move was in fact impending; and clearly England was going to have to either do more or leave France at Philip's mercy. The result was two new theaters of conflict. An English force commanded by John Norris (Essex had begged for the assignment and been refused) was sent to Brittany in France's northwest to block the army that Philip had placed there. Almost simultaneously the governor-general of the Netherlands, the Alessandro Farnese who was now Duke of Parma, led a Spanish army from the Low Countries into Normandy. This last move was a boon to the Dutch rebels, easing the pressure on them just at the point where Parma appeared to be on the verge of victory. With the Spanish now in Brittany and Normandy, Henry IV (who was at war with his own country's Catholic League as well) faced the danger of being caught in a vise and crushed. Regardless of the fate of the Huguenots, for England it was unthinkable that the French Channel ports should fall into Parma's, and Philip's, hands. Yet another expeditionary force, this one responsible for dealing with Parma, had become imperative. Elizabeth asked Willoughby to take command once again. But both his health and his finances had been impaired by the campaign of the previous year—Willoughby, like Dudley before him, paid dearly for the privilege of fighting the queen's wars—and he begged off. He recommended that the assignment be given to his friend Essex, who was lobbying to the same purpose on his own behalf. The queen finally consented, if reluctantly, and once again the earl was eagerly off to war.

At about this same time, in another echo of the career of his stepfather, Essex secretly married Frances Walsingham Sidney, who was both the daughter of Elizabeth's recently deceased secretary and (what is likely to have mattered more to the romantic young earl) the widow of his late friend Sir Philip Sidney. Sidney had left his sword to Essex when he died; now Essex had his wife as well. The marriage would remain secret until the birth of the couple's son, news of which drove Elizabeth into the vengeful rage that had to be expected whenever one of her favorites or some member of the privy chamber became seriously involved in an affair of the heart. Essex was able to save himself from banishment only by pledging to keep his wife away from court. He was helped by the fact that his great rival Sir Walter Ralegh now impregnated and married one of Elizabeth's maids of honor. Ralegh had the worst of it by far: he and his bride were imprisoned in the Tower.

Essex's marriage was happy enough by all appearances, producing a number of children over the next decade, but it brought none of the political or financial advantages that a more calculating man might have sought in a wife. Sir Francis Walsingham had left a surprisingly modest estate aside from tens of thousands of pounds owed him by the Crown for expenses incurred in the performance of his varied duties—a debt that would remain unpaid to the end of Elizabeth's life. The banishment of Essex's bride meant that he could never possess that most valuable of political weapons, a spouse whose position at court enabled her to serve as an advocate and a trustworthy set of eyes and ears. Young Robert Cecil, by contrast, was newly and wisely married to a goddaughter of the queen and lady of the privy chamber, and he had had the good sense to get the queen's approval before marrying.

Ambrose, Earl of Warwick, the last of the Dudleys, died in 1590. The next year brought the death of one of Elizabeth's oldest and closest favorites and friends, Sir Christopher Hatton, a kind of tame Robert Dudley who had devoted himself so unreservedly to the queen's service that he never married or is even known to have considered marriage. He had been first brought to court because he amused the queen with his talent for dancing and theatricals, but as their friendship developed he was made a gentleman of the privy chamber; this was the rarest of honors, affording access to the innermost royal sanctum, a place otherwise off limits except to women. He also became a member of the Privy Council, then finally lord chancellor and chancellor of Oxford University. He receives scant attention in histories of the reign, perhaps because unlike the other men in Elizabeth's life he never provoked her to jealousy or anger and was unfailingly satisfied to do her bidding. His passing must have been a painful loss; one by one the people who had long been closest to the queen—ladies of the chamber as well as veterans of the council—were dropping away. Now only one was left, really—William Cecil, Lord Burghley, who was growing so feeble that increasingly he had to be carried about in a chair but still kept his hands on the levers of power. The circle around Burghley and Elizabeth was growing both younger and smaller. The question of who might ascend to Burghley's supreme position when he too died remained as unresolved as the royal succession. The most obvious possibilities were the dashing young favorites— Essex and even Ralegh in spite of his current eclipse. A somewhat darker horse was the distinctly unglamorous Robert Cecil. A faintly grotesque little man, bent of back and spindly of leg, Cecil was the antithesis of Essex, following his father's example in working quietly but tirelessly to make himself indispensable, patiently maintaining a focus on the big picture and the long term.

As 1592 opened, Essex appeared to have the advantage. In January he returned from Normandy, where his first experience of independent command had left a bitter aftertaste but done him no grievous political harm. The Normandy campaign is sometimes described as a farcical affair in which Essex marched his four-thousand-man army hither and yon to no purpose except to impress Henry IV and to no effect beyond the wasting of the queen's money. In fact it was a failure and an expensive one, but that Essex should be blamed is not clear. His instructions were to remain in France for only two months, and upon landing his little army at Dieppe he was to be met by and begin joint operations with Henry. The French king was not at Dieppe, however, so that to effect a union Essex had to move his troops a hundred miles in bad weather. He soon learned what Dudley, Norris, and Willoughby had learned before him about what it was to command an army in the name of Elizabeth Tudor: the queen, too far away to have much grasp of the realities on the ground, barraged him with instructions, criticism, and complaints. Also characteristically, she refused to provide enough troops or money to reap the benefits of her initial investment. Twice Essex hurried back to England to explain his situation and beg for more time and resources. He attempted repeatedly to put spirit into his demoralized and disease-ridden troops with daring attacks in which he exposed himself unnecessarily to danger. None of it was enough. By year-end he and Henry IV were bogged down in what seemed certain to be an interminable siege of the city of Rouen. Lashed by the queen's angry letters, annoyed to learn that while he was fighting in France Robert Cecil had been appointed to the Privy Council, he finally gave up and returned home. He had been shown something about the importance of being physically at court if one wanted to keep the queen's affection and influence her thinking. He had not, unfortunately for himself, taken the lesson sufficiently to heart.

WINNING BIG

THOMAS WOLSEY, THOMAS CROMWELL, EDWARD SEYMOUR, John Dudley, Thomas Cranmer—the history of the Tudor era is littered with the wreckage of more or less briefly brilliant careers. To rise too high or too swiftly, clearly, was to tempt the fates.

Slow and steady was the way to win the race. This is the lesson of the Cecils, who entered our story at its beginning, stayed in the background through two generations, and finally during Elizabeth's long reign not only attained the political, financial, and social heights but managed to entrench there two distinct branches of their family tree.

We noted in passing, in dealing with the first Henry Tudor's invasion of England in 1485, that among those who joined him on his march from Wales into England was a young man named David Cecil. Little is known of his background except that he appears to have been the son of a minor gentry family from the Welsh marches. After the victory at Bosworth Field he shows up in the records as a member of Henry VII's bodyguard, a yeoman of the chamber (which means he had access to the king's private quarters), and finally sergeant at arms (a kind of security officer with authority over others). He became a landowner, though not an important one, in Lancashire in the north.

This David Cecil used his position at court to secure an appointment for his son Richard as a page in Henry VIII's privy chamber. Richard in his turn rose to become a groom of the chamber and yeoman of the wardrobe, a position of sufficient respectability to permit him to make an advantageous marriage, get himself appointed to various offices in Nottinghamshire, and add to the landholdings accumulated by his father. Obviously he understood that the world was changing and the route to advancement was changing with it: though he brought his son William to court at an early age as page of the robes, the boy was later sent off to Cambridge University, an expensive undertaking. In six years at Cambridge young William, while somehow failing to take a degree, became proficient in Latin, Greek, Italian, French, and Spanish, thus making himself capable of dealing on equal terms with the Tudor court's elite. While still at university he married the sister of John Cheke, a rising star among England's classical scholars and a prominent young Protestant. Richard Cecil is not likely to have been greatly pleased with this marriage; union with the Cheke family offered no financial advantages and few if any political ones. Nevertheless, upon leaving Cambridge William was permitted to take up the study of law at Gray's Inn in London; obviously his father remained willing to invest heavily in his preparations for a career. The investment began to pay dividends as early as 1542, the year William became twenty-two. Thanks no doubt to his father's access to Henry VIII as well as his own attainments, William was not only appointed to the Court of Common Pleas but made a member of Parliament. His wife died the following year, having given birth to a son, and after two years of widowhood he married the eldest daughter of Sir Anthony Cooke, a leading courtier, humanist scholar, and educator. This marriage should have pleased Richard mightily; the Cookes, being exceptionally well connected, provided William with entry to the circle led by Edward Seymour, uncle to the little Prince Edward and leader of the evangelical faction at court.

Cecil, with his intelligence and education and understanding of court life, was soon noticed and put to use. He became secretary to Seymour—now the Duke of Somerset—in 1548. The following year he spent two months as a prisoner in the Tower in the aftermath of Somerset's fall, negotiating that crisis with all the skill that Cromwell had shown after the fall of Wolsey almost two decades before. In 1550 he became a member of the Privy Council, one of King Edward's two secretaries, and "surveyor" (general business manager) of Princess Elizabeth's estates. Having definitely arrived, he allied himself with Archbishop Cranmer and so impressed Lord Protector John Dudley that he was knighted.

The religious restoration that came with the accession of Mary I created grave difficulties for the evangelical party and everyone connected with Dudley, as we have seen, but Cecil does not appear ever to have been in danger. The queen respected him, he continued to sit in Parliament, and Cardinal Pole used him in diplomatic missions to the continent. In all likelihood he could have played a substantial role in the new regime, but he chose instead to withdraw to his estate at Wimbledon, maintaining contact with Elizabeth and like her going to occasionally ridiculous lengths (ostentatiously displaying his rosary beads, for example) to demonstrate that he was a faithful and practicing Catholic. Elizabeth was fortunate, when Mary died, to have close at hand an experienced politician who was also as dependable a friend as Cecil. In immediately appointing him her principal secretary, she was showing her basic good sense.

Cecil used his new position to take control of all communications to and from the queen and make himself head of the Privy Council and minister-in-chief. He and Elizabeth were, in important respects, a strangely matched pair. Cecil, once in power, showed himself to be a statesman of some vision, capable of formulating strategic objectives and acting decisively when presented with opportunities to achieve them. Elizabeth, with her focus on trying to maintain a stable status quo, on surviving, was chronically reluctant to make irrevocable commitments. The difference between the two became manifest almost at the beginning, when Cecil correctly saw his opportunity to drive the French out of Scotland but had to threaten to resign before the queen would allow him to act. This set the pattern for the next forty years: Cecil generally knew what he wanted to do next and why, and he repeatedly found it difficult or impossible to get a decision out of the queen. In no way, however, can the partnership be dismissed as a failure for either party. The shrewd and patient Cecil, himself a cautious man but able to take carefully calculated risks, learned to swallow his frustration and wait. In the end he accomplished more than a little. And Elizabeth got what she wanted: she survived, and rather handsomely.

Cecil had been born too late to get in on the great scattering of wealth triggered by the suppression of the monasteries, but his father had benefited in a small way, and during the reign of Edward VI both were able to buy up church lands at insider prices. He was already a fairly rich man when Elizabeth became queen, but the best was yet to come. In the aftermath of his great success in Scotland he was given the lucrative post of master of the Court of Wards and granted extensive tracts of land in Lincolnshire, Rutland, and Northamptonshire. Elizabeth also gave him licenses to trade in beer and cloth—licenses that he could then sell to eager merchants. For the rest of his life he was able to put himself first in line whenever royal largesse was being dispensed.

On the dynastic front, by contrast, things did not seem to be going particularly well for Cecil. In 1561 he sent his only son, Thomas, who was then nineteen years old, on a two-year grand tour of Europe, during which the youth was reported to be neglecting his prayers and studies to such an extent, and devoting so much time to gambling and sport, that his father threatened to have him forcibly confined. Actually Thomas appears to have been nothing worse than high-spirited and mischievous, his conduct intolerable only by the standards of his father and his strait-laced stepmother. After returning to England he was given a seat in Commons and married to a baron's daughter. (William Cecil was careful to find spouses among the nobility for all his children, thereby condemning one of his daughters to a disastrously unhappy marriage to an earl.) The court, and the whole world of politics, now lay wide open to Thomas Cecil. His father must have been disappointed when he showed himself to be less interested in life at court than in making a career as a soldier.

In 1563, after eighteen years of marriage, Mildred Cooke Cecil presented William with their first and only son, a boy who was given the name Robert. As with Thomas, however, paternity brought disappointment and worry: the child was not only frail but misshapen, with a humped back and feet that pointed outward; all his life he would walk with a crablike shuffle. Rather obviously, this boy was never going to be a soldier. His father must have feared that he might never prosper in the image-obsessed world of the court, either.

But William now had two heirs a generation apart in age, and it became part of his life's work to place both of them high among the elite. The age, as we saw earlier in connection with food, was one of conspicuous consumption, and of a growing gulf between rich and poor. All across England, families newly rich on church land were building lavish country homes; it was a way of showing off, of proving wealth and power, of staking a claim to aristocratic status. Probably it is only natural that William, as alert as his own father had been to what would be required for success in the next generation, now set out to build for his sons the grandest nonroyal palaces of the age. From his father he had inherited a Staffordshire estate stitched together from onetime monastic lands and an old manor called Burghley, and during Queen Mary's reign he had begun building a house commensurate with his new wealth. Upon the birth of his second son he had bought a property called Theobalds only about a dozen miles from London and begun building there as well, and as his fortune increased his plans for both places became more and more grandiose. Work went on at what was named Burghley House for thirty-two years, culminating in the late 1580s in the completion of the most stupendous of the so-called "prodigy houses" of the Elizabethan period. The house's main part had thirty-five major rooms on two floors plus another eighty more or less ordinary rooms, with east and west wings nearly equal in size, and it was all set in a park of ten thousand acres. The plans for Theobalds were expanded after Elizabeth paid a first visit in the 1560s and declared her intention to return. She visited ten more times between 1571 and 1594 (each visit cost the proud owner between £2,000 and £3,000—money very well spent), and each time she found the place more imposing than before. In the end it had five interior courts, the largest 110 feet on each side with a huge fountain of black and white marble as its centerpiece. The next largest was eighty-six feet square and abutted presence, privy, bed, and coffer chambers specially built for the queen. The land that Burleigh acquired around it eventually had a circumference of eight miles. When Elizabeth created him Baron Burghley in 1573, there could be no doubt about his having resources appropriate to his new rank.

And neither son proved to be a disappointment. Thomas got the military career he had wanted and distinguished himself, participating in putting down the revolt of the northern earls in 1569 and in an English foray into Scotland in 1573. He was knighted in 1575, went with Robert Dudley and the young Earl of Essex to the Netherlands war in 1585, and was wealthy enough to establish his wife and five sons and eight daughters in a prodigy house of his own at Wimbledon. Though Robert's disabilities could not be outgrown, and though he was educated at home rather than being sent to university, he grew up to be intelligent, hardworking, ambitious, and cunning. His father placed him in Parliament when he was twenty-one and arranged his marriage to a lady close to the queen. When Francis Walsingham died in 1590 and Elizabeth procrastinated in naming a replacement, William Cecil arranged for Robert to take up the duties of secretary without being able to give him the title.

The question of whether he or someone else would ultimately be appointed gave rise to much court gossip.

Ultimately the question was one of succession: who would take charge when Burghley was finally gone? Essex obviously regarded himself as entitled to do so. And it was he, obviously, whom the queen loved. But it was Robert Cecil whom she appointed to the council in 1591, when Essex was away in France. Nobody knew what to expect, which was exactly the way Elizabeth wanted it.

12

A Seat at the Table

The value of staying home, of keeping close to the queen and flirting with her and becoming as adept as Christopher Hatton at appearing to worship her as an unattainably perfect woman, was soon made plain to Essex. In just a year he was given a seat on the council. That made him a player at the table where policy was decided, and it did so at a time when great questions urgently needed to be answered. After Essex's departure from France, Alessandro Farnese had forced Henry IV to break off the siege of Rouen, which thus remained in control of France's Catholic League. But then Farnese suffered a wound that at first did not seem dangerous and abruptly died, not yet forty-eight years old. His passing cost Philip II possibly the best soldier-diplomat of his time. William of Orange's son and heir, the capable Maurice of Nassau, was able to nurse the Dutch rebellion back to vigor with the help of a continuing English military presence. In Brittany, at the same time, John Norris with his little army succeeded in fighting the Spanish to a standstill—an admirable achievement in light of the difficulties he had experienced in trying to get Elizabeth and Burghley to send him men and money. If Norris was a more effective beggar than Essex in addition to being the better general, he had the advantage of a mother who was a lady of the privy chamber. In any case, having accomplished far more than Essex ever had on the continent, Norris received typical Tudor thanks, returning home sick and seriously in debt only to be ordered against his will to depart again, this time with orders to crush a rebellion now boiling in Ireland. He was all soldier, gruff and charmless, and though his mother helped to shield him from taking all the blame for disappointments that were not his fault, she was unable to make the queen enjoy his company.

Thanks in part to the queen's approval, thanks as well to the force of his own personality and to Burghley's ability to wait patiently for conditions to ripen to the advantage of his son, Essex found himself not only taking an active part in the council's deliberations but second only to Burghley himself among its members. An informal division of labor was established: the lord treasurer continued his customary dominance over domestic politics and matters financial, while Essex, not yet thirty, was able to take charge of military and foreign affairs. This arrangement created the impression, and certainly encouraged Essex to expect, that when Burghley passed from the scene (surely he could not last long now!) he would be succeeded by the earl as minister-in-chief. The situation was not without difficulty, but it put Essex at odds less with Burghley than with Elizabeth. Essex made himself the council's great champion of the continental Protestants and therefore of his friend Henry of France. Like Dudley before him, he wanted an English war on Spain and on Spain's friends in France. Elizabeth, however, not only wanted but needed reduced commitments—and much less military spending. Burghley must have been pleased to remain on the margins of this debate. As treasurer, he was obliged to struggle with an increasingly restless Parliament to find the hundreds of thousands—ultimately the millions—of pounds needed to sustain a conflict that had metastasized from the Netherlands into France and was now threatening to worsen the situation in Ireland as well. However strong his sympathy for the beleaguered Protestants across the Channel, however convinced he may have been that Spain was too dangerous a threat not to be confronted, the old man cannot have been displeased to see Essex become the object of the queen's displeasure.

Essex had been on the council less than a year when Henry IV brought France's religious wars to an abrupt end by the simple but shocking expedient of becoming a Roman Catholic. His Huguenot followers, along with the Puritans of England, were of course horrified at such an utterly cynical conversion—"Paris is worth a mass," Henry famously declared—but the Catholic League dissolved in confusion mixed with relief. Even the Spanish were at first baffled. Soon the Spanish army was gone from Brittany, its presence there having been rendered pointless, and England was able to withdraw all its troops from the continent except for the small force supporting Maurice of Nassau in the seven Dutch provinces that he now controlled. There could be no general peace, however, so long as England remained engaged in the Low Countries. The relationship between England and Spain deteriorated further as Philip awoke to the possibility of repaying the English for the trouble they had caused him in the Netherlands by making similar trouble in Ireland. The limitations of religion as a determining factor in international relations were demonstrated afresh when Henry IV, securely in command in France as a result of his conversion, declared war on Spain and allied himself with England (thereby allying himself as well, if a bit obliquely, with the Dutch Protestants).

It was time once again for direct action against the Spanish homeland, which meant naval action, and Essex of course insisted on a prominent part. By 1596 he had been at home for several years and had been sharing power with Burghley for two. He was restless, satisfied neither that he was being adequately rewarded for his services nor that his abilities were being put to full use. The idealist in him had always found the artificial life of the court to be faintly contemptible, especially under an aged queen who persisted in wearing low-cut gowns, demanded to be wooed, and expected every man at court to pretend that she was still as fresh and desirable as a girl of twenty. What was real by Essex's romantically aristocratic code, what required genuine courage and sacrifice and provided a true test of a man's worth, was *war*. And England was in need of heroes: nearly a decade had passed since the death of Philip Sidney, and no comparably chivalrous figure had arisen to take his place. (Essex would have said he had not yet had a chance to do so.) In 1595 those old salts Drake and Hawkins had died on a wretchedly unsuccessful last voyage to the West Indies, where improved Spanish defenses had made their tactics obsolete. The time was ripe for new exploits and new men, and Essex set out to provide both. He partnered with Howard of Effingham, the admiral of what there was of an English navy, and Francis Vere, who had long and successfully commanded the queen's forces in the Netherlands, to find investors for an assault on the Spanish port city of Cádiz. Getting the queen's approval was difficult as usual, but when the assault force set out at the beginning of June it was formidable: more than a hundred ships carrying twenty thousand men. Howard commanded the fleet and Essex the troops, with Vere and Ralegh in prominent positions. (For all his faults, Essex was not petty or mean-spirited. Upon getting the upper hand in his long rivalry with Ralegh he had become generous, even serving as godfather to Sir Walter's son.) The Cádiz expedition turned out to be a stupendous success, one of the greatest achieved by either side in the course of this long and generally sterile war. The defenders were taken by surprise, some three dozen ships including several of Spain's finest fighting galleons were captured or destroyed, and to the profound humiliation of the Spanish Crown, Cádiz itself was occupied. Essex achieved his dream of becoming a national hero, leading the assault and putting the Spanish to flight. He wanted to fortify the city and make it a base from which to prey on the enemy's coast and shipping, and perhaps attack inland as well, but was overruled by Howard and the other leaders. They set Cádiz ablaze and sailed home in triumph, only to find upon arrival that Elizabeth was unhappy because so much Spanish cargo had been destroyed rather than brought to England. (Her complaint was justified: the English had carelessly given the Spanish admiral an opportunity to burn his ships rather than handing them over.) Essex was further chagrined to learn that in his absence Robert Cecil had been appointed secretary. Essex himself had no interest in the position; a less suitable appointment for a man of his restless temperament could hardly be imagined. But he was intensely jealous of the Cecils now, and in his quixotic fashion he had somehow decided that he was honor bound to deliver the job to William Davison, who had lost his place in the administration (as well as being sent to the Tower) when Elizabeth used him as a scapegoat, pretending that he was responsible for the execution of Mary, Queen of Scots. Her choice of Robert Cecil seemed to Essex both a gratuitous rebuke and confirmation that Lord Burghley was so committed to his son's advancement that he had to be considered a rival, even an enemy. As with his Normandy expedition of 1591, from which he had returned to find the younger Cecil seated on the Privy Council, Essex felt that he had gone abroad to perform services of real value only to see the finest rewards in the queen's gift bestowed upon the paper-shuffling time-servers at court. Something like paranoia began to fester in his mind and spirit. With each new slight or perceived slight his suspicions would grow more pronounced, generating helpless fury, for example, when Howard of Effingham was made Earl of Nottingham, placed above Essex in the hierarchy of nobility, and given sole credit (or so it seemed to Essex) for the success of the Cádiz venture.

That autumn, in an effort to take revenge for the destruction of Cádiz, Philip II sent another Armada to pillage the English coast. Even more quickly than its predecessor, this new fleet was dispersed by storms, so that once again it was England's turn to strike a blow. Essex, who had by this time stopped sulking and secured his own appointment as master of ordnance, began preparations for an expedition to be modeled on, but strategically more ambitious than, Cádiz. The original plan was to attack the Spanish port of Ferrol, where many of the ships involved in the abortive 1596 attack were known to have put in for refitting, garrison it as a permanent foothold on the Spanish mainland, and then proceed westward to the Azores for the purpose of intercepting that summer's treasure fleet from America. This time, however, nothing went smoothly. When Essex set sail in July he ran into viciously foul weather and had to return home. By the time he could set out again his army had been savaged by plague, so reduced in numbers that attacking a target as formidable as Ferrol was out of the question. Probably the entire enterprise should have been abandoned, but the fleet was manned and equipped, there remained every reason for confidence that the Spanish treasure convoy could be found and taken, and Essex badly needed a return on all the money he had invested not only in this venture but in the previous year's as well. So the flotilla charted a course for the Azores, where angry disagreements broke out between the earl and his vice-admiral, Ralegh, and the Spanish treasure ships managed to slip into the port of Terceira just hours ahead of the English. By the time Essex gave up hope of accomplishing anything and was making his empty-handed way home, the Spanish ships at Ferrol had completed their refitting and put to sea under orders to do to the English port of Falmouth what the English had done to Cádiz. With Essex still too far away to intercept them, the Spaniards faced almost no opposition. But once again Philip's plans were undone by storms that scattered those of his ships that did not sink and sent them struggling back toward home.

It had been a near thing all the same, and it put a scare into the English court. The fact that Essex's expedition had left the Spanish fleet not only intact but free to move unopposed against England increased Elizabeth's disgust at the failure of what would come to be called derisively, as though it had been a holiday excursion, Essex's "island voyage."

In the following year, 1598, Henry IV decided that he had had enough of a war that was bankrupting France and bringing severe hardship to many of her people. (The Dutch rebels, he observed sourly, could not expect all of northern Europe to be "miserable in perpetuity" for their sake.) Elizabeth was not pleased with his change of heart, troubled no doubt by the old fear that an end to hostilities could lead to an alliance between the Catholic powers. She decided to send an embassy to France in an attempt to change the king's mind, and it is rather surprising that her choice to head this mission was not Essex, an old friend of the French king's, but her secretary Robert Cecil. Possibly this was a measure of her displeasure with the earl after the disappointment of his Azores venture; just as possibly, she remained unwilling to allow her favorite to absent himself from court for months yet again. Essex for his part was undoubtedly mindful that he could ill afford to set forth on new adventures while leaving his enemies at court.

A deal was worked out: Essex agreed to take on the duties of secretary while Cecil was out of the country and pledged not to use the office for the benefit of himself and his friends or to the disadvantage of Burghley (who was in failing health and no longer much at court), Cecil, or any of their faction. During two months on the continent Cecil saw firsthand how severely war had ravaged northern France and how hungry the French were for peace. He saw, too, that the king was determined to make peace and abandoned the idea of changing his mind. Cecil found himself inclined to agree with the king; the status quo was difficult for England as well as for France, and he, unlike Essex, was prepared to let go the dream of destroying Spanish power on its home ground. He returned home in April to find that Essex had not only kept his word to make no mischief but had—much to the surprise of his detractors—done a competent job of managing the queen's affairs. If this had been the great test of his ability to function responsibly and effectively at the highest levels of administration, he had passed with distinction.

Cecil's return, however, brought a revival of the old half-submerged tension between himself and Essex and the two camps whose leaders they were. The strength of the Cecil party lay in the unchallengeable authority of its patron Burghley, who had enjoyed the queen's confidence longer than most of the courtiers of 1598 had been alive. Thanks to Burghley, it enjoyed a decided advantage in terms of ability to bestow offices and incomes on its friends. Essex on the other hand attracted, more or less by default, those upon whom Burghley (and therefore the queen) had declined to bestow favors: alienated and disaffected nobles and gentleman-adventurers who hoped that when Burleigh died the tables could be turned. Ultimately it would all depend upon Elizabeth, of course. The people who allied themselves with Essex put their hope less in his aristocratic flair or his not-quite-stable brilliance than in the simple fact that even after years of turbulence the queen remained in some deep way powerfully attached to him. Whether he was Rob Dudley reborn for her, or a surrogate son, or proof that she could still win the adoration of the most sublimely elegant young nobleman in the kingdom—there was no need to speculate about such things so long as whatever it was that bound the queen to her last favorite remained intact.

The bond was fraying, however. A month after Cecil's return from France, the inevitable happened: France and Spain signed the Treaty of Vervins, by which Philip II formally acknowledged Henry IV as rightful king of France and ended hostilities against him. The pact compromised, if it did not violate outright, the terms of the existing understanding between France and England. It came as a keen disappointment to those Protestants (Essex being the most prominent) who regarded themselves as locked in a war to the death with Spain and had no qualms about allying themselves with a Catholic French king for the sake of victory. It also—with consequences that would prove more fateful for Essex than for anyone else at court—freed queen and council to give the Irish problem the attention that it now urgently required.

Ireland had been a problem for centuries, not least because of its way of absorbing the Englishmen sent to subdue it and gradually turning their descendants into Irishmen. But the problem took on new dimensions when England became Protestant and added a new system of religious belief to the political control it had long sought to impose on its neighbor island. Ironies proliferated. The Irish, who if anything had been less loyally Roman Catholic than the English over the centuries,

learned from the 1540s to associate the Reformation with foreign oppression and to resist it ferociously, simultaneously embracing the old
religion with a devotion they had not previously displayed. And at the
very time when England claimed to be fighting in the Netherlands to defend the religious liberty of the Protestants, it found itself trying to impose its church on Ireland by main force. The Netherlands revolt had
been England's one great opportunity to threaten and torment Philip of
Spain, and Elizabeth's government had seized the opportunity. In the
1590s Ireland was Philip's best chance to play tit for tat, and though he
was perhaps slow to awaken to the possibilities, by 1598 he had done so.

At the end of June 1598 Elizabeth met with her councilors to discuss
the worsening of the English position in Ireland. Hugh O'Neill, Earl of
Tyrone, was mounting a rebellion bigger and better organized than
anything the Irish had previously managed, and, poor worn-out John
Norris having died on active service, the council was going to have to
dispatch a new commander to restore order. When the queen suggested
William Knollys, Essex's uncle, the earl interpreted this as an attempt to
weaken his position at court by removing one of his supporters. In reply,
no doubt in an arrogant and even disdainful tone, he proposed a member of the Cecil party. When the queen dismissed this suggestion as
ridiculous, a shocking scene unfolded. Essex turned his back on Elizabeth, an unthinkable breach of etiquette. Elizabeth stepped forward and
struck him across the head—hit him hard, apparently. Cecil then
clutched at the hilt of his sword, but regained control of himself before
doing anything more. He stormed out proclaiming that he would accept
no such insult from anyone, possibly even saying (historians have been
understandably hesitant to believe that even he was capable of such
words) that Elizabeth was "as crooked in her disposition as in her car-
cass." The witnesses must have looked on in stunned silence.

During the month that followed, while queen and council struggled
with the Irish problem, Essex stayed away from court in a deep, self-
destructive sulk. He was needed both as the council's acknowledged
military authority and in his capacity as master of ordnance, but he continued to ignore even summonses from the queen herself. Finally he
won the test of wills: Elizabeth appointed him earl marshal, which
salved his delicate ego by putting him once again above the Earl of Nottingham in order of precedence, and when she heard that he was ill she

dispatched her own physician. At last, like an indulged child, Essex was drawn back to court with flattery and favors—but not until, and largely because, an English army had been ambushed and massacred at Yellow Ford in the north of Ireland. That happened on August 14. Ten days earlier Burghley had died. Essex returned to court to find that he, and therefore the men whose patron he was, had missed out on the great redistribution of offices and honors that the lord treasurer's death had occasioned. The discovery heightened his already poisonous sense of alienation and grievance.

At this point Essex fell into a trap that may or may not have been of his own making. In the wake of the disaster of Yellow Ford, where half the English army had been left dead on the field, Tyrone and his rebels controlled nearly all of Ireland. Unless England decided to give up the fight—but that was unthinkable—*somebody* was going to have to take a new and bigger army across the Irish Sea. There could hardly have been a more dangerous assignment—Ireland was a notorious graveyard for English reputations and fortunes, those of Essex's own father included—and Essex knew that his departure would leave Cecil in control of almost everything, including access to the queen.

But he was England's leading living soldier, or regarded himself as such and was so regarded by many others, and no one in the kingdom had a stronger sense of noblesse oblige. If his queen needed him, he could not do other than serve. Hardly foolish enough to want the job, in effect he talked himself into it by finding every other candidate unacceptable. Whether Cecil and the earl's other rivals were nudging him on, and were doing so for the purpose of destroying him, it is impossible to say. By early spring 1599 thousands of troops had been sent to Ireland, but they still had no commander. What was perhaps inevitable happened on April 12: Essex was commissioned to depart for Ireland, not as a mere lord deputy but with the grander title of lord lieutenant, and there take command.

His fate was sealed.

A DIAMOND OF ENGLAND

EARLY ONE SUNDAY MORNING IN JULY 1581 A MAN NAMED
George Eliot, who had once gone to prison for rape and homicide but
was released by the queen's government to take up a commission as
hunter of priests, arrived on horseback at the gates of a country house
called Lyford Grange some miles south of Oxford. It was a casual visit, a
sort of fishing expedition prompted by the fact that Lyford Grange was
locally notorious as a center of underground Catholic activity, its owner
currently in a London prison for refusing to repudiate the bishop of
Rome. Eliot, earlier in his life, had been employed in Catholic house-
holds, even that of Thomas More's son-in-law. He had become adept at
pretending to be Catholic himself, acquiring a knowledge of papist practice and a network of Catholic acquaintances that was proving useful in
his new career. Happening to pass through the neighborhood on this
Sabbath day, he had thought it worthwhile to stop at Lyford Grange on
the off chance of snagging a fugitive priest.

Immediately upon arriving, Eliot began to suspect that something unusual might be afoot: a guard was on duty atop the house's watchtower,
and the gates leading to its courtyard were barred. He was received war-
ily at first, but when he called up that he had come to see the cook and
asked for him by name, the guard left his post to fetch him. The cook,
who had once worked with Eliot and believed him to be Catholic, welcomed him warmly and ushered him inside. Eliot and his assistant were
given ale and invited to stay for a meal. With the assistant remaining behind in the kitchen, Eliot was led through several rooms to a large chamber where—no doubt to his delight—he found a mass in process before
a congregation of several dozen men and women, among them two
nuns in the habits of their order. When the service was concluded, a second priest went to the altar and began another mass. Eliot remained for
it, and for what must have seemed to him an interminable sermon on the

subject of "Jerusalem, Jerusalem, thou that killest the prophets." As soon as the mass was over, Eliot collected his assistant, gave thanks for the hospitality, said that he was now too late to remain to eat, and hurriedly departed. By early afternoon he was back with a force of armed and mounted men.

The house was searched all that day and into the night, and though many incriminating discoveries were made (rosaries and other forbidden religious objects, the habits out of which the nuns had changed upon learning of Eliot's return, even the wanted brother of Lyford Grange's owner), priests were not among them. The search resumed the following morning, but even stripping away paneling in a number of rooms failed to turn up anything more. The searchers, who had been reinforced the preceding night and now numbered about sixty (Lyford, obviously, was a sprawling and complicated structure), finally concluded that the priests must have been alarmed by Eliot's swift departure and made their escape before his return. Just as they were preparing to leave, however, Eliot's assistant noticed a tiny sliver of sunlight in a crack above a stairwell. Using a crowbar to pry an opening, he found not one or two but *three* priests lying side by side in a tight space along with a supply of food and drink. For Eliot it was a triumph, a bonanza. All the more so when it was established that among the three was the most notorious papist in all of England, a member of that alien and sinister new brotherhood known as the Jesuits, the infamous turncoat Edmund Campion. The following Saturday, his hands tied in front of him and his elbows behind and his feet bound under the belly of his horse, a sign bearing the words "CAMPION THE SEDITIOUS JESUIT" pinned to his hat, Eliot's prize was put on display in the crowded marketplaces of London. Then he was taken to the Tower and locked in the space known as the Little Ease, where there was no window and not enough room to stand erect or lie down at full length.

His capture was a coup for the government even more than for Eliot. Campion had been in England only a little more than a year, and during that time he had been only one of the dozens of priests moving in secret from one place to another. But his activities had made him an improbably prominent public figure, the most wanted man in the kingdom, an intolerable embarrassment for the government and its church. Not even Catholics could challenge the fact that, according to the statutes as they stood in the 1580s, Campion was guilty of high treason. Now that he was in custody, neither he nor anyone else could be in doubt about his fate: he was a doomed man. As for what exactly he and his fellow priests and the people who harbored them were guilty of, what kind of threat they actually posed—understanding that requires an examination not only of Campion's activities during the year before his capture and his conduct afterward, but of his life before he became an outlaw.

He was born into very ordinary circumstances, one of several children of a London bookseller, but his talents set him apart from an early age. He became a scholarship boy, his education financed by London's Worshipful Company of Grocers, and was still in his early teens when selected to deliver a Latin oration to Mary Tudor as she entered London for her coronation. He was sent to Oxford at age seventeen, rose with unusual speed to positions of prominence, and was a fellow and proctor when, at twenty-six, he was chosen to deliver a formal address before Queen Elizabeth during her visit to the university in 1566. The queen not only noticed Campion but singled him out for praise. Her church being in need of distinguished young candidates for advancement in the aftermath of the purging of the Marian hierarchy, this royal attention led to Campion's being offered the patronage of both William Cecil and Robert Dudley. He became Dudley's protégé—Dudley was chancellor of Oxford at the time—and was called upon to deliver orations on occasions of state and at events including Amy Robsart's funeral (which must have been an excruciatingly delicate affair for everyone involved). As part of his preparation for the great things that clearly lay ahead, Campion took holy orders as a deacon in the Anglican church in 1568. He must have been suspected of leaning in the direction of Rome, however, because as part of the government's reaction to the revolt of the northern earls and the pope's excommunication of Elizabeth he came under pressure to demonstrate his willingness to conform. Upon declining to do so he was repudiated by the Grocers Company and departed for Ireland, where he found influential patrons including the queen's deputy Sir Henry Sidney and his son Philip and hoped to become involved in the refounding of Dublin University. The stern measures enacted in England in response to the queen's excommunication—it was made high treason to "absolve or reconcile" anyone in accordance with the Roman rite, or to be absolved or reconciled—were soon extended to the parts of Ire-

land that England controlled. The authorities were ordered to arrest anyone suspected of being Catholic. Campion, though not yet a professed
Catholic, once again came under suspicion and found it advisable to
move on. He quietly returned to England for a time, then crossed the
Channel. He traveled to Douai, where he was received into the Catholic
Church and entered the college that William Allen had established three
years earlier for the education of English refugees seeking to become
priests. Lord Burghley, upon learning of Campion's conversion, lamented
the loss of "one of the diamonds of England."

There followed a decade of study and teaching. In three years at
Douai—where the discussion of current politics, incidentally, was absolutely forbidden—Campion taught rhetoric while adding a degree in
theology to his two Oxford diplomas. He then proceeded to Rome,
where he requested and was granted admission to the young, phenom-
enally fast-growing Society of Jesus, the Jesuits. The order naturally not
having a presence in England, he was assigned to its Austrian province.
After another six years of preparation in Moravia, Vienna, and Prague, he
was ordained a priest, and in 1580 he was called back to Rome to join
the faculty of the English seminary recently established there. It happened that at just this time the Jesuits were being asked to send priests
into England, to join those who year after year were crossing the Channel after graduating from Allen's seminaries and one after another were
being captured and killed. The Dutchman who was then general of the
Jesuits hesitated before agreeing. He feared (with good reason, as time
would prove) that even English members of a religious order about
which England's people knew nothing except its evil reputation among
Protestants would be all too easily depicted as aliens, subversives, and
traitors. That they would, having joined an order founded by the
Spaniard Ignatius Loyola, be entering an England whose government
was relentless in depicting Spain not only as the nation's arch-enemy but
as the principal agent of the Antichrist. And that they were therefore certain to be accused of having come on a political mission. Campion is
said to have shared these concerns, and at no point in his career had he
shown the smallest interest in anything more than a life of quiet scholarship. Nevertheless, when it was finally decided that Jesuits would be
going to England—the general's agreement was probably inevitable, it
having been part of Loyola's vision that his men should go wherever they

were most needed—Campion along with another product of Oxford, the thirty-four-year-old Robert Persons, was chosen to be the first.

Campion and Persons were given highly specific instructions. Their purpose, the "preservation and augmentation of the faith of Catholics in England," was to be accomplished through the delivery of the sacraments exclusively. They were not to attempt to convert Protestants or engage in disputation. As with Allen's seminary priests, they were forbidden to give attention to political questions, to send reports on the English political situation back to the continent, or to permit anything to be said against Elizabeth in their presence. Their experience was harrowing from the start. The government was on the lookout for Campion even before his arrival, its agents on the continent having learned of his assignment, and upon landing at Dover he was detained and taken to the mayor for questioning. At first the mayor seemed inclined to disbelieve his claim to be a traveling merchant and to send him to London in custody, but in the end, somehow, Campion was let go. He reconnected with Persons, was taken into the care of the Catholic underground, and was never again out of danger.

Campion was a brilliant rhetorician, a master of Latin and English composition. It was his writing that made him the most talked-about man in England and the living symbol of the old church, the hero of his cause and a monstrously seductive liar to the enemies of that cause. The first thing that he wrote after reaching England, a short piece dashed off in half an hour, was a message to the Privy Council. Campion and Persons both wrote such messages. They did so at the request of a lay member of the underground, solely for the purpose of leaving behind, as they moved out of London and began their travels, a statement of their purpose in England that could be made public if they were captured and had no opportunity to explain themselves before being killed. In his statement, Campion defends his adherence to the old faith and asserts that he and his fellow missionaries seek only to preach the gospel and deliver the sacraments to England's Catholics. He asks to be given a hearing before the masters of the universities (to consider his theology), the kingdom's high judges (where the subject would be the legality of his actions), and the Privy Council (for a defense of his loyalty to the queen). The man to whom Campion entrusted the message, instead of holding it for use in case of capture as instructed, made copies and sent them to others. Soon it was being reproduced and circulated everywhere. To its Catholic readers, long without leadership and treated as criminals, it was an inspiration. To the government it was a tissue of lies woven as a cover for conspiracy. Wherever copies were found they were destroyed. It became known by the name given by those who scorned it: "Campion's Brag."

Later, while traveling in the heavily Catholic north, Campion produced a longer statement in response to the Protestant pamphleteers who were, under government auspices, flooding England with condemnations of the church of Rome. He titled it *Decem Rationes,* because it sketched out ten reasons why he believed as he did. It was printed by Persons at a secret press in the Thames valley and given wide distribution: dignitaries arriving for Oxford University's commencement exercises in June 1581 were shocked to find copies on their chairs. The resulting hubbub made Campion the personification of Catholicism in England, his elimination a matter of urgency for the Burghley administration.

The government disgraced itself with its treatment of Campion after his capture. After some days in the Little Ease he was taken to Leicester House, where his onetime patron Dudley and other officials questioned him about his actions before and after coming to England. Having heard him out, they told him they could fault him for nothing beyond his acceptance of Rome. "Which is my greatest glory," Campion replied. He was offered not only his freedom but preferment in the Church of England if he would change his allegiance. Upon declining—one is reminded of Reginald Pole at the time of Henry VIII's divorce—he was returned to the Tower. At the end of July he was stretched on the rack (evidently his fingernails were also torn out), his examiners trying to make him confess that he had taken the immense sum of £30,000 to Ireland to support rebellion there. He was tortured still more savagely some three weeks later, just before being put on display in a series of so-called "conferences" at which senior members of the Anglican clergy presented their positions on various theological and ecclesiastical questions, invited him to respond, and repeatedly interrupted his attempts to do so. In spite of having been given no opportunity to prepare and being allowed neither books nor pen and paper nor even a table or chair, Campion was sufficiently effective in rebuttal, and public revulsion at his mistreatment was so strong, that a scheduled fifth session was abruptly called off and the conferences brought to an end. He was then given a third racking, saying later that he thought the man in charge, the sadist Richard Topcliffe, had intended to kill him. (Asked how he felt after Topcliffe had finished with him, Campion replied, "Not ill, because not at all.") Even three weeks later, when with other captured priests he was brought to court to face charges of high treason, he was unable to raise his right hand to take the required oath. One of his codefendants took his hand, kissed it, and elevated it for him.

The trial was more of the same, a travesty no less outrageous than the show trials of Henry VIII half a century before. Campion and others were charged with having conspired, at Rome and later at Reims, to murder the queen, encourage a foreign invasion, and incite rebellion in support of the invasion. It was easily established that some of the accused had never been in Rome or in Reims, and that some had never set eyes on each other before being brought together in court. Such facts counted for nothing, as did an absence of evidence that would have been laughable under less appalling circumstances. Campion conducted the defense in spite of his shattered health, and by all accounts he was once again impressive. He was helped by the fact that the Crown's witnesses were an unsavory crew of demonstrably bad moral character, and by the prosecution's inability to provide corroboration of transparently perjured testimony. Though some observers naïvely thought it inconceivable that such proceedings could possibly end in conviction, a finding of guilty was never less than inevitable.

"In condemning us you condemn all your own ancestors—all the ancient priests, bishops and kings—all that was once the glory of England, the island of saints and the most devoted child of the See of Peter," Campion told the court before he and the others were sentenced. "For what have we taught, however you may qualify it with the odious name of treason, that they did not uniformly teach?" When condemned to death he began to lead the others in singing the Te Deum, the old song of thanksgiving, and they continued to sing while being led away. He lay in chains and in darkness for eleven more days, at the end of which he was lashed to a hurdle and dragged through muddy streets to Tyburn. There, as the implements of butchery were being made ready, one of the members of the Privy Council who had turned out to witness the event suggested that Campion might best end his life by asking the queen's forgiveness.

"Wherein have I offended her?" Campion replied. "In this I am innocent. This is my last speech. In this give me credit—I have and do pray for her."

Lord Howard of Effingham, no doubt thinking of Mary, Queen of Scots, and suspecting that Campion was being as devious as all Jesuits were supposedly trained to be, asked him just what queen it was for whom he prayed.

"Yea," came the answer, "for Elizabeth your queen and my queen, unto whom I wish a long quiet reign with all prosperity."

With that the cart on which he stood was rolled away, and Campion fell to the end of the rope around his neck. In short order he was cut down, and the executioner, knife in hand, began the horrible part of his work. Throughout the four centuries since, the story of how Elizabeth and her government were ahead of their time in wishing for religious toleration, of how they would never have killed hundreds of priests if those priests had not persisted in seeking their destruction, has remained central to the mythology of the Tudor era. But Campion himself showed that story to be a fable. He did so at his own trial, pointing out that not only he but all the defendants, men whom the government supposedly believed had devoted their lives to the conquest of England by foreign powers and the killing of England's queen, had been offered full pardons in return for nothing more than attending Anglican services.

13

The Last Act

The England that the Earl of Essex left behind when he set out for Ireland bore all too little resemblance to the merry, prosperous, and even glamorous Renaissance kingdom that television and the movies persist in offering us as the glorious culmination of the Elizabethan age.

The country's economy was not only primitive by the standards of later times—that could go without saying—but provided most of its people with a lower standard of living than they had experienced not just in decades but in centuries. The royal treasury, which had never recovered from the profligate spending of Henry VIII, was chronically bare after a decade and a half of inconclusive and arguably unnecessary war. Five Parliaments had had to be called between 1586 and 1597 to vote the special subsidies (the double, triple, and even quadruple subsidies) without which the Crown's credit would have been ruined. Hundreds of thousands of pounds had been extracted from a church that no longer had anything approaching its pre-Reformation resources, and even all this was not nearly enough. Elizabeth and her council levied taxes whenever and wherever they thought it safe to do so, sold monopolies and licenses that gave special (not to say flagrantly unfair) advantage to a lucky few while burdening everyone else, and borrowed at home and abroad. As these measures too proved insufficient, attention turned to sale of the Crown lands that were the centerpiece of the queen's inheritance, assets that if husbanded could have ensured the security and autonomy of untold generations of her successors.

No one could remember a time when conditions had been so miserable for the population at large. The rise in taxes became particularly onerous as market conditions changed, reducing, for example, continental demand for English wool. This combined with the disruptive effects of war to increase unemployment and reduce incomes. Starting in 1594 there had been an unbroken sequence of wet summers leading first to crop failures, then to chronic and widespread hunger, and finally to rioting by the desperate poor and a savage response by frightened authorities. Prices of necessities soared, malnutrition increased the death rate, and the income of a common laborer had not bought so little since the mid-1300s.

The Tudor propaganda machine worked hard (underwriting and promoting the work of friendly poets and balladeers, for example) to keep the people mindful of how devoted their queen was to them and how much they presumably loved her. Her acts of charity, infrequent and niggardly as they generally were, were aggressively publicized. Behind the theatrics, however, there was ample reason for cynicism, and disillusion was widespread. The nobility became a minority as pampered as it was tiny and, by the meager standards of the day, fabulously wealthy. In 1534, at the dawn of the English Reformation, the average amount paid by holders of hereditary titles when Parliament voted a subsidy was £921, and fifteen nobles paid more than £1,000 each. The average declined to £487 by 1571 and would be down to £311 by 1601, when in all of England only one nobleman was assessed more than £1,000. This change—between Elizabeth's first Parliament and her last it amounted to a 38 percent drop—is especially striking in light of the 500 percent inflation experienced in England during the sixteenth century, and the increasing tax burden imposed on the rest of the population. Elizabeth's government remained fearful enough of the landowning magnates to be unwilling to risk offending them even when the Crown's need for revenue was urgent.

Subjects lacking the ability to retaliate when aggrieved, on the other hand, could count themselves fortunate if they were merely ignored. By the 1590s a long generation had passed since Queen Mary's brief restoration of the old religion, decades of officially prescribed preaching had persuaded increasing numbers of churchgoers that to be Catholic was to be pro-Spanish and therefore disloyal, and the fear of Catholic resistance with which Elizabeth had begun her reign was no longer necessary. A statute passed in 1593 took religious repression in new directions, forbidding Catholics to travel more than five miles from their homes and making exile the penalty for failure to pay the ruinous fines imposed on recusants—those refusing to attend Church of England services. There was some easing of pressure between 1595 and 1598, when England was allied with France in opposition to Spain. When Henry IV of France issued the Edict of Nantes, with its broad grant of freedom to the Huguenots, English Catholics briefly hoped for similar treatment by their government. Exactly the opposite happened, however: the government resumed the aggressive hunting down, torture, and killing of priests and the harsh punishment of anyone who harbored them. The regime was sufficiently secure by this point to be able also to complete its expulsion of militant Puritans from the established church and the destruction of Presbyterianism as an open expression of Puritan belief.

Elizabeth herself, from her position at the privileged center of a national network of misery and exclusion, continued to bend the economic, religious, and political life of the whole kingdom to whatever shapes seemed best suited to ensure her own safety. Approaching seventy now, she had already lived much longer than any other member of the dynasty and was still in good enough health to ride ten miles. At close range, however, she was a wretched approximation of Gloriana, the Virgin Queen celebrated in the poetry of the likes of Edmund Spenser and Philip Sidney. Even as a young woman she had been comically, almost childishly insecure about her appearance and desperately needful of praise. (At thirty, upon being told that Mary Stuart was taller than herself, she had exclaimed in jealous triumph that the queen of Scots was therefore obviously "too high—I myself am neither too high nor too low!") Forty years later foreign visitors were writing home of their encounters with a haggard crone, her wig off center and her face a stiff white mask of makeup, who persisted in dressing like a young woman, had lost so many teeth that she was impossible to understand when she spoke rapidly, but remained so hungry for flattery that when it was not offered freely she would call herself an old and foolish woman and wait eagerly to be contradicted. Insiders described the experience of serving an evil-tempered harridan, a thrower of shoes who could bear no signs of independence in the people around her. It took two hours of preparation every morning, the ladies attending the queen noted, before she was in a condition to be seen outside the privy chamber. Before receiving visitors she would stuff a perfume-soaked handkerchief into her mouth in the hope of taming her breath.

Four decades of painstakingly building and maintaining a theatrically regal persona, of projecting a manufactured image across not only her kingdom but all of Europe in order to compensate for being a female monarch in a world ruled by men, had reduced Elizabeth to the tiresome shabbiness of a trouper whose prime was long past. The show went on—her wardrobe at the end included 102 French gowns, 67 "round" gowns (dresses not opening in the front), 100 loose gowns, 126 kirtles or skirts, 96 cloaks, and more than two dozen fans—but it no longer carried much conviction. The audience, no longer impressed, was looking forward to the next act whatever it might turn out to be. The queen herself, however, not only showed no interest in removing herself from center stage but forbade her councilors to so much as raise the question of what, or who, might follow her final bow.

Throughout her reign Elizabeth had been careful to maintain her own authority by balancing faction against faction, party against party, at court and in council. Thus she had prevented any one group (William Cecil's circle, for example, or even that of Robert Dudley) from becoming dominant. Now, however, she appeared to have lost the energy for such calculations, or to have ceased to find them necessary. She was allowing her world to grow narrower; only eleven men remained on the Privy Council by 1597, all of them either aged associates of long standing or the sons of personages from the early days of the reign. Virtually all authority over the setting and execution of policy had been gathered into the hands of the Cecils. Perhaps she was satisfied that Robert Cecil, the careful and hardworking little son of Lord Burghley, was too much the bureaucrat ever to dare to threaten her authority, never mind her survival. No doubt she was confident that she had in him a chief of staff who, if even more attentive to the filling of his own pockets than his father had been, could be depended upon to manage the affairs of the Crown with sufficient care to free her of the burden of having to pay close and sustained attention. Elizabeth had never been willing to sacrifice for the sake of any grander goal than simply keeping herself on the throne, and Cecil was perfectly suited to making sure that she could do that with minimal difficulty. That she had little interest—no discernible interest at all, really—in what would happen to England's government or people after her passing became all too apparent as old age settled upon her. It was obvious in her willingness to sell off the assets of the Crown. It was even clearer in her failure to make a will or otherwise prepare for a transfer of power after her death, her refusal even in her final decline to so much as suggest whom she wished to succeed her.

This was the queen—irascible, distrustful, incorrigibly selfish—who sent the Earl of Essex off to Dublin. She sent him because she understood that an Ireland free of English domination could become a platform for her continental enemies. She understood too, however, that there was no money for another long war like the one that had still not ended in the Netherlands. She wanted, therefore, a quick and decisive victory, she wanted it on the cheap, and she was prepared to tolerate nothing less. Essex knew this from the start; his understanding of the queen's expectations, and of her certain reaction if those expectations were not met, is the only possible explanation for his later behavior. He was certainly capable of understanding that in taking on the Irish mission he was putting himself at mortal risk, and it was not paranoid of him to suspect that his rivals at court rejoiced to think that in going to Ireland he was embracing his own destruction. But by 1599 his situation was so bad as to justify desperate measures. Every mark of favor that the queen had bestowed on Burghley and then Cecil—putting them into the most powerful and lucrative positions, allowing them to share the royal bounty with their friends and supporters—had been another nail in the coffin of Essex's aspirations, another affront to his sense of entitlement. By 1599 he was the leader less of a faction on the Privy Council than of a gang made up largely of outsiders and misfits—men who shared his sense of being unfairly excluded and were therefore more disposed than they otherwise might have been to resent the status quo and seek opportunities to challenge it. He still had friends and family connections at court, but he consistently failed in his efforts to boost their careers. He tried repeatedly to win the office of attorney-general for his cousin Francis Bacon, for example, but never came close to succeeding.

It was long customary to interpret what happened to Essex in Ireland as the necessary consequence of arrogance, incompetence, and sheer foolishness. Such a verdict, however, is more easily delivered than defended. The earl encountered daunting obstacles almost from the day of his arrival in Dublin, and his conduct remained rational even as the pressures on him mounted. The Ireland that he entered was, and long had been, a cesspit of ethnic and religious hatred. Attitudes and behaviors that would endure for half a millennium were already in place: the English, seen inevitably as invaders and oppressors, regarded the Irish as not only uncivilized but barely human. The Reformation's success in England became a reason for its rejection by Ireland, giving both sides rich new reasons to despise each other. Rebellions had been brutally crushed in the 1570s and 1580s (at the same time that Essex's father, Walter Devereux, was coming to ruin with his failed effort to establish English settlements), only to be followed by the much bigger, better organized rising led by the charismatic, tactically adroit Hugh O'Neill, Earl of Tyrone. Tyrone's bloody victory at Yellow Ford had caused Irishmen to think that it might be possible to expel the English altogether.

By the time of Essex's arrival, Tyrone had under his command a larger, better-equipped and -led, more modern rebel force than any the English had ever encountered in Ireland. Essex for his part commanded the largest English army ever sent there: sixteen thousand foot soldiers and thirteen hundred horse. Nevertheless, the council responsible for the management of the English "pale" centered on Dublin, upon meeting with the new lord lieutenant, advised him that conditions were not yet right for a direct attack. Essex, seeing that he possessed neither the ships nor the draft horses that an offensive against Tyrone would require—the geography was such that in order to engage the Irish he would have to move his troops by water—wrote to the queen to request more of both. While waiting for a reply he moved part of his force through the northern counties of Munster and Leinster to relieve besieged garrisons, establish new ones, and so secure his rear against a rumored Spanish landing. (This move is sometimes characterized as a flagrant act of disobedience on Essex's part, but in fact he had requested and received permission for it before leaving England.) As time passed and Essex received little of what he had asked, he and the queen began an acrimonious exchange of letters. The earl's requests became complaints, and Elizabeth responded with angry demands that he get on with his assignment and stop squandering her money. Almost certainly it was the sharpness of the queen's words that caused Essex to launch an offensive that she would regard as too little too late and that he believed to be premature; he undertook it only because to refuse would be to risk recall and a disgrace from which there might be no recovery. And so in September, with the problematic weather of autumn beginning, he took his available troops, by now greatly reduced in number, northward into Ulster in search of Tyrone. The only alternative would have been to suspend operations until the end of winter, and it was inconceivable that Elizabeth would accept such a delay. (Maintaining Essex's army had cost £300,000 in the five months since his arrival in Ireland.) In the end he was unable to bring the rebels to battle. Instead he had to settle for a parley at a river crossing; the unarmed Tyrone sat on a horse that was belly-deep in midstream while Essex stood on the bank and the two talked for half an hour. They agreed on a truce, the details of which hardly matter because a furious Elizabeth repudiated the agreement as soon as she was informed of it. She sent off an order for Essex to remain where he was pending further instructions.

At this point, no doubt because he thought that Elizabeth's rejection of his truce meant that she had given up on him, something snapped in Essex. He lost control of himself and his destiny. Fear of the queen's wrath, certainty that Cecil and others must be encouraging the queen to be wrathful, news that in his absence Cecil had been given the lucrative mastership of wards that he himself had badly wanted—perhaps all these things together drove the earl to decide that unless he seized the initiative he was lost. He had already been talking recklessly of taking his army back across the Irish Sea to Wales and advancing from there to London and a showdown with the rivals who—or so he told himself—had gained control of the queen and needed only to destroy him in order to ensure their mastery of the kingdom. Such an undertaking would have been as difficult as dangerous, however, and Essex put it aside in favor of a headlong dash back to court and the mistress who had so often forgiven him in the past. He must have hoped that if he could see Elizabeth, talk with her and explain himself, all would be well.

And so on September 24 he sailed back from Ireland accompanied by only a small party of companions. Once across, he began the long, hard gallop across Wales, the marches, and the midlands to where the queen and court were gathered at Nonsuch Palace, the massive folly begun so many years before by Henry VIII. He arrived, having left a long string of spent horses in his wake, on the morning of September 28. Still filthy from what under happier circumstances might have been considered an epically heroic ride, he burst into the queen's privy chamber and found her neither dressed nor bewigged. She induced him to leave, promising that they could meet again an hour later, when both had had an opportunity to compose themselves. The day became a sequence of meetings in which Essex talked first with the queen, then with the queen and members of the council, finally with his fellow councilors only. Thus Elizabeth gradually extracted herself from a situation that she must have found intensely uncomfortable, leaving it to Cecil and others to question Essex about the conduct of his campaign in Ireland and the meaning of his disobedience.

The day ended with the earl under arrest and sinking into a state of physical and emotional collapse from which he would never entirely recover. Preparations were put in motion to try him for treason, but they were suspended when he became so ill that (much to Elizabeth's annoyance) his admirers had church bells rung in anticipatory mourning. His recovery was followed by a renewal of planning for a trial, but this time Essex saved himself by sending the queen a letter sufficiently submissive and repentant to drain off the worst of her fury. After a thirteen-hour hearing at which Essex found the strength to mount an eloquent defense against numerous charges of misconduct—a defense that inspired his followers and increased the popularity that the Cecil party found so threatening—he was "sequestered" from all his offices, meaning that until further notice he could neither perform their duties nor draw income from them. He was returned to house arrest under restraints that were gradually relaxed until at last, in August, his liberty was restored.

He had, by the narrowest of margins, been spared permanent imprisonment or worse. But he had not emerged undamaged. Indeed he was, in almost every sense, mortally wounded: his health shattered, his nerves in disarray, his political career at a dead end, and his financial position nearly hopeless. The conditions under which he was freed included a prohibition against his appearing at court; this destroyed any possibility that he might charm his way back into the queen's good graces, and shows just how great a danger he seemed to the Cecil party.

Theoretically, the way remained open for Essex to retreat gracefully to a life of rural retirement, but in practical terms not even that was possible. Like his stepfather Dudley, he had incurred unmanageable debts in the service of the Crown. Being left at the mercy of his creditors would mean the lowest depths of humiliation not only for the earl himself but for his wife and their children.

Essex's only hope—literally his *last* hope—lay in the income generated by his monopoly on imports of sweet wines. This "concession" must have seemed like something very close to family property by 1600: it had originally belonged to Dudley, and after bestowing it on Essex in 1589 the queen had routinely renewed it in 1593 and 1597. It was up for renewal yet again in 1601, but this time the decision was in no way routine. It put into Elizabeth's hands the power to save her onetime favorite, whom she had in so many ways encouraged to expect so much, or to crush him utterly. Any inclination that the queen might have felt to allow Essex to withdraw into dignified failure would have been discouraged by Cecil himself. Cecil had long since arrived at the conclusion that the only plausible successor to the aging queen was James VI of Scotland, and he knew that Essex in his younger days had taken pains to cultivate a friendly long-distance relationship with James on the basis of their shared Protestantism. The possibility that as king of England James might rehabilitate the fallen earl was both real and, from Cecil's perspective, ominous.

The decision therefore was to show no mercy, and it brought the Essex story to a swift, dramatic, and pathetic close. The final chapter opened with the queen's refusal to renew the sweet-wine concession, which left the earl with no way of extracting himself from his financial predicament. His London residence, Essex House (it had been Leicester House when owned by Robert Dudley), was by this point a gathering place for all the malcontents and adventurers who had not won places for themselves at the Cecil court and found all routes to advancement blocked as a result. Like Essex himself, those men were easily persuaded that Robert Cecil and his cohorts were not only their enemies but, because of their unwillingness to keep the struggle against Spain at a fever pitch whatever the cost, the enemies of England and Elizabeth and the whole Protestant cause. They had no difficulty believing that the queen had become the prisoner and the tool of self-serving schemers, and that those who knew the truth had a duty to free her. Essex with his medieval-romantic code of honor was particularly vulnerable to being seduced by such thinking, especially now that he was cornered. He embraced the delusion that if he rose against the council, the people of London would rise with him.

Robert Cecil was aware that Essex House had become a hotbed of sedition (though the "Essexians" would have denied being guilty of any such thing), and he had infiltrated the place with his agents. He could have moved early to arrest the ringleaders and scatter their followers, but that might not have been sufficient to ensure the earl's destruction. He waited until February 8, 1601, more than three months after the termination of Essex's monopoly, before sending a delegation of Privy Council members with a summons for him to appear at court for questioning. Essex panicked. After making prisoners of his visitors—itself an outrageous act, considering their eminence—he rallied his followers and took to the streets, proclaiming his loyalty to the queen and declaring that he had been forced to take up arms because of a plot against his life. At no point was there the smallest possibility of his succeeding, and within a few hours he was under arrest. Thomas Cecil, himself Lord Burghley now that his father was dead, commanded the troops that rounded up Essex and his companions and was made a knight of the garter as his reward. (The first Lord Burghley would have regarded his whole career as justified if he had witnessed this triumph of his two sons—both of whom would become earls during the next reign, and both of whom have descendants who are marquesses today.)

Essex, at the end of a trial in which he responded to charges of treason with icy contempt, was found guilty and condemned to death. The situation remained explosive, however. A member of Essex's circle managed to burst in on the queen and demand that she grant the earl an audience; his reward was immediate execution. Essex remained so popular a hero, however, that the council ordered the preachers of London to denounce him from their pulpits. He was beheaded not at Tower Hill, where crowds of his admirers might have gathered, but in one of the Tower's interior courtyards, in the presence of only a few witnesses.

The end of Essex was in a real sense the end for Elizabeth as well. There would be no more favorites; Walter Ralegh, once Essex's chief rival for the queen's affection, was again at court but, perhaps because he was alive and Essex was not, he was no longer doted on by the queen. Elizabeth showed a marked aversion to almost everyone known to have played a part in bringing Essex to ruin or to have denounced him after his fall, telling the French ambassador that she knew she had a share in responsibility for his death. War continued in the Netherlands and in Ireland; though Essex's successor in Ireland was slowly getting the upper hand over Tyrone, he was doing so in ways that ensured perpetual Irish hatred. The costs continued to be nearly insupportable. A Parliament summoned in 1601 was asked to vote a quadruple subsidy, one twice as onerous as the double subsidies extracted from its two immediate predecessors. The news that a Spanish force had been landed in Ireland made it impossible for members to refuse. They did, however, mount an unprecedented challenge to Elizabeth's view of her prerogatives, demanding an end to the monopolies that she had long been either selling to the highest bidder or (as with Dudley and Essex and their wine concession) giving to those she wished to enrich at no direct cost to herself. These monopolies were a burden on the public and had a distorting effect on the economy, and when Parliament first complained of them in 1597 the queen had promised corrective action but done nothing. This time Commons was determined, and when the queen resisted it began work on a bill that would have taken the matter out of her hands and possibly precipitated a crisis. Faced with this defiance, Elizabeth delivered a speech in which she claimed to be surprised to learn that the monopolies had caused so much unhappiness. She committed herself to their elimination. This has often been represented as a victory for the queen, a climactic demonstration of her political skill. Such a verdict is mystifying. She avoided a showdown by surrendering, abandoned a cherished prerogative at the insistence of Parliament, and established no precedent that did her or her successors the slightest good.

In spite of Parliament's approval of unprecedented subsidies, the state of the treasury remained so alarming that the government was selling not only great expanses of Crown land but the queen's jewels. Revenues from the land sales totaled some £800,000 over the last two years of the reign, and even that did not save the government from remaining hundreds of thousands in debt. That much if not all of this land was sold for less than fair market value is suggested by the behavior of Robert Cecil. In 1601 and 1602 he became the leading speculator in the kingdom, using £30,000 of his own money to buy up as much as possible of the property being sold by the government he headed and borrowing heavily to buy still more. Meanwhile he had quietly taken up Essex's old lines of communication with James of Scotland, positioning himself for the next reign by making himself the mastermind behind a transfer of power that the queen had never approved.

Death, when it came, was an enigmatic affair. Elizabeth remained in excellent health through almost all of 1602, continuing to ride, to hunt, and even on occasion to dance. But in December an abrupt decline began, and by the time she moved to Richmond Palace the following month she needed help dismounting her horse and could not climb stairs without the help of a walking stick. Her hands began to swell so badly that the coronation ring she had never removed in four and a half decades had to be cut off. (A second ring, one given to her by Essex, remained.) By March she was feverish, chronically unable to sleep, and unwilling to take nourishment or allow her physicians to attend her. We have already observed her strange final days: the long hours spent standing in a kind of semi-trance, the days and nights on the floor with her finger in her mouth, the final removal to the deathbed when she lost the ability to resist. Though it was later claimed that in her final moments she signaled her wish to be succeeded by the king of Scotland, the people who said so were the very ones who had arranged things that way.

Her passing was not nearly as lamented as legend would have us believe. One wonders what her grandfather would have thought of the dynasty he had started at Bosworth, of what it had wrought and how it ended. One wonders too what her father would have thought. Whether he possibly could have cared.

An Epilogue in Two Parts

Τhe world, as is its way, got along perfectly well without the Tudors. England in particular—which is to say the thin but highly visible slice of the population that reaped the fruit of the Tudor revolution—did very well indeed, not least over the very long term. If it took two centuries to turn the descendants of looters and speculators into the ladies and gentlemen of Jane Austen's novels, for the lucky few the transformation process was as agreeable as it was prolonged. As for the mass of the people, their numbers, their poverty, and their power-lessness simply added to the comforts of the comfortable, providing a virtually limitless supply of desperately needy, all-but-free domestic and agricultural labor. Those unable to find work in the houses and fields of the gentlefolk would become the manpower—and womanpower and childpower—for the "dark Satanic mills" of the Industrial Revolution, which could never have proliferated as they did or been so staggeringly profitable without them. Those unable to do even that work would eventually populate the underworld described by Dickens in *Oliver Twist*.

The Tudor juggernaut left problems of ideology in its wake, but time dissolved most of them. First to go was the Catholic-Protestant split. When James VI of Scotland became James I of England, many of his subjects still retained an at least sentimental attachment to the old religion, and a considerable number took it more seriously than that. But before he had been king three years, the exposure of the Gunpowder

Plot—a plan by despairing and fanatically foolish Catholics to blow up the royal family and the entire Protestant establishment—quickly and permanently changed everything. Catholicism became indefensible, the long campaign to eradicate it accepted as not only justifiable but necessary. Anti-Catholicism became integral with British patriotism. (Catholics were long barred from the universities and from public office, and even today any member of the royal family who so much as married a Catholic would be removed from the line of succession.) Though the Catholic part of the population did not disappear entirely, it became tiny, peculiar, and politically irrelevant. The old religion became the hereditary foible of a minuscule minority of stubbornly eccentric noble and gentry families. Catholics continued to be persecuted, often with brutal harshness, but from now on the only religious differences that mattered would be among Protestants of various kinds.

Less easily settled was the conflict between the Tudor theory of kingship—Henry VIII's expansive view of the authority of the Crown—and the economic and political power that Henry's plundering of the church had bestowed upon a new landowning elite. When James and then his son Charles I persisted in claiming that they, like Henry, were accountable to God only, and when a Parliament now dominated by the gentry refused to agree, a showdown became almost inevitable. It came in the form of the years-long unpleasantness known as the English Civil War, the cutting off of King Charles's head, and Parliament's triumphal emergence as the most powerful institution in the kingdom. By the time all this was sorted out, England was beginning to assemble its global empire. It had begun its rise to a position of astounding preeminence in the family of nations.

Meanwhile the Tudors—not all the Tudors, but Henry VIII and Elizabeth—were not receding into the background as historical personages usually do. Instead they were showing themselves to be the two most durably vivid figures in the whole long saga of English royalty. Henry struck deep roots in the world's imagination as something more than, or at least other than, human, a kind of sacred monster: as pitiless as a viper, a killer not only of enemies but of the utterly innocent as well as of his own best servants and even his wives, but at the same time the magnificently manly centerpiece of Holbein's larger-than-life portraits. Though there was no way to deny his awfulness, throughout the

English-speaking (and Protestant) world it remained impossible to condemn him outright; to do so would be to bring into question the English
Reformation and—what continued to matter most—the legitimacy of
the people who now owned and governed the empire. No matter that
three-plus centuries of Plantagenet rule had produced any number of
stronger, braver, *better* kings. Henry had proclaimed himself greater
than any of them, bought agreement where he could and coerced it
when he had to, and resorted to murder if all else failed. What with one
thing and another, the story he told about himself stuck. Every king before him was a pale and shadowy figure by comparison, and no later
king ever rivaled his fame. The nature of that fame was deeply ambiguous, however, which is perhaps one reason why it continues to fascinate.
Henry remained both sacred (to his beneficiaries certainly, and to all
who regarded the Reformation as God's own work) *and* a monster. He
has held the world's interest in part because of the question of how such
a gifted and fortunate man could have committed such crimes. And because of the related, troubling question of how it is possible for such a
thoroughly vicious character to be so . . . *attractive.*

With Elizabeth things are both simpler and more complicated. She is
more understandable in ordinary human terms than her father, but at
the same time her personality is no less opaque; it is often impossible to
be confident that we know what she wanted, what she felt, or what (if
anything) she intended in making (or refusing to make) particular decisions. Her image has been much more fluid over the centuries than her
father's, and it is undergoing a profound change even now, more than
four centuries after her death. Her reputation certainly got off to a fast
start: upon becoming queen, she was exalted as the restorer and protector of true religion, and she was still a fairly young woman when the an-
niversary of her accession was made an official public holiday. But she
disappointed and even alienated many of her most ardent early supporters (the proto-Puritans, for example), and the whole last third of her
reign was a time of deepening general misery. By the end of her life
most of her subjects were pleased to have seen the last of her, and to
have what they regarded as the natural order restored in the person of a
male monarch. But the Stuarts in their turn proved a disappointment
too—a disappointment above all to the landowning gentry, whose
agents in the House of Commons were unwilling to tolerate Henrician

assertions of unlimited royal power. Praising Elizabeth, depicting her reign as England's golden age, became an effective if oblique way of cutting the Stuarts down to size. Her first biographer, William Camden, laid down the tracks along which Elizabethan historiography would run almost up to our own time. In volumes published first in Latin and then in English between 1615 and 1629, he depicted Elizabeth's reign as a half century of peace, prosperity, and true religion harmoniously achieved. It mattered little that the picture he painted could have been scarcely recognizable to anyone alive in England from 1559 to 1603. The figure of Elizabeth became sacred in its way, too, and thanks to the disregarding of certain inconvenient facts it was never nearly as dark as her father's. She became part saint and part goddess, the highest expression of what England was coming to see as its own quasi-sacred place in the world.

The pedestal on which she had been placed was given a vigorous shake in the nineteenth century by historical writers as esteemed (in their own time) as Macaulay and Froude, and by the better historian John Lingard, but it was too firmly planted to topple. To the contrary, these early challenges were followed by decades in which the study of Elizabethan England was dominated by scholars whose belief in the queen's greatness and the glory of her reign was little more qualified than Camden's had been three centuries before. Possibly in unconscious reaction to a decline in England's global stature, A. F. Pollard, A. L. Rowse, John Neale, and Conyers Read together erected a fortress of hagiography so formidable that for a time it must have seemed that there could never be anything more to say. Gloriana was not only greater than ever but evidently more secure in her greatness.

There is always something more to say when the subject is history, however; time passes and perspectives change. The chief vulnerability of the Pollard-Rowse-Neale-Conyers consensus was its close connection to the old Whig school of history, according to which everything that had happened was to be celebrated because all of it was part of the (divinely ordained?) process by which England had ascended inexorably to greatness. Membership in this school required believing that the English were fortunate—and had also always been grateful, most of them—to be rid of everything the Tudors had cast aside. Such a subjective judgment was by definition unprovable at best, and the work of a new generation of scholars has rendered it untenable. The cooling of ancient religious passions—the evolution of Britain into an essentially secular, post-Christian culture—has made a dispassionate examination of the past possible at last. The result has been—still is—a literally radical revaluation of Elizabeth, her reign, her times, and their meaning. One could cite many examples, but for present purposes one will stand in for all: Eamon Duffy's *The Stripping of the Altars.* This single book, since its first edition was published by Yale University Press in 1992, has made it impossible to responsibly assert that at the time of Henry VIII's revolution the English church was a decadent, moribund, obsolete, or obsolescent institution that had lost its central place in the everyday lives of the English people.

Elizabeth—and with her the whole Tudor story—looks very different today than she did half a century ago. She appears likely to change at least as much again when another twenty or fifty years have passed. The process is still at full flood. Whether or when it will end, whether and to what extent the popular image of the Tudors will be reshaped by all the fresh scholarship, we can only wait to see.

It is somehow impossible to resist ending on an admittedly minor note, by making a final visit to the amazing Dudleys.

Edmund Dudley had risen high in the reign of Henry VII only to be destroyed. His son John had risen even higher in the reign of Edward VI only to be destroyed also. One of John's sons was married to a queen of England (even if she was queen for only nine days), another had come close to marrying a much longer-lasting queen, but in the end it had all come to nothing. When we left them, the Dudleys appeared to have become extinct. The last of the line, Ambrose Dudley, Earl of Warwick, had a long marriage but no children. His brother Robert, Earl of Leicester—Elizabeth's beloved Rob—had died in 1588 and had been preceded to the grave by his little son Lord Denbigh, the only child of his late marriage to Lettice Knollys Devereux. (A very Dudleyesque footnote: Leicester had hoped to marry Denbigh to Arabella Stuart, a descendant of Henry VIII's sister Margaret. If James VI and I had died without children, Arabella Stuart would have had a strong claim to the English throne and the Dudleys might have had a *third* chance to become kings through marriage.)

But in fact the story was not over. In 1574, five years before the birth of Denbigh, Leicester had had a son with Lady Douglas Sheffield, a daughter of the queen's admiral Lord Howard of Effingham and therefore a royal cousin through the Boleyn connection. Lady Sheffield would later claim that she and Leicester had been married, but he would always deny this and she could produce no documentary evidence. (Possibly there had been a sham ceremony as part of an elaborate seduction scheme.) Leicester did, however, recognize the boy, whose name was Robert, as "my base son," enrolling him at Oxford as *filius comiti* or earl's son and providing for him in his will.

By the time of Elizabeth's death, this new Robert Dudley was in his late twenties and, having married very young, was the father of a family that would soon grow to include six daughters. He was a true Dudley—tall and handsome, skilled not only in handling horses and dogs and the sports of the aristocracy but at mathematics as well—who at age seventeen had been temporarily exiled from court for kissing the maid of honor who later became his wife. Shortly after Elizabeth died, taking her jealous resentment of any wives and offspring of the Earl of Leicester with her, Dudley asked the Court of the Star Chamber to affirm that his parents had in fact been married and that he was, therefore, rightful heir to the earldoms of Warwick and Leicester. Whatever the merits of his case (they have been in dispute ever since), a finding in Dudley's favor would have given rise to horrendous complications having to do with property already distributed to other heirs. (Among those other heirs were the Sidney family—Sir Philip Sidney, that most perfect of Elizabethan soldier-poet-courtiers, had a Dudley as his mother.) The court never ruled on Dudley's legitimacy or lack thereof, instead taking an easy way out by dismissing his suit on technical grounds, locking up the evidence, and forbidding him to pursue the matter further.

Dudley then requested and received King James's permission to go traveling. He departed for the continent, secretly taking with him his beautiful young cousin Elizabeth Southwell, who went disguised as a boy. In short order the pair reported from Lyon, France, that they had converted to Catholicism and married. It was one of the great scandals of the age.

Dudley and his bride proceeded to Florence, where he entered the service of the Medici grand dukes. His career there was long and distinguished: he became a respected authority on all things maritime—sailing to the New World, designing and building ships and harbors, writing books on navigation—while also developing a "curative powder" of some kind and receiving a patent for a silk-weaving machine. He and Elizabeth had half a dozen sons, a fresh crop of Dudleys but now named Carlo, Fernando, Cosmo, and the like. At that point we lose track of them. If there are still Dudleys in Italy today, it is easy to believe that they must be dashing figures, and having fabulous adventures.

Sources and Notes

Nothing could be easier, in connection with the Tudors, than the assembly of an impressively weighty bibliography. The available literature, even the fairly *recent* literature, is so vast as to bring the concept of infinity to mind. And few exercises could be of less real value to the general reader for whom this book is intended. What may have some value—at least in a book that is an attempt at synthesis, without any claim to plowing new ground in original source materials—is an indication of which works the author has found to be particularly useful.

As to source notes, to the extent that the facts of the Tudor story are knowable (many are not, and after more than four centuries it is unlikely that they ever will be) they have by now been sifted and settled by something like fifteen generations of scholars and writers. Many of the facts, often the most significant or just plain interesting, recur so frequently in the literature of the Tudor era that to give sources for them would (while requiring dozens of pages) be no less pointless than a comprehensive bibliography. The author of the current work has elected, therefore, to provide sources in particular cases only: for quotations that do not appear to have become widely familiar as a result of frequent previous use, and—what seems especially necessary—for those facts and opinions that are most likely to challenge the reader's preconceptions because they are most at variance with popular views of the Tudors. The resulting source notes appear below, along with citations of those books to which the author feels particularly indebted. Both things are arranged under headings corresponding to the four parts of this book.

In assembling and verifying the facts out of which his narrative has been constructed—dates and biographical details, for example—the author has relied heavily on one of the world's most awesomely comprehensive and authoritative resources: the sixty-volume 2004 edition of the *Oxford Dictionary of National Biography* (*DNB* in the notes below). Use has also been made of *The*

Encyclopaedia Britannica, and for the same reasons. Readers seeking to confirm statements of fact for which sources have not been provided, or to pursue additional information, are encouraged to begin by consulting those two works.

The Subject Overall

Studies dealing in depth with the reigns of all five Tudor monarchs have always been rare, at least in comparison to biographies of individual figures, and some of those that were once well known are now discredited and largely forgotten. Examples are the works of Macaulay and Froude, who survive as masters of style and of storytelling, but not of scholarship. An exception is the relevant part (volumes 4, 5, and 6) of John Lingard's *History of England* (New York: Publication Society of America, 1912). Though inevitably superseded in many details since it first appeared early in the nineteenth century, this remarkable work (pioneering in its use and sophisticated evaluation of original source material) remains a fruitful and broadly reliable guide to sixteenth-century England, rich both in facts and insights. Lingard is obscure today mainly because he has *always* been obscure. He was too far ahead of his time, replacing fable with fact more than a century before England was ready for so much objectivity.

Noteworthy among much more recent treatments of the whole dynasty are works by G. R. Elton, especially *England Under the Tudors* (Methuen, 1955) and *The Tudor Constitution* (Cambridge University Press, 1960); John Guy's *Tudor England* (Oxford, 1988); and Penry Williams's *The Tudor Regime* (Oxford, 1979). These are scholarly achievements of a very high order and immensely useful, though not well suited—or indeed intended—for a general audience.

PART ONE
A King Too Soon and a Queen Too Late

The author is grateful to have been able to make use of:

Erickson, Carrolly. *Bloody Mary: The Life of Mary Tudor.* Robson, 1995.

Loades, D. M. *Mary Tudor.* National Archives, 2006.

———. *Two Tudor Conspiracies.* Cambridge, 1965.

MacCulloch, Diarmaid. *Tudor Church Militant: Edward VI and the Protestant Reformation.* Penguin, 1999.

Skidmore, Chris. *Edward VI: The Lost King of England.* Weidenfeld & Nicolson, 2007.

Wilson, Derek. *The Uncrowned Kings of England: The Black Legend of the Dudleys.* Constable, no date given.

Notes

PAGE

20 *The main points of dispute were familiar* . . . : Religious divisions as of the start of Edward's reign are examined in MacCulloch, *Church Militant*, pp. 2 and 63; Skidmore, *Edward VI*, p. 7; and Mackie, *Earlier Tudors*, p. 426.

21 *This had become more true than ever* . . . : The difficulties faced by the more ambitious reformers late in Henry's reign are addressed in Smith, *Mask of Power*, pp. 147 and 159, and Mackie, *Earlier Tudors*, p. 429.

21 *Even if they had been left free to express* . . . : MacCulloch, *Church Militant*, p. 59.

27 *Surrey, whose hopes for a military career* . . . : Mackie, *Earlier Tudors*, p. 420.

27 *They ensnared Gardiner in a clumsy* . . . : Scarisbrick, *Henry VIII*, p. 490.

28 *It was by no means clear that the jury* . . . : Mackie, *Earlier Tudors*, p. 422.

28 *Thereafter Norfolk, in an effort* . . . : *DNB* entry on Thomas Howard, third Duke of Norfolk.

29 *So was anyone too closely* . . . : Henry's rejection and distrust of Gardiner is in Erickson, *Great Harry*, p. 371.

29 *It is not certain that this was a usurpation* . . . : Lingard, *History of England*, p. 5:235.

30 *He was given four manors* . . . : *DNB* entry for Edward Seymour, Duke of Somerset.

31 *Overall this splendid payday* . . . : Guy, *Tudor England*, p. 199.

32 *He also empowered himself to assemble* . . . : Skidmore, *Edward VI*, p. 66.

33 *Edward was a lad of above-average intelligence* . . . : Skidmore, *Edward VI*, p. 62, and Lingard, *History of England*, p. 5:237.

34 *"Peace and concord" were promised* . . . : Skidmore, *Edward VI*, p. 61.

34 *It was, "as God's viceregent and Christ's vicar* . . .*"*: Lingard, *History of England*, p. 5:238.

35   *It is more pathetic than impressive* . . . : Skidmore, *Edward VI*, p. 149.

35   *The coronation of the new king* . . . : MacCulloch, *Church Militant*, p. 126, and Skidmore, *Edward VI*, p. 69.

36   *Even more provocatively, the visitors* . . . : Lingard, *History of England*, p. 5:251; MacCulloch, *Church Militant*, p. 70; and Skidmore, *Edward VI*, p. 89.

44   *In the six years following Henry VIII's death* . . . : The numbers in this paragraph are from Guy, *Tudor England*, p. 203.

44   *Statistical precision is impossible* . . . : Ibid., p. 204.

45   *According to various reports he set his sights* . . . : Skidmore, *Edward VI*, p. 71.

46   *At Seymour's direction, Edward wrote a letter* . . . : *DNB* entry for Thomas Seymour.

49   *Gardiner, accused of disobeying his instructions* . . . : Lingard, *History of England*, p. 5:264.

49   *The number of bishops who followed* . . . : Mackie, *Earlier Tudors*, p. 518.

50   *It would also explain his fumbling* . . . : Skidmore, *Edward VI*, p. 113, and Roger Turvey and Nigel Heard, *Edward VI and Mary* (Hodder Murray, 2006), p. 48.

50   *Though they accomplished little or nothing* . . . : Skidmore, *Edward VI*, p. 91.

53   *None of which might have mattered* . . . : Lingard, *History of England*, p. 5:285.

53   *In Devon in the far west* . . . : MacCulloch, *Church Militant*, pp. 43 and 119, and Guy, *Tudor England*, p. 208.

54   *As many as four thousand men were dead* . . . : Lingard, *History of England*, p. 5:289.

55   *An extraordinary figure named Robert Kett* . . . : The demands are in Turvey and Heard, *Edward and Mary*, p. 135; Kett's words are in Lingard, *History of England*, p. 5:290.

55   *With one proclamation he condemned destruction* . . . : Skidmore, *Edward VI*, p. 113.

56   *When Somerset cried out* . . . : The duke's concessions to the rebels are in ibid., p. 45.

59   *And so Dudley advanced on Norwich* . . . : Lingard, *History of England*, p. 5:290.

59   *After first and briefly allying himself* . . . : MacCulloch, *Church Militant*, p. 95.

61   *The conservatives were required to absorb* . . . : Lingard, *History of England*, p. 5:342.

69   *Francis van der Delft, the Catholic* . . . : Skidmore, *Edward VI*, p. 162.

69   *The narrowness of its base is suggested* . . . : MacCulloch, *Church Militant*, p. 163.

70   *He achieved perhaps the greatest triumph* . . . : Elton, *Tudor Constitution*, p. 396.

70   *Harsh penalties were imposed* . . . : MacCulloch, *Church Militant*, p. 141, and Lingard, *History of England*, p. 5:342.

70   *Once again it was made treason to deny* . . . : Skidmore, *Edward VI*, p. 82.

70   *Henceforth the death penalty could be imposed* . . . : Ibid.

70   *Seven of Henry's bishops were replaced . . .*: MacCulloch, *Church Militant*, pp. 96 and 154.

73   *He had never been an impressive physical specimen . . .*: Skidmore, *Edward VI*, p. 240.

76   *In the first, a draft in Edward's own hand . . .*: Ibid., p. 247, and Lingard, *History of England*, p. 5:357.

78   *Two days later, in reporting to the Privy Council . . .*: Lingard, *History of England*, p. 5:358.

79   *"He has not the strength to stir . . ."*: Skidmore, *Edward VI*, p. 255.

80   *He died in the arms of a Dudley son-in-law . . .*: Wilson, *Uncrowned Kings*, p. 226.

81   *The crown, Jane declared . . .*: *DNB* entry for Jane Grey.

83   *When Mary sent a messenger to the council . . .*: Mackie, *Earlier Tudors*, p. 527.

85   *Quite the contrary: the French ambassador . . .*: Loades, *Mary Tudor*, p. 26.

87   *She said disingenuously . . .*: Loades, *Elizabeth I*, p. 28.

88   *One of the most poignant scenes . . .*: Erickson, *Bloody Mary*, p. 118.

88   *When Parliament's passage . . .*: Loades, *Mary Tudor*, p. 41.

89   *Nothing came of this . . .*: This and "grief and despair" are in the *DNB* entry for Mary I.

90   *She wrote directly to the king . . .*: Loades, *Mary Tudor*, p. 47.

90   *Therefore, though he removed members of the Privy Council . . .*: Ibid., p. 48.

91   *Ordered to provide the names . . .*: Erickson, *Bloody Mary*, p. 242, and Lingard, *History of England*, p. 5:80.

92   *(In fact Henry, in futile pursuit . . .*: Loades, *Mary Tudor*, p. 52.

92   *Under the terms of her father's will . . .*: Ibid., p. 66.

94   *By 1549, when the new reign's first Act of Uniformity . . .*: Ibid., p. 75.

97   *Mary declared that she "wished to constrain . . ."*: Erickson, *Bloody Mary*, p. 309.

98   *When that old champion of reform . . .*: Lingard, *History of England*, p. 5:390.

98   *By 1553 he had had ready for Parliament's attention . . .*: Skidmore, *Edward VI*, p. 232.

98   *Anyone accused of such offenses . . .*: Lingard, *History of England*, p. 5:462.

99   *Cranmer exploded in rage when informed . . .*: This and the following statement about Cranmer "spreading abroad seditious bills" are in Lingard, *History of England*, p. 5:401.

100   *Pole was so well respected . . .*: Erickson, *Bloody Mary*, p. 389.

103   *Two days before, in an even more forceful . . .*: Ibid., p. 320.

105   *By repealing Henry VIII's Succession Act . . .*: Guy, *Tudor England*, p. 233.

106   *If Mary and Philip had a son . . .*: Mackie, *Earlier Tudors*, p. 537.

107   *Philip himself, when he learned . . .*: Erickson, *Bloody Mary*, p. 348, and *DNB* notes for entry on Philip II.

109   *"As for this marriage," she said . . .*: Lingard, *History of England*, p. 5:425.

110   *In all some 480 men were convicted . . .*: Loades, *Two Tudor Conspiracies*, p. 127.

110   *Not only when put on trial but before . . .*: Ibid., p. 16.

115   *London, where there had been only three . . .* : Penry Williams, *Life*, p. 129.

117   *"His way with the lords is so . . ."*: Erickson, *Bloody Mary*, p. 380.

118   *"If the English find out how hard up . . ."*: Ibid., p. 382.

122   *Mary even allowed herself . . .* : Loades, *Mary Tudor*, p. 168.

122   *Protestant preachers who had not fled . . .* : Erickson, *Bloody Mary*, p. 397.

123   *What is clear is that it was controversial . . .* : Lingard, *History of England*, p. 5:469.

124   *It was long and widely believed . . .* : Ibid., p. 5:464.

124   *Something on the order of three hundred individuals . . .* : Mackie, *Earlier Tudors*, p. 553.

128   *She had more success in restoring . . .* : Lingard, *History of England*, p. 5:494.

128   *Mary and Gardiner wanted to introduce . . .* : Loades, *Tudor Conspiracies*, p. 260.

129   *But Pole's position was still . . .* : *DNB* entry for Reginald Pole.

129   *This gathering, by the time of its adjournment . . .* : Mackie, *Earlier Tudors*, p. 555.

129   *Philip, inevitably but unfairly . . .* : Loades, *Mary Tudor*, p. 175; Guy, *Tudor England*, p. 248; Lingard, *History of England*, p. 5:521; Loades, *Mary Tudor*, p. 175, and Guy, *Tudor England*, p. 248.

136   *Elizabeth had only recently repeated her assurances . . .* : Lingard, *History of*
136   *England*, p. 5:525, and Erickson, *Bloody Mary*, p. 480.

PART TWO
Survivor

Though the enormous number of biographies of Elizabeth I continues to grow decade by decade, no single work is recognized as definitive. Three generations have brought a movement from J. E. Neale's *Queen Elizabeth I* (Jonathan Cape, 1934), regarded originally as authoritative but now as hagiographic, to gradually less worshipful and finally rigorously critical works. Biographies of value include:

Haigh, Christopher. *Elizabeth I*, 2nd ed. Longman, 1998.

Hibbert, Christopher. *The Virgin Queen*. Viking, 1990.

Loades, David. *Elizabeth I*. Hambledon & London, 2003.

Neale, J. E. *Queen Elizabeth I*. Pelican, 1960.

Smith, Lacey Baldwin. *Elizabeth Tudor*. Little, Brown, 1975.

Williams, Neville. *Elizabeth I*. Weidenfeld & Nicolson, 1972.

Notes

PAGE

141   *Her decline began with a refusal . . .* : An exceptionally detailed and vivid account of Elizabeth's last days appears in the opening pages of Evelyn Waugh's *Edmund Campion* (Little, Brown, 1946).

141   When begged to get some sleep . . . : Lingard, *History of England*, p. 6:647.

142   At a time when the Crown's ordinary revenues . . . : Elton, *England Under*, p. 362.

142   Even the most glorious event of the reign . . . : The cost figure is in Haigh, *Elizabeth I*, p. 138.

142   Ferocious inflation has combined with falling wages . . . : Data on living standards and death sentences are ibid., p. 166.

144   Though of course we have no data . . . : As noted above, Duffy's *Stripping of Altars* is an exhaustive demonstration of the lingering popularity of the old religion.

145   Queen Mary herself suspected . . . : Erickson, *Bloody Mary*, p. 346.

146   The coronation took place on January 15 . . . : The cost figure is in the *DNB* entry for Elizabeth I.

149   The Privy Council opened the legislative . . . : Elton, *England Under*, p. 271.

150   When Parliament reconvened on April 3 . . . : The change to supreme "governor" is in Hibbert, *Virgin Queen*, p. 92.

151   A uniformity bill outlawing the mass . . . : Elton, *Tudor Constitution*, presents the words of the bill on p. 401 and a brief discussion of it on p. 388.

151   Thanks to the breakdown in relations . . . : Loades, *Elizabeth I*, p. 134.

151   She found, however, that almost to a man . . . : Lingard, *History of England*, pp. 6:9 and 14.

153   The point of conflict . . . : Haigh, *Elizabeth I*, p. 47.

154   She allowed the Diocese of Ely to remain without a bishop . . . : Ibid., p. 49.

154   Out of the eight thousand priests in England . . . : Elton, *England Under*, p. 276.

154   The persecution was relaxed as soon as . . . : Haigh, *Elizabeth I*, p. 42.

164   Elizabeth herself, though she never forgave . . . : Hibbert, *Virgin Queen*, p. 67.

171   Even people close to the queen . . . : Haigh, *Elizabeth I*, p. 16.

177   Henry Sidney, Dudley's brother-in-law . . . : Milton Waldman, *Elizabeth and Leicester* (Collins, 1946), p. 103.

178   What appears to have happened . . . : Haigh, *Elizabeth I*, p. 16.

185   It was perhaps in response . . . : Elton, *England Under*, p. 298.

185   It was a monumental blunder nevertheless . . . : Ibid., p. 303; Lingard, *History of England*, p. 6:225; and Loades, *Elizabeth I*, p. 169.

186   They were exasperated, therefore, when Elizabeth . . . : Haigh, *Elizabeth I*, p. 38.

       The worst of their mistakes was to overreact . . . : Elton, *England Under*, p. 279.

198   The Privy Council then fell into an angry dispute . . . : Wilson, *Uncrowned Kings*, p. 303.

199   Anjou definitely had no interest . . . : Hibbert, *Virgin Queen*, p. 181, and Lingard, *History of England*, p. 6:241, note 1.

202   In that same year the increasingly discontented . . . : Elton, *England Under*, p. 300.

204   In actuality it was all talk . . . : Loades, *Elizabeth I*, p. 176, and Smith, *Elizabeth Tudor*, p. 143.

211   Somewhat oddly for a Protestant . . . : Guy, *Tudor England*, p. 262.

212   It was her good fortune to have two . . . : Lingard, *History of England*, p. 6:328.

217   Much of the trouble grew out of the determination . . . : Smith, *Elizabeth Tudor,* p. 172; Haigh, *Elizabeth I,* pp. 122 and 149; and *DNB* entries on Francis Walsingham and Mary, Queen of Scots.

217   As early as 1581 Walsingham was asking . . . : Haigh, *Elizabeth I,* p. 76.

217   An innovation called "compounding" . . . : Loades, *Elizabeth I,* p. 234.

226   Her navy had barely broken off its pursuit . . . : Smith, *Elizabeth Tudor,* pp. 66 and 72.

227   Her admiral, Lord Howard of Effingham . . . : Howard's words are in Loades, *Elizabeth I,* p. 252.

227   Here she supposedly delivered . . . : Loades, *Elizabeth I,* p. 252, observes that the queen "is alleged to have made" the Tilbury speech.

228   During the period when invasion seemed imminent . . . : Hibbert, *Virgin Queen,* p. 220, and Lingard, *History of England,* p. 6:505.

228   Between July and November twenty-one imprisoned priests . . . : Lingard, *History of England,* p. 6:520.

229   Though theologically Whitgift was . . . : Elton, *England Under,* p. 428.

232   When the fleet finally set out again . . . : Drake's instructions, and the number of lives lost on the expedition, are in Guy, *Tudor England,* p. 349.

248   Getting the queen's approval was difficult . . . : Loades, *Elizabeth I,* p. 265, and Haigh, *Elizabeth I,* p. 142.

250   The Dutch rebels, he observed sourly . . . : The words in quotes are in the *DNB* entry for Robert Cecil.

252   He stormed out proclaiming . . . : The words in quotes are in the *DNB* entry for Robert Devereux, second Earl of Essex.

262   Five Parliaments had had to be called . . . : Loades, *Elizabeth I,* p. 292; Elton, *England Under,* pp. 362 and 461; and Haigh, *Elizabeth I,* p. 166.

263   Prices of necessities soared . . . : Haigh, *Elizabeth I,* p. 166.

263   In 1534, at the dawn of the English Reformation . . . : The numbers in this paragraph are from ibid.

264   (At thirty, upon being told . . . : Smith, *Elizabeth Tudor,* p. 73.

265   The show went on—her wardrobe . . . : Haigh, *Elizabeth I,* p. 90. Lingard, *History of England,* p. 6:657, says the number of the queen's gowns was in the thousands.

265   She was allowing her world . . . : The number of Privy Council members is in Haigh, *Elizabeth I,* p. 107.

267   It was long customary to interpret . . . : Loades, *Elizabeth I,* p. 274.

268   He had already been talking recklessly . . . : Lingard, *History of England,* pp. 6:597 and 600, and *DNB* entry on Robert Devereux, second Earl of Essex.

272   Elizabeth showed a marked aversion . . . : *DNB* entry for Robert Devereux.

272   This has often been represented . . . : Lingard, *History of England,* p. 6:629, suggests that the queen's "victory" lay in the fact that the royal prerogative on monopolies had not been positively surrendered.

272   Revenues from the land sales totaled . . . : Smith, *Elizabeth Tudor,* p. 203.

273   In 1601 and 1602 he became the leading . . . : Hibbert, *Virgin Queen,* p. 244; Elton, *England Under,* p. 411; and Guy, *Tudor England,* p. 396.

Also available from Amberley Publishing

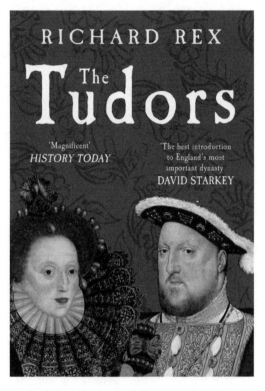

An intimate history of England's most infamous royal family

'The best introduction to England's most important dynasty' DAVID STARKEY
'A lively overview... Rex is a wry commentator on the game on monarchy' THE GUARDIAN
'Gripping and told with enviable narrative skill. This is a model of popular history... a delight' THES
'Vivid, entertaining and carrying its learning lightly' EAMON DUFFY

The Tudor Age began in August 1485 when Henry Tudor landed with 2000 men at Milford Haven
intent on snatching the English throne from Richard III. For more than a hundred years England was
to be dominated by the personalities of the five Tudor monarchs, ranging from the brilliance and
brutality of Henry VIII to the shrewdness and vanity of the virgin queen, Elizabeth I.

£14.99 Paperback
143 illustrations (66 colour)
272 pages
978-1-4456-0280-6

Available from all good bookshops or to order direct
Please call **01285-760-030**
www.amberleybooks.com

Also available from Amberley Publishing

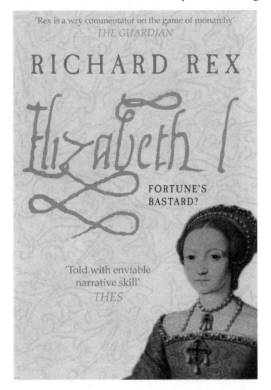

'Rex is a wry commentator on the game of monarchy'
THE GUARDIAN

RICHARD REX

Elizabeth I

FORTUNE'S BASTARD?

'Told with enviable narrative skill'
THES

An accessible biography of Elizabeth I by a leading Tudor expert

Richard Rex highlights the vivid and contrary personality of a Queen who could both baffle and bedazzle her subjects, her courtiers, and her rivals: at one moment flirting outrageously with a favourite or courting some foreign prince, and at another vowing perpetual virginity; at one time agonising over the execution of her cousin, Mary Queen of Scots, then ordering the slaughter of hundreds of poor men after a half-cock rebellion. Too many biographies of Elizabeth merely perpetuate the flattery she enjoyed from her courtiers, this biography also reflects more critical voices, such as those of the Irish, the Catholics and those who lived on the wrong side of the emerging North/South divide. To them she showed a different face.

£9.99 Paperback
75 illustrations
192 pages
978-1-84868-423-2

Available from all good bookshops or to order direct
Please call **01285-760-030**
www.amberleybooks.com

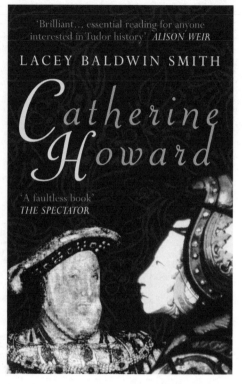

Also available from Amberley Publishing

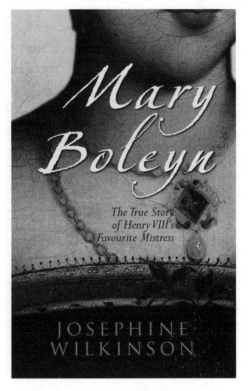

The scandalous true story of Mary Boleyn, infamous sister of Anne, and mistress of Henry VIII

Mary Boleyn, 'the infamous other Boleyn girl', began her court career as the mistress of the king of France. François I of France would later call her 'The Great Prostitute' and the slur stuck. The bête-noir of her family, Mary was married off to a minor courtier but it was not long before she caught the eye of Henry VIII and a new affair began.

Mary would emerge the sole survivor of a family torn apart by lust and ambition, and it is in Mary and her progeny that the Boleyn legacy rests.

£9.99 Paperback
22 illustrations (10 colour)
224 pages
978-1-84868-525-3

Available from all good bookshops or to order direct
Please call **01285-760-030**
www.amberleybooks.com

Available from March 2011 from Amberley Publishing

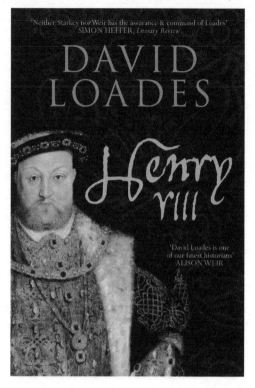

A major new biography of the most infamous king of England

'David Loades is one of our finest Tudor historians' ALISON WEIR

'David Loades Tudor biographies are both highly enjoyable and instructive, the perfect combination'
ANTONIA FRASER

Professor David Loades has spent most of his life investigating the remains, literary, archival and archaeological, of Henry VIII, and this monumental new biography book is the result. His portrait of Henry is distinctive, he was neither a genius nor a tyrant, but a man' like any other', except for the extraordinary circumstances in which he found himself. As a youth, he was a magnificent specimen of manhood, and in age a gargantuan wreck, but even in his prime he was never the 'ladies man' which legend, and his own imagination, created. Sexual insecurity undermined him, and gave his will that irascible edge which proved fatal to Anne Boleyn and Thomas Cromwell alike.

£25 Hardback
113 illustrations (49 colour)
512 pages
978-1-84868-532-1

Available from March 2011 from all good bookshops or to order direct
Please call **01285-760-030**
www.amberleybooks.com

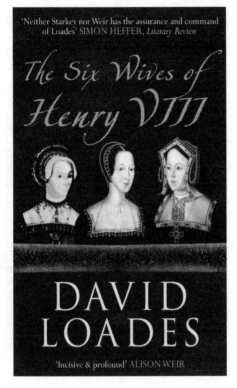

Also available from Amberley Publishing

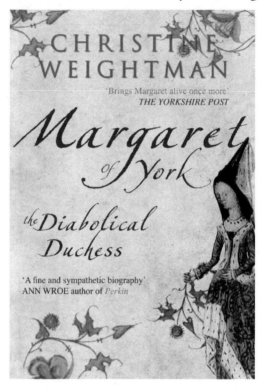

The amazing life of Margaret of York, the woman who tried to overthrow the Tudors

Also available from Amberley Publishing

The tragic love affair that changed English history forever

Anne Boleyn was the most controversial and scandalous woman ever to sit on the throne of England. From her early days at the imposing Hever Castle in Kent, to the glittering courts of Paris and London, Anne caused a stir wherever she went. Alluring but not beautiful, Anne's wit and poise won her numerous admirers at the English court, and caught the roving eye of King Henry.

Their love affair was as extreme as it was deadly, from Henry's 'mine own sweetheart' to 'cursed and poisoning whore' her fall from grace was total.

£9.99 Paperback
47 illustrations (26 colour)
264 pages
978-1-84868-514-7

Available from all good bookshops or to order direct
Please call **01285-760-030**
www.amberleybooks.com

Also available from Amberley Publishing

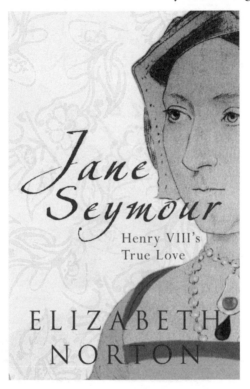

The first ever biography of Jane Seymour, Henry VIII's third wife, who died in childbirth giving the king what he craved most – a son and heir

Jane Seymour is often portrayed as meek and mild and as the most successful, but one of the least significant, of Henry VIII's wives. The real Jane was a very different character, demure and submissive yet with a ruthless streak.

Elizabeth Norton tells the thrilling life of a country girl from rural Wiltshire who rose to the throne of England and became the ideal Tudor woman.

£9.99 Paperback
53 illustrations (26 colour)
288 pages
978-1-84868-527-7

Available from all good bookshops or to order direct
Please call **01285-760-030**
www.amberleybooks.com

Available from November 2010 from Amberley Publishing

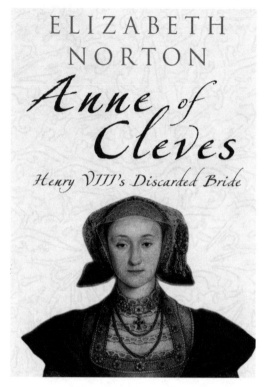

ELIZABETH
NORTON

Anne of Cleves

Henry VIII's Discarded Bride

The first major biography of Henry VIII least favourite wife –
but the one who outlived them all...

'I like her not!' was the verdict of Henry VIII on meeting his fourth wife, Anne of Cleves, for the first time.
Anne could have said something similar on meeting Henry and, having been promised the most handsome
prince in Europe, she was destined to be disappointed in the elderly and corpulent king.

Thomas Cromwell lost his head for his role in the Cleves marriage, but Anne's shrewdness ensured she
kept hers. Anne of Cleves led a dramatic and often dangerous life but, for all this, of Henry VIII's six
wives, she is truly the wife that survived.

£9.99 Paperback
54 illustrations (27 colour)
224 pages
978-1-4456-0183-0

Available from November 2010 from all good bookshops or to order direct
Please call **01285-760-030**
www.amberleybooks.com

Also available from Amberley Publishing

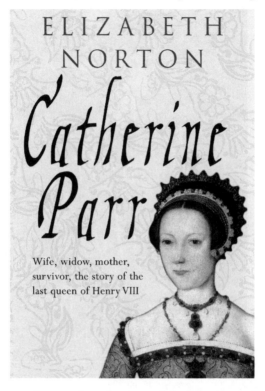

ELIZABETH
NORTON

*Catherine
Parr*

Wife, widow, mother,
survivor, the story of the
last queen of Henry VIII

Wife, widow, mother, survivor, the story of the last queen of Henry VIII

'Scintillating' THE FINANCIAL TIMES
'Norton cuts an admirably clear path through the tangled Tudor intrigues' JENNY UGLOW
'Wonderful, an excellent book, a joy to read' HERSTORIA

The sixth wife of Henry VIII was also the most married queen of England, outliving three husbands
before finally marrying for love. Catherine Parr was enjoying her freedom after her first two arranged
marriages when she caught the attention of the elderly Henry VIII. She was the most reluctant of all
Henry's wives, offering to become his mistress rather than submit herself to the dangers of becoming
Henry's queen. This only served to increase Henry's enthusiasm for the young widow and Catherine
was forced to abandon her lover for the decrepit king.

£18.99 Hardback
40 illustrations (20 colour)
240 pages
978-1-84868-582-6

Available from all good bookshops or to order direct
Please call **01285-760-030**
www.amberleybooks.com

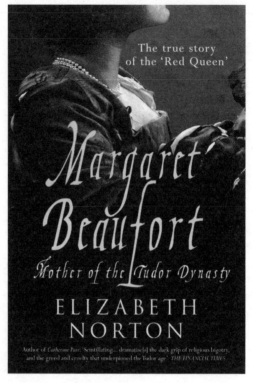

Available from April 2011 from Amberley Publishing

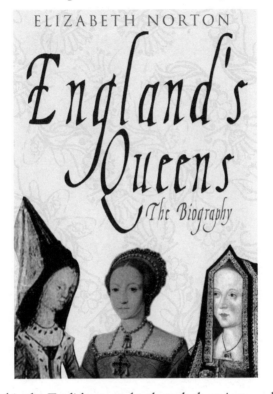

Her story not his, the English monarchy through the private and public lives of the queens of England

Nearly eighty women have sat on the throne of England, either as queen regnant or queen consort and the voices of all of them survive through their own writings and those of their contemporaries.

For the first time, the voice of each individual queen can be heard together, charting the course of English queenship through nearly two thousand years of history. Each queen played her own part in shaping what the role of queen would become and it developed through the lives and actions of each of the women in turn.

£25 Hardback
150 illustrations (100 colour)
384 pages
978-1-84868-193-4

Available from April 2011 from all good bookshops or to order direct
Please call **01285-760-030**
www.amberleybooks.com

Available from March 2011 from Amberley Publishing

The complete letters, dispatches and chronicles that tell the real story of Anne Boleyn

Through the chronicles, letters and dispatches written by both Anne and her contemporaries, it is possible to see her life and thoughts as she struggled to become queen of England, ultimately ending her life on the scaffold. Only through the original sources is it truly possible to evaluate the real Anne. George Wyatt's *Life of Queen Anne* provided the first detailed account of the queen, based on the testimony of those that knew her. The poems of Anne's supposed lover, Thomas Wyatt, as well as accounts such as Cavendish's *Life of Wolsey* also give details of her life, as do the hostile dispatches of the Imperial Ambassador, Eustace Chapuys and the later works of the slanderous Nicholas Slander and Nicholas Harpsfield. Henry VIII's love letters and many of Anne's own letters survive, providing an insight into the love affair that changed England forever. The reports on Anne's conduct in the Tower of London show the queen's shock and despair when she realised that she was to die. Collected together for the first time, these and other sources make it possible to view the real Anne Boleyn through her own words and those of her contemporaries.

£20 Hardback
45 illustrations
352 pages
978-1-4456-0043-7

Available from March 2011 from all good bookshops or to order direct
Please call **01285–760–030**
www.amberleybooks.com

Available from June 2011 from Amberley Publishing

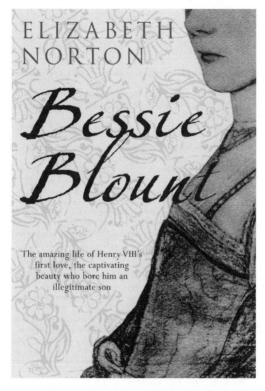

*eautiful, young, exuberant, the amazing life of Elizabeth Blount, Henry
'III's mistress and mother to his first son who came tantalizingly close to
succeeding him as King Henry IX*

Sidelined by historians until now, Bessie and the son she had by the king are one of the great 'what ifs' of
English history. If Jane Seymour had not produced a male heir and Bessie's son had not died young aged
17, in all likelihood Henry Fitzroy could have followed his father as King Henry IX and Bessie propelled to
the status of mother of the king.

£20 Hardback
30 illustrations (20 colour)
288 pages
978-1-84868-870-4

Available from June 2011 from all good bookshops or to order direct
Please call **01285-760-030**
www.amberleybooks.com

List of Illustrations

showing her aged about twelve. © Jonathan Reeve JR997b66fp40 15001600.

29. Prayers written out by Elizabeth (then aged thirteen) in a little volume she presented to her father, Henry VIII, as a New Year's gift for 1546. © Jonathan Reeve JR221b5fp286 15501600.

30. The Tower of London *c.*1550 and Traitors' Gate through which Elizabeth passed on her way to prison in 1554. © Jonathan Reeve JRCD3b20p1025 15501600 and © Elizabeth Norton and the Amberley Archive.

31. The Entrance of Queen Elizabeth. Queen Elizabeth's accession (or 'entrance') came to be celebrated as a religious festival. © Jonathan Reeve JR201b5p2 15501600.

32. Although in Mary's reign Elizabeth had affected the simplest and plainest fashions in dress (in order to distinguish herself from her overdressed sister and to allude to the Protestant aesthetic of plain simplicity), once she became queen Elizabeth re-invented herself with the aid of spectacularly ornate dresses such as this. © Jonathan Reeve JR1006b66fp144 15001600.

33. Sketch for a portrait of Elizabeth I. © Jonathan Reeve JR978b65p61 15001600.

34. Signature of Elizabeth I. © Jonathan Reeve JR1013b66fp196 15001600.

35. Great Seal of Elizabeth I. © Jonathan Reeve JR1009b66p181 15001600.

36. Robert Dudley was a favourite of the queen's from the start of the reign, and was given the prestigious Court position of Master of the Horse. In the early 1560s Elizabeth was widely reckoned to be in love with him, even though he was already married. By kind permission of Ripon Cathedral Chapter.

37. Elizabeth I at prayer is the frontispiece to *Christian Prayers* (1569). © Jonathan Reeve JR1168b4fp747 15501600.

38. Elizabeth I and the Three Goddesses, 1569. © Jonathan Reeve JR999b66fp64 15001600.

39. Elizabeth's falcon downs a heron. Illustration from George Turberville, *The Book of Faulconrie or Hauking* (1575), p.81. © Jonathan Reeve JR172b4p740 15501600

40. Francis, Duke of Alençon, came closer than anyone else to securing Elizabeth's hand in marriage. He first visited Elizabeth's court in 1576 and to everyone's surprise, Elizabeth appeared completely smitten with him. © Jonathan Reeve JR1003b66fp112 15001600.

41. 'A Hieroglyphic of Britain', which John Dee himself designed as the frontispiece to his *General and Rare Memorials Pertayning to the Perfect Arte of Navigation* (1577). John Dee (1527–1608), alchemist, geographer, mathematician and astrologer to the queen, wrote the *Arte of Navigation* as a manifesto for Elizabethan naval imperialism. © Jonathan Reeve JR174b4p743 15501600.

42. Sir Walter Ralegh and his son. Ralegh became the latest in the long line of the queen's favourites in the early 1580s. © Jonathan Reeve JR1008b66fp166 15001600.

43. Robert Devereux (1565-1601), the second Earl of Essex. Pushed forward at Elizabeth's Court by his stepfather, the Earl of Leicester, in the justified hope that he might displace Ralegh as the queen's foremost favourite. Neither his talents nor his means quite matched his ambitions, however, and after losing royal favour he gambled and lost everything in a desperate attempted coup. He was executed in 1601. © Jonathan Reeve JR1005b66fp133 15001600.

44. Mary Queen of Scots, a prisoner throughout the two decades preceding her execution at age forty-four in 1586. © Jonathan Reeve JR1178b2fp440 15001550.

45. In 1586, the Derbyshire gentleman Anthony Babington was the central figure in a plot to liberate Mary Queen of Scots and assassinate Elizabeth. © Jonathan Reeve JR204b5p9 15501600.

46. The Spanish Armada off the French coast, 1588. © Jonathan Reeve JR216b5p148 15501600.

47. Sir Francis Drake. © Jonathan Reeve JR191b4p830 15501600.

48. The 'Ermine Portrait', from 1585, show Elizabeth aged about 52. © Jonathan Reeve JR1000 b66fp92 15001600.

49. The 'Procession Picture' from Elizabeth's last years. © Jonathan Reeve JR200b5pii 15501600.

50. Engraved portrait of Elizabeth I by William Rogers *c.*1595. © Jonathan Reeve JR1016b5fp26 15001600.

51. The 'Ditchley Portrait' (*c.*1590, but not showing the queen's nearly 60 years). © Jonathan Reeve JR1017b5fp86 15001600.

52. Elizabeth I in old age. © Jonathan Reeve JR1719b89fpiii16001700.

53. Funeral of Elizabeth. © Jonathan Reeve JR1099b2p581 16001650.

Index

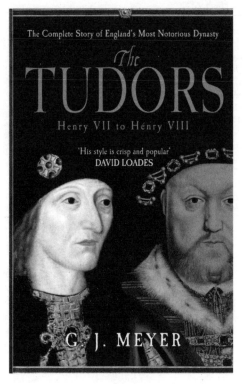